A DARK PATH TO FREEDOM

ENVER ALTAYLI

A Dark Path to Freedom

Ruzi Nazar, from the Red Army to the CIA

Translated by
David Barchard

HURST & COMPANY, LONDON

First published in the United Kingdom in 2017 by
C. Hurst & Co. (Publishers) Ltd.,
41 Great Russell Street, London, WC1B 3PL
© Enver Altayli, 2017
Translation © David Barchard
All rights reserved.
Printed in the United Kingdom by Bell & Bain Ltd, Glasgow

Distributed in the United States, Canada and Latin America by
Oxford University Press, 198 Madison Avenue, New York, NY 10016,
United States of America.

The right of Enver Altayli to be identified as the author of
this publication is asserted by him in accordance with the
Copyright, Designs and Patents Act, 1988.

A Cataloguing-in-Publication data record for this book is
available from the British Library.

ISBN: 9781849046978 *hardback*

This book is printed using paper from registered sustainable
and managed sources.

www.hurstpublishers.com

CONTENTS

v

FOREWORD

The failed coup in Moscow in August 1991 heralded a period of monumental change in Central and South Asia. Within a couple of years, the whole political geography of the region seemed to have been redrawn. The abolition of the Soviet Union on 26 December 1991 completed the emergence as independent states of the USSR's Muslim-majority republics. The erstwhile Soviet-backed regime in Kabul collapsed in April 1992 and the next month a bitter civil war broke out in Tajikistan, while Azerbaijan and Armenia clashed over the fate of Ngorno-Karabagh.

Living and travelling in the region at the time, I had a chance to witness some of the human dimensions of this great upheaval. From outside the region, the end of the Cold War was understood primarily in terms of the collapse of a political system and the end of an empire. But the demise of the Soviet Union also opened the way for the lands north of the Oxus River to reconnect with South Asia and the world, for people to pick up relationships that had been frozen for most of the twentieth century. Suddenly it was possible for artisans, painters and dancers from the new republics to gather in Islamabad for a Silk Road festival. One could drive across the Oxus at Heiraton and onto the old Timurid capital of Samarkhand, to admire Ulugh Beg's fifteenth-century observatory. The Oxus, or Amu Darya in the vernacular, was imbued with historical and political significance. Once on the northern bank you were definitively in the cultural zone of Turkistan. Through most of the Cold War era the Oxus represented the Iron Curtain in the East. But even in the thirties, the British traveller Byron described being thwarted in his attempts to reach the Oxus. He was refused permission by the Afghan authorities to approach such a sensitive feature.[1]

FOREWORD

My most vivid recollection of the upheaval relates to days spent in sub-zero temperatures on the Afghan bank of the Oxus, in December 1992. A wave of humanity had crossed the river on barges, to seek sanctuary in Afghanistan from the fighting which then raged in Tajikistan's Kulyab region. The first night of the exodus, scattered across a frosty field, family groups clasped their few possessions and huddled together with no protection from the bitter cold. As I walked from family to family, with a few blankets to distribute, the openness with which the new arrivals launched into their stories was striking. A *kolhoz* manager started to explain the running of a collective farm. A couple of men recalled how Stalin had uprooted their community to work on new cotton plantations—they wanted to know where they could grow cotton in Afghanistan. An older man described himself as a veteran of the Red Army's heroic stand at Stalingrad. It was as if these refugees from Turkestan wanted to share all their stories of seventy years of life under the Soviets before a dawn that, in those freezing temperatures, some might not live to see.

The subject of *A Dark Path to Freedom*, Ruzi Nazar, was a hero of Turkestan, whose life journey and career reached their climax in the period when I first glimpsed Central Asia. He epitomises the saga of the people of Turkestan, snippets of which the refugees had shared on the banks of the Oxus. His story is the prequel to Central Asian independence, the deep currents that eventually washed those refugees up on the banks of the Oxus. Ruzi Nazar was a twentieth-century Uzbek Ulysses. However, as a Muslim wandering in the lands that bridge Asia and Europe, he should rather be thought of as an Amir Hamza.[2] His is a life narrative of the young man journeying out of the village and witnessing half a century of tumult in the Stalinist terror, the Second World War and the Cold War, before eventually returning as an acclaimed national figure. His story is of a life of purpose and morality, of choosing the correct path, even when navigating through the moral swamps of the Stalinist terror and Nazi totalitarianism. While Ruzi is famous for the part he played in the great global confrontations of the twentieth century, his moral character as a hero is shaped by the sage woman, whose advice he carries with him. Ruzi recalls his mother's guidance:

> You will often come to crossroads in your life. If on one side of you there is the right path, albeit one whose outcome is uncertain and full of dan-

viii

gers, and on your other a path crooked and wrong but full of material riches, choose the right path, even if it is full of dangers.

There is also an historical significance to the geography of Ruzi's career. As a Turkestan patriot, Ruzi was mainly concerned with the lands east of the Black Sea, north of the Himalayas and south of the Urals, where Turkic tribes have settled and built a series of empires since the sixth century. Much of this territory has now been shaped into the post-Soviet Central Asian republics. But Ruzi's story captures an idea of Eurasia, in the sense that his efforts on behalf of the people of Turkestan saw him based variously in Ukraine, Austria, Germany, Italy, Turkey and of course the United States. Each of these places was connected with events in the homeland and in each of them Ruzi encountered both compatriots and hosts who engaged with developments in Turkestan. The wide-ranging familiarity makes sense in terms of recent scholarship, which has reminded us of the connectivity across the Eurasian super-continent. Historic East-West trade routes have long acted as vectors for the transmission of ideas, technology and political and military power. Europe has been far more connected to and shaped by Ruzi's Turkestan than was ever acknowledged by those who dreamed that civilisation was forged in Greece and Rome alone.[3]

If Ruzi's journey physically spanned Eurasia, thematically his engagement encompassed the grand issues of the twentieth century. He lived through one manifestation of European colonialism, that of the Russian empire in Asia. This, of course, was the theme that Ruzi pursued throughout his life. He travelled as far as the Bandung Conference to shape global awareness that the Soviet Union, while presenting itself as an ally of the Afro-Asian liberation movements, was itself a colonial power. The pivotal period in which Ruzi built his personal reputation as a patriot and intellectual was his time with the Turkestan Legion, from 1942 to 1945. By embracing German support, Ruzi and the other Turkestan nationalists inserted themselves into the confrontation between Nazi and Soviet totalitarianism. But Ruzi experienced a different fate from his contemporary Subhash Chandra Bose, who received German and Japanese backing for his Indian National Army in the East. After the collapse of Fascism, the United States needed allies against the Soviets in the Cold War. Ruzi was uniquely qualified to pioneer cultural resistance and espionage in the new confrontation. For Ruzi, participation in the Cold War simply meant accepting a new backer for the latest phase of the struggle for Turkestan independence. Ruzi's career also touched on the theme of what independence would look like, as he espoused a vision of a democratic Turkestan, beyond the Soviet yoke. During his stint in coup-prone Turkey in the 1960s, he had the opportunity to grapple with the challenge of sustaining democracy and stability in a country courted by East and West. He even pops up with a role in the Iran hostage crisis and used his briefings to US policy-makers to advocate reliance on brain rather than brawn.

Along with these grand historical themes, Ruzi's life also brings out timeless personal and idiosyncratic themes. How do you survive under an authoritarian regime, saving your life, honour and soul, while still playing a part in public affairs? Part of the answer is principled hypoc-risy. Toe the party line in public while sharing your true beliefs only in the presence of those you can trust and fellow dissidents. This system-atic double-speak helped Ruzi to survive both the Soviets and the Nazis. But I find it eerily familiar from my dialogue with the Taliban. One struggles to understand what people really mean in a situation where loose words can have them killed. More broadly, Ruzi's time with the Turkestan Legion and its political counterpart, the National Turkestan Unity Committee (NTUC), provides a case study in the moral limits of collaboration. The Turkestanis wore German uniforms but manoeuvred to avoid being absorbed by the genocidal SS. They embraced the war against the Soviets but resisted attempts to fight their own people with a new front in Turkestan itself. Eventually the Nuremburg trials had to scrutinise the collaboration, asking whether the men who accepted Nazi patronage had contributed to the geno-cide. Efforts to protect Central Asian Jews helped tilt the scales and clear the Turkestanis of complicity in the genocide. But Ruzi's most recurrent personal theme was that of the obligation to engage in pri-vate acts of humanity, even when you are surrounded by carnage. Share food, drink and kind words, even on the battlefield. Ruzi's mother told him: 'A good action has as much value with God as the degree to which it is kept secret'.

Ruzi's story, set as it is against the cataclysmic events of the twenti-eth century, was supposed to be safely placed in the past. We refer to such tales to remind ourselves of that which we have left behind. Ruzi himself lived on in retirement until 2016, almost completing his century. But it turns out that the current affairs of the twenty-first century hark back to his journey to a troubling degree. A new generation of demagogues successfully challenged the notion that a liberal consensus could shape the world. The idea of 'post-truth' has shattered any notion that empirical reality must shape dominant narratives. In Russia, the idea of Eurasia has been re-discovered, rationalising a new Russian expansionism, championed by Aleksandr Dugin.[4] Patriotism and nationalism have been dusted off to challenge global collectivism. And those involved in politics in the Muslim world must still juggle to maintain their legitimacy, balancing the compulsions of international alliances with appeals to Muslim and national identity. Ruzi Nazar, in his heroic journey, navigated through these multiple Scyllas and Charybdises. Enver Bey Altayli was a protégé of Ruzi, who shares his Uzbek roots and his experience of the Cold War and the Central Asian states' struggle for independence. A vote of thanks to Altayli for bringing us his own narrative of the Ruzi journey, so disturbingly relevant to our times.

Michael Semple,
Research Professor, George Mitchell Institute for Global Peace,
Security and Justice, Queen's University Belfast
talkforpeace@gmail.com

CHILDHOOD IN TURKESTAN

Margilan

When, in the year 332 BC, Alexander the Great arrived with his 55,000 soldiers at the Plain of Issos, near what is today the town of Iskenderun, the Persian king Darius was waiting for him. The arrogant Darius, ruler of one of the biggest empires the world had ever seen, commanded an army whose numbers ran into hundreds of thousands. Yet the battle ended in victory for Alexander. Having thus overcome the last big obstacle on the road to Asia, Alexander entered the lands of the king of Sogdia, who ruled what is today Uzbekistan and Tajikistan. This time he found himself opposed by the heroic warriors of Central Asia. Far from home and utterly exhausted, Alexander's army found itself facing starvation. The waters were poisoned. Herds of animals had been driven away onto the mountain slopes, and the grain and rice stores had been torched.

According to legend, Alexander and his weary army arrived on the outskirts of the town which we today call Margilan, in the Fergana valley. He was met by an aged woman leading hundreds of other women. The old woman offered the commander some bread and cooked chicken, which Alexander ate with relish. There were thousands more portions prepared for his hungry troops. The people of the town had been cooking for days. Delighted at this hospitality, Alexander declared, 'From now on, this place shall be called *murg u nan*'—in Tajik, *murg* means chicken and *nan* bread, and so from this incident the town of Margilan is said to have taken its name. Alexander spared the lives of the townspeople. Moreover, he pardoned the king of Sogdia and married his daughter, who had fallen in love with him.[1]

The 2,000th anniversary of this historic town's foundation was celebrated in September 2007 according to a resolution taken by UNESCO. Across the world, in capitals like Paris, Berlin, Washington and Ankara, meetings and seminars were held about the town of Margilan and its importance in the history of Central Asia. This Silk Road town was officially recognised as the centre of an ancient civilisation.

In his book *Turkestan at the Time of the Mongol Invasions* (1898–1900), V.V. Barthold mentions Margilan. Zahir-ud-Din Muhammad Babur, who was the great-grandson of the Turko-Mongol conqueror Timur and who established an empire in India in the sixteenth century, describes Margilan in his memoirs, referring to its beauty and to its orchards with their great variety of fruits.[2] But, above all, when Margilan is mentioned, it is silk which comes to mind.

In ancient Arabic and Chinese sources, Margilan is referred to as an important centre of trade and culture on the Silk Road. Margilan silk fabrics in particular were much sought after in the great cities of the West during the Middle Ages. These textiles, woven from the highest-quality silk of the East and decorated with natural colours and motifs, were transported by caravan from Margilan to the ports of the Mediterranean and from there by boat to the cities of Europe.[3]

Ruzi Nazar was born in Margilan on 21 January 1917, the son of a family which had been engaged in silk production for centuries. It was a year in which the world was turned upside down, and no one could have known what was in store either for the infant Ruzi or for Central Asia. There seemed to be two likelihoods. The first was that, despite the protective silken chrysalis which his family had woven around him, he would perish in the scalding atmosphere of Russian colonialism. The other was that he would pierce a hole in the chrysalis and proceed on his own way.

Ruzi's birth coincided with an extremely painful and bloody period in human history. The countries of Europe and Asia were in the midst

2

of the First World War. Ruzi's homeland, Turkestan, then a colony of Russia, and particularly the Fergana valley, was being pillaged by the colonists and also racked by the fire and bloodshed of internal rebellions.

To understand Ruzi's later life, one must look more closely at the social and economic conditions of his early years. During the Middle Ages, a brilliant civilisation flourished in Central Asia. The cities of Samarkand, Khiva and Bukhara were centres of learning and the arts. At at time when most of the world believed in a geostatic model the central Asian scholar Al-Biruni (973–1048) was entertaining the possibility of the earth's movement. Ulugh Beg (1394–1449), the ruler of Samarkand, observed the heavens from the largest and most advanced telescope of the day and drew a flawless map of the night sky. Another son of Samarkand, Ibn Sina (or Avicenna) (980–1037), wrote works of medical science which were used as basic textbooks in the West until the seventeenth century. The mathematician al-Khwarizmi (780–850) brought algebra to the world in his work *Hisab al-jabr wa'l-muqabala*. In the centre of Samarkand, three magnificent universities, which people today still visit with admiration, carried out scientific work, and the Central Asian cities were home to the Sufi tradition which put human love above the radical interpretation of Islam and regarded compassion as the essence of divinity. Ruy Gonzales de Clavijo, who visited Samarkand at the start of the fifteenth century as the ambassador of King Henry III of Castile, reported on the magnificent civilisation which he had observed and lavished praise on its architecture.[4]

Although his country was under occupation by Tsarist Russia and then by the Soviet Union, Ruzi was well aware during his childhood of the rich legacy bequeathed by the great men of Turkestan. Even under the conditions which then prevailed, this heritage was transmitted from one generation to the next by whatever means were possible. Ruzi received his earliest education from his mother, Tajinissa.

Tajinissa came from Kokand in the Fergana valley. Before Kokand was occupied by the Russians towards the end of the nineteenth century, her father, Halmat, had been commander of the garrison kept by the khanate of Kokand in Margilan. As a girl she had been taught Arabic, Farsi and Russian language and literature by private tutors and as a result she had a full command of the classics of Eastern literature and Chagatay divan poetry; indeed, she could be called a poet herself. It was she who first awoke intellectual excitement in Ruzi.

Tajinissa Hanim taught the girls of Margilan to read and write. She was also in contact with the Jadid movement, which promoted modern attitudes among the Turkic and Muslim peoples of the Russian empire and which published a large number of newspapers and magazines.[5] She was aware of what was going on in the world, and it was she who instilled a love of his country in Ruzi, which was to guide his actions throughout his life: his basic principles, such as his ideals of independence and of opposition to colonialism, all sprang from his mother.

Ruzi's father, Jamshid Umirzakoghlu, was a master of his profession. The people of Margilan regarded him as a 'magician in silk' and called him 'Master-craftsman' and 'Jamshid Ata' ('Father'), for he was both of these things. He was totally preoccupied with getting the moths to lay their eggs, the hatching of the caterpillars, the spinning of the silk threads from the chrysalises, and their transformation into fabric. He had no time to devote to intellectual pursuits; instead, he was passionate about his craft. However, he once heard that a fifteen-year-old apprentice called Mamurjon in the local butcher's shop had a wonderful singing voice. One day, when he was buying his meat there and saw the boy sweeping the shop floor, he asked Mamurjon to sing a song for him. The boy was shy, and so Jamshid said that he had a headache and hearing someone sing would help relieve it. Mamurjon did not want to disappoint him and so he burst into a heart-tugging, passionate Central Asian folksong. When it was over, Jamshid turned to the butcher and asked if he could have Mamurjon as his foster child. Thus Mamurjon Uzakov became a member of the family. Initially he sang in Jamshid's house, but later he attracted the attention of senior state figures in the Soviet period who were interested in music. Eventually he became one of the greatest masters of Uzbek Turkish classical music in Central Asia.

Ruzi thus received his intellectual and literary education from his mother and his love of music and art from his father. The music of Mamurjon and other performers was a constant part of his early life. But the region in which he grew up was about to change even faster than he himself would.

The New Regime

In the nineteenth century, Turkestan became the scene of the 'Great Game', the name given to the rivalry between Great Britain and Tsarist Russia in Central Asia.[6] At that time the British empire had encompassed India and was advancing northwards. As for the Russian empire, Ivan IV ('the Terrible') had conquered Kazan in 1552 and Astrakhan in 1554–6 and had then begun the occupation of Siberia. This brought the Russians to the frontiers of Turkestan.[7] Peter I (r. 1682–1725), known in Turkey as 'Mad Petro', had dreamed of making Moscow into the Third Rome and believed that to do so it was necessary to conquer India. The gateway to India was Turkestan.[8]

Until 1852 Russia occupied the lands in northern Turkestan where nomads lived. In the 1820s it abolished the Kazakh khanates of the Middle Horde and Lesser Horde, followed by the Great Horde in 1848, turning them into the Governor-Generalship of the Steppes. Thus northern Turkestan became a Russian colony. A series of military operations up to 1884 destroyed the forces of the three states in Turkestan: Kokand, Khiva and Bukhara. The armies of the khanates lacked modern artillery and machine guns and had no chance against their well-equipped attackers. Despite this the people of Turkestan stubbornly defended their country, suffering heavy losses. Kokand became part of Russia, while Khiva and Bukhara were made into vassal states. Southern Turkestan became part of a newly established Governor-Generalship of Turkestan. A governor-general appointed by the tsar resided at Tashkent and ruled the colony from there.[9]

By 1917, some 1,221,000 Russian peasants and 327,000 Cossacks had been settled in the Steppes and 427,000 Russian migrants in the territories of the Governor-Generalship of Turkestan. All land inside these frontiers was declared to belong to the state. The farmers of Turkestan, who had previously owned their land, were now reduced to being tenants. In the north, the number of flocks owned by the nomads was reduced. In the south, farmers were forced to grow cotton instead of corn. A Russian official noted in 1913: 'Every grain of corn grown in Turkestan competes with Russian wheat, while every ton of cotton grown there competes with American cotton.'[10]

This completed Turkestan's transformation into a colony. Its vast territories, covering more than six million square kilometres, were mercilessly plundered by Tsarist Russia.[11] Cultural policies were applied which aimed at Russifying and Christianising the area. The military administration in Tashkent issued the following instruction to its education minister: 'To permit education in this territory in the mother tongue would conflict fundamentally with the interests of the Russian state. Consequently only Russian is to be used as the language of education in the territory.'[12]

Although it appeared that relative stability had been attained, disorder steadily grew within the Tsarist empire from the second half of the nineteenth century. The social and economic activity which had begun in Europe as a result of industrialisation reached a level at which it shook the internal balance within the Russian empire, and this was exacerbated by the growth of politically libertarian movements. Tsar Alexander II led the way with a large number of reforms, including the granting of freedom to the Russian empire's serfs in 1861, but in 1881 he was assassinated. Alexander III, who succeeded him, resorted to the harshest possible measures in the administration of the country. After his death in 1894 he was succeeded by his son, the final representative of the Romanov dynasty, Nicholas II, but by now the empire was beset by problems at home and abroad.

It was impossible for the Russian empire to make territorial gains in Europe at the start of the twentieth century, and so, after the colonisation of Central Asia, it turned its attention to Korea and Manchuria. This brought it into conflict with Japan, which was also trying to expand into mainland Asia, and in 1904 war erupted when the Japanese navy launched an attack on the Russian fleet. American mediation eventually enabled Nicholas II to sit down to peace talks after a heavy defeat.

In the same year, the growing strength of the liberal and socialist parties in domestic politics forced the tsar to take the decision to transform Russia into a constitutional monarchy. Beginning that November, a series of strikes and workers' demonstrations in St Petersburg were put down at great cost in lives, triggering protests and demonstrations against Tsarist rule all across Russia. Nationalist and pro-independence movements rose in the Caucasus, with bloody clashes between Armenians and Azeris; Baku was ransacked. In Poland 400,000 workers went on strike. In October 1905 the Petersburg People's Soviet announced a general strike and called on people not to pay taxes and to withdraw their money from the banks.

CHILDHOOD IN TURKESTAN

In February 1906 Nicholas II ratified the establishment of the Duma, or Russian parliament. Liberals were satisfied with this decision, but socialist-inspired unrest continued, spreading among soldiers returning home from the Russo-Japanese War. The first Bolshevik uprising in Russia took place in April and was only put down after the deaths of 16,000 people and the arrest of 75,000 more. But the disorders across the country did not stop, and attempts to put down the rising opposition with bloodshed only made the tension worse. Step by step, the combination of a frail economy and the organisational strength of the Bolsheviks brought the end of the Romanov dynasty closer.

When the First World War began, Russia sided with the Allied powers (Britain, France, Belgium, Serbia and Montenegro) against the Entente countries (Germany, Austria-Hungary, the Ottoman Empire and Bulgaria). The harsh effects of the war were soon felt by soldiers at the front and by ordinary people at home. A set of events collectively described as the February Revolution of 1917 spread in waves to the east of the country. A provisional Soviet government was formed, taking power on 25 October. It began by withdrawing Russia from the war and then announced that it would distribute the estates of large landowners among poor peasants.

The progress of the Russian revolutions between 1905 and 1917 was greeted with great joy in Russia's colonies. For the people of Turkestan the years of the First World War in particular were very painful. Tsarist Russia did not accept Turkestanis in its armies, as it was thought too risky to give Central Asians a military training. Despite this, uprisings against the occupying Tsarist forces never stopped.[13] Between 1899 and 1916, there were 4,922 armed attacks on Russian military units in the territory of the Turkestan Governor-Generalship.[14] During the First World War, however, the Tsarist army needed supporting manpower, and so young men were taken from every Central Asian family and employed behind the lines. The conscripts suffered from hunger, cold and constant maltreatment, and hundreds of thousands died. Only old people, women and children remained behind to work in the cotton fields, and they were set to work under the whiplash. The colonial authorities seized the cotton they grew for army use, paying only a pittance for it and forcing the population to live on the edge of starvation.

In 1916, the Bala Aldi uprising spread to every part of Turkestan but was bloodily suppressed with the execution of 347 rebels.[15] Mustafa

Shokay, one of leaders of the Turkestani independence movement, would later write of this period: 'After the Bala Aldi rebellion, the 1917 February Revolution broke out in the centre of Russia and a provisional government was established. The new government proclaimed that it accepted the principle of self-determination for national peoples and that the new system would be democratic. But the colonial authorities in Turkestan began to search for ways of maintaining their authority here. In their view representatives of the local population had no right to a say in the administration of Turkestan. At a meeting held in Tashkent at the building of the Governor-General, someone called Nicholas, who was a member of the Popular Socialists Group, asked to speak and declared: "Russian workers and Russian soldiers have made this revolution. For that reason, the administration and government of Turkestan belongs to us, that is the Russians. The local people should be satisfied with what we give them."' [16]

On 9 March 1917, a telegram arrived in the main post office in Tashkent from St Petersburg stating that the tsar had been deposed. Alexei Kuropatkin, the governor-general of Turkestan, announced on 12 March that a democratic republic had been established in Russia.

This was the turbulent time into which Ruzi was born. Life still went on, even though in Turkestan and, indeed, throughout the whole world it was full of uncertainties.

Ruzi's parents wanted their son to receive a good education. But they doubted whether the classical religious schools in the masjids and mosques would be adequate. They thought hard about what they should do and eventually reached a decision. A new kind of school for Muslims had been set up in Margilan, beside the town's post office, by a Crimean Tatar called Nogay Hodja, a member of the Jadid movement and follower of Ismail Gaspirali, the Turkic writer and intellectual leader in the Crimea. Ruzi started his education at the Nogay School in 1923 and it was from Nogay that he received his first instruction both in patriotism and in discipline. But when Ruzi entered the third grade, Nogay Hodja himself was no longer there. Although it was rumoured that he had been arrested as an opponent of the new Soviet regime, nothing more was ever heard of him again. There were only two possibilities. He had died either in front of a firing squad or in a concentration camp in Siberia.

CHILDHOOD IN TURKESTAN

Ruzi was a clever, hard-working and energetic little boy and by the age of nine he had already become acquainted with the new official ideology of the state. Mr Abdullayev, Ruzi's third-grade language and literature teacher, explained the Communist ideology to the class in words that they could understand. 'There is no God. Religion is the opium of the people. Religion is a heap of superstitious beliefs invented by the people who control the means of production: in other words it is intended to make it easier for rich people to exploit poor ones.' When Ruzi first heard these words, he was astonished. But there was more to follow. The next year, when Ruzi went into the fourth grade, a Godless People's Club was formed in the school. Some of the teachers wanted him, as a successful student, to join it. Ruzi went home and poured out his feelings to his mother and father. Many years later, he described that moment. 'My father was a quiet and cautious man. He was well aware that a new historical period had begun. But both my mother and father were very upset. They advised me to give a reasonable excuse, such as that I could not join the club because I could not spare the time from my lessons. For a ten-year-old boy, this was not an easy situation to be in. I was living in two separate worlds. In one I had a family who were attached to traditional values and believed in God. On the other there was my school which was giving me an atheist education opposed to these values. If I chose to prefer one side, it meant I would be denying the other. My heart and mind told me that my parents were right and that my Communist teachers were wrong. So I would believe my mother and father and try to get round the people at school.'[17]

Ruzi could be a mischievous boy. His father had set up a small trapeze for him, attached to an apricot tree in the garden of their home. Ruzi used to swing from it and do acrobatics. One day he climbed the tree to pick apricots for some neighbourhood girls. But at the very top, he started to perform the acrobatics which he used to do on the trapeze below. Eventually he got tired and could only dangle from a high branch. The women who were watching at the foot of the tree thought he was going to fall and began screaming. One of them told Ruzi to grasp the branch he was hanging from with his legs, just as he did on the trapeze. Ruzi did what she suggested, managing to get on top of the branch with a nimble movement. After taking a deep breath, he laughed at the people down below him. This last feat was also part of the game: Ruzi had won the admiration of the little girls of the neighbourhood, but he also wanted to attract the attention of the women.

Like most children at that age, Ruzi was keen to dress well. His mother bought him a red winter jacket. One night when the house was covered in snow, he left the jacket outside in the garden. When he tried to put it on the next morning, he found that it was stiff with ice. Despite warnings from his mother, he put it on. Soon afterwards, he began to shiver with cold, but in order not to spoil his tough guy image, he did not take the jacket off in case anyone was watching. As soon as he left home, he took off the jacket and threw it into the house through a back window.

As he grew up, Ruzi tried hard to make sense of what was going on in politics. His mother and father were his main sources of information. But Ruzi also had a half-brother, Yoldash Kari, fifteen years older than himself, the child of Jamshid Ata's first wife, who had died after an illness. Yoldash Kari was tall, handsome, black-haired—a typical Uzbek youth. Like most of the well-educated young people of the time, he followed politics closely, and he explained the history of the country to Ruzi: what had happened in the past, how Turkestan had become a colony, and the need for liberation. The people had suffered for years in the fight for independence, and the men who carried out the October Revolution of 1917 had deceived them.[18]

Ruzi was still only ten years old, but he and his brother were able to discuss the contradictions between what his parents and elders told him and what he was taught at school. Slowly he began to grasp the meaning of what he was being told.

Red Years

When Ruzi was playing at home one day, he found a flag in his elder brother's bedroom. It wasn't the red flag he knew, with its sickle and crescent. He asked his brother about it. 'It's our flag,' Kari replied, meaning the flag of the people of Turkestan. 'But don't tell anyone about it. We would have big problems if they heard we had a flag like that here.' But when Ruzi kept on asking questions, Kari explained to him about the Turkestani republic which had been set up in Kokand immediately after the October Revolution. The flag belonged to that state.

CHILDHOOD IN TURKESTAN

From 4 to 8 April 1917, against the background of revolution throughout the Russian empire, a First Congress of the Muslims of Turkestan had met in Tashkent and chosen Mustafa Shokay as its president. At this gathering, the first national congress since the occupation of the country,[19] autonomy was declared for the people of Turkestan within the democratic Russian Federation. A congress in Kokand on 25 November 1917 set up a permanent assembly consisting of thirty-six Muslim and eighteen Russian members and established a twelve-member provisional government. On 27 November it proclaimed the National Autonomous Area of Turkestan.

The Red Army regarded this as a serious threat to Soviet rule. Forces composed of General Frunze's Red Guards and Armenian militia attacked Kokand on 14 February 1918.[20] After four days of street fighting, the new national government fell. Frunze's troops then carried out a large-scale massacre in the city, looting it and murdering around 50,000 civilians.

On 30 April 1918, another congress gathered in Tashkent, mostly composed of Russian Communists. It approved a resolution proclaiming the First Congress of April 1917 to be illegitimate and invalidating its decisions. On 5 May 1918, it proclaimed the foundation of the Turkestan Autonomous Soviet Socialist Republic. Thus Russian Communist rule began in place of Russian Tsarist rule.[21]

The fate of the Alash Orda government, which had been founded in Northern Turkestan (what is today Kazakhstan) in December 1917 and which also demanded autonomy, was no different. In January 1920 it was broken up by the forces of the Red Army. Thus government power in the north, too, passed into the hands of the Communists.[22]

The Communist regime in Russia proceeded mercilessly with military operations aimed at consolidating the former Tsarist colonies within the Soviet empire. An army commanded by Frunze occupied Bukhara at the start of September 1920 and replaced the khanate with the People's Republic of Bukhara. In October the same year, units of the Red Army entered Khiva and set up the Khwarezmian People's Republic in place of the khanate there. But all these actions were simply temporary solutions. The growing activities in both republics of nationalist intellectuals, known as Jadidists, made Moscow nervous. In September 1924 the Red Army launched a further operation against

Bukhara and Khwarezm. The two republics were abolished and their territory was shared out among other newly established Soviet republics.[23] The people of Turkestan saw that they would never obtain their rights by peaceful means and took up arms. The struggle dragged on until the middle years of the decade.

When Ruzi began school in 1923 the new regime was in control of most of the country. Most of his brother Yoldash Kari's older friends had taken to the mountains. They had refused to let him go with them as he was not old enough.

Young men from every household took part in the armed resistance. Prayers were said for them every night in their homes and, when news of deaths came through, families secretly read the Koran and prayed for their souls. Mothers who lost their sons wept soundless tears. One might say, 'I have lost my son. He is with the angels in God's sight. Tomorrow when I go there too in death, he will take my hands and take me through into the beautiful paradise where he now is.'[24]

On 13 June 1920 Lenin instructed the Turkestan Commission, headed by General Frunze, to divide Turkestan up into tribally based republics.[25] According to Stalin in his 1913 work on socialism, any community possessing a common language, geography, economic unity, and moral and cultural characteristics constituted a nation.[26] The people of Turkestan were a community with a shared language, a shared fatherland and economy, and shared cultural and moral values. Yet on 24 March 1924 the Central Committee of the Communist Party of the Soviet Union overruled its own principles and took a decision to break up Turkestan. It was applying the old imperialist principle of 'divide and rule'. Thus in 1925 the Soviet Republics of Uzbekistan and Turkmenistan were created, followed by the Soviet Republics of Tajikistan, Kyrgyzstan and Kazakhstan.

The years of civil war in Russia had been harsh. After the Soviets consolidated their rule and the war came to an end, a kind of calm reigned in the country, albeit temporary and imposed. During the years of the New Economic Policy, in an effort to diminish popular opposition to the regime, the Soviet government gave permission for its merchants and businessmen to engage in trade with neighbouring countries like Afghanistan, Iran and East Turkestan (today called Xinjiang, the Uyghur Autonomous Region of China).[27] Though Ruzi was still a small boy at this time, he was able to sense the relaxation when they went shopping in the market. The father of one of Ruzi's classmates, Tashpolat, traded the valuable silks of Margilan in East Turkestan, buying flocks of sheep there which he would bring home with the help of shepherds. Tashpolat was fond of jokes, cheerful and plump. He would tell Ruzi how his father had counted the money he made, coin by coin, saying to his wife, 'Madame, look: we're rich. We can make Uzbek pilaf every day from now on.'[28]

Tashpolat's uncle, Isakjan Halmat, was one of those who would frequently visit Ruzi's family home in those days to discuss politics. Another of Jamshid's friends was Safican Eke, who was extremely clever, well educated and fluent in Russian. He had had polio and so walked on crutches. Safican Eke closely followed developments in central Russia and Tashkent, and one day he said, 'Jamshid Bey, the abundance which exists in the country at the moment, the favourable economic situation, the calm environment, is not going to continue for very long. The Communists are implementing this new policy in order to pacify people and to get the rich to bring out the money they have been keeping hidden. This situation is going to end very soon. They will confiscate the goods and wealth of rich people. So be careful. Take precautions.'

Jamshid was a craftsman who was imbued with his family's long tradition of silk production. He understood that in the new system no possibility remained for doing business as an entrepreneur, but it would be to the regime's advantage for production to continue, and he was confident that his professional knowledge and expertise would be needed. He was quite right. Jamshid's success in the Margilan Silk Factory continued to the end of his life.

However, on this occasion he was quick to follow the advice of his far-sighted friend. He pulled down the guesthouse and workshop at his home. He did not trust Soviet safe-deposit boxes and banks and so he had an underground store constructed, where he concealed his most valuable silks, and covered it over with earth so that no one could detect it. Time proved Safican Eke right.[29] Soon after their conversation the homes of wealthy families began to be pillaged.

When the young people of Margilan got married, gold bracelets and necklaces would be given to the bride. If they were in financial need, the married couple would be able to sell part or all of these assets. The new regime was well aware of this tradition and resorted to every means it could to find out what gold, jewels or other valuables there were in people's homes. They even made use of small children to do this. Ruzi's teacher said one day, 'Come on, children, let's see whose mother has got the most jewellery! Everyone whose mother has got any gold, raise your hand.' The class was confused for a moment. Some pupils raised their hands.

Ruzi, who took in everything going on around him, kept his hand down and looked straight ahead without saying anything—but he felt bad, because his mother had once told him, 'Even if it means death, never tell a lie.' While he was wrestling with his feelings, he remembered another proverb which his mother had often told him: 'Tell the truth, even if you have a sword hanging over your neck. Liars leave no good reputation behind them and none of their works last.' At the last moment he raised his hand and said, 'My mother has a golden earring.' This way he had both told the truth and kept quiet about the bracelets and other gold jewellery in the house.

Soon afterwards, officials conducted raids on all their homes, acting on the information the children had given. They took all the jewellery they could get their hands on. But Ruzi's mother lost only her golden earring. All her other valuables were saved.[30]

The fate of Ruzi's brother was worse. In 1927 he had been working as a clerk in Uzbekistan's Ministry of Justice when he was arrested by NKVD men, the Soviet security police, and accused of being a pan-Turkist, a counter-revolutionary and a bourgeois nationalist. After a brief trial he was executed by firing squad.

News of his execution devastated both his father and Ruzi's mother, who had shown her stepchild even more affection than her own son. A sense of mourning enveloped their home. While everyone wept, the ten-year-old Ruzi wandered around, sharing his grief for his elder brother, whom he had loved so much and from whom he had learnt so many things, with his mother, father and sister, Shemsihan. His father called him over, telling him to come immediately. He took out a packet of cigarettes which a friend had brought him and gave it to his son. Then he filled up a glass with vodka and told Ruzi, 'Take out a cigarette and light it. Then drink this vodka to the bottom.' Ruzi was astonished and hesitated. But when his father said, 'Get on with it. Do what I tell you!' he lit a cigarette with difficulty and began to drink. The smoke made him cough and the vodka went to his head. Jamshid pressed his son to his chest and held his little hands. 'Neither I nor your late brother ever let either a cigarette or alcohol get into our mouths,' he said. 'Now, as your father, I am leaving you this lesson. If your elder brother had smoked cigarettes and drunk vodka, perhaps he would be alive today.' In this way Jamshid gave his one remaining son a symbolic but intense lesson that instilled in him a spirit of courage and resistance.[31] For the rest of his life, Ruzi never forgot the things that had taken place that night.

Contradictions

Ruzi found himself leading a double life from the day he started school. At school there was atheism, at home belief in God. Though he was only a child, Ruzi was certain that the love and faith of his father and mother represented the true reality. At home people talked with praise and wonder about the heroic exploits of those who had fought for the independence of Turkestan between 1918 and 1925. But in school not a word was spared to denounce their banditry and describe every single one of them as a thief and a robber. At home, the fighters who had been caught and executed by firing squad were regarded as martyrs and saints. At school, they were described as traitors, enemies of Communism, and agents of the capitalist states.

Ruzi's mind was shaped by these rival realities and at school he became a bit like an actor in a play. His real identity was the one he lived out at home, but he never slipped up at school; quite the contrary. He was successful and popular. This last feature attracted the attention of the school authorities and they registered him as a member of Komsomol, the Communist Party's youth wing. Before long, the administrators of the school and the Party selected him to be secretary of the school committee, and Ruzi continued to carry out this role until he left school in 1932, when he was fifteen. He was now no longer a child but a youth whose mind had already absorbed many things.[32]

For hundreds of years, the people of the Fergana valley had worked as farmers. There were irrigation canals in the valley that were 3,000 years old but still in working order. Soviet ideology had from the outset, however, regarded farmers as a threat to the regime, who were at risk of becoming bourgeois capitalists. The only way to overcome this threat was for agriculture to pass from the control of the bourgeoisie into that of the proletariat.[33] A programme was drawn up with this goal in mind. The first stage involved proclaiming most of the large land-owners to be enemies of the people and arresting them. Their estates were then distributed among landless peasants.

The condition of children whose family lands had been confiscated was pitiful. One day a child would arrive at school as a member of a wealthy and privileged family. The next, he or she would have fallen into the position of a child of an enemy of the regime and of the people. Ruzi would console these children, hug them and try to share their pain. After a while, these children would vanish from the school. Most of them, even at that age, moved to other Central Asian republics and tried to survive there under different names.[34]

In the second stage of the programme, the land was taken back from its new peasant owners and combined into collective farms known as *kolkhozes* and *sovkhozes*. The herds belonging to nomads were confiscated. Each nomad who had owned perhaps thousands of animals was now forced to live hand to mouth as the shepherd of his own former livestock. Kollektivatsiya, the policy of collectivisation instituted by Stalin at the end of the 1920s and continued during the 1930s, cost the lives of millions through hunger and poverty.[35] During these years, famine killed about eight million people in Central Asia.[36]

As Ruzi finished high school he stood on the threshold of a decision about his future. The Komsomol Committee of Margilan decided that he was to work in its Candidates for Pioneers section, preparing children to join the youth wing of the Communist Party. Even at that tender age, Ruzi had learnt about the need for secrecy and discretion, and the huge problems which careless talk could bring down on people's heads. As a requirement of his new job, he taught the children how to play games, but he also tried to instil in them, in a way they would understand, the moral education he had received at home.

Ruzi's work on the committee lasted a year, and at the end of it he had reached his decision. He wanted to study. He realised that the only way to stay afloat in this life was to get a good education and learn a decent occupation. He talked to his mother and father, obtained their consent, and then set off for Tashkent.[37]

STUDENT YEARS IN STALIN'S CENTRAL ASIA

Tashkent

Tashkent is a tree-lined city, one of the greenest in the world. The earliest settlement in the region was the town of Ming Urik, its name meaning 'a thousand plum trees', founded around 200 BC. Later it was called Shash, Chash and Shashkent. In the earliest dictionary of Turkish, the *Divanü Lugati'i Türk*, the town is called both Shash and Tashkend.

In AD 751 Tashkent was conquered by the Arabs. In the tenth century it belonged to Sassanid Iran and in the thirteenth and fourteenth centuries it lay inside the frontiers of the Turkish Karahanli state. At the end of the fourteenth century it became part of the Timurid empire and was one of its cultural and commercial centres. It was adorned with a wide variety of mosques, madrasas and caravanserais. Subsequently it was governed by the Turkish khanates of Central Asia.

As the khanate of Kokand was weakened by attacks from Tsarist Russia, Tashkent was annexed and made into the headquarters of the Russian governor-general appointed from St Petersburg. To the north, 25,000 kilometres away, lay Orenburg, the headquarters of the governor-general of the Steppes, and when a railway was constructed between Orenburg and Tashkent, the latter become one of the most important communication centres in Central Asia. After the October Revolution, Tashkent became the capital, first of the Turkestan Soviet

Socialist Republic, established within the Russian Federation in 1918, and then, from 1924, of the Uzbekistan Soviet Socialist Republic. Since the break-up of the Soviet Union in 1991 it has been the capital of an independent Uzbekistan.[1]

When Ruzi arrived, his wooden suitcase in his hand, to study in Tashkent in 1933, he was a youngster whose moustache had only just begun to sprout. He had grasped the nature of the Soviet system in outline. There was no free enterprise in the country. It was the state which set the rules for economic life. For that reason he wanted to study economics. Because he had finished school with excellent marks and was a good Komsomol member, he was accepted into the preparatory class of the Economic Planning Institute in the Technical School. With the help of family friends from Margilan who were living in Tashkent, he soon adjusted to the life of the big city.

The first chairman of the Praesidium of Uzbekistan, Yoldash Ahunbayev, was from Margilan too. He was a relatively uneducated ordinary worker by background, fatherly, good-hearted and much loved by the people. He was aware of what was going on but helpless to do anything about it. He knew and liked Jamshid Ata's handsome and clever son. However, Ahunbayev had a cross-eyed and rather plain niece whom he wanted Ruzi to marry. Every time he suggested this, Ruzi would excuse himself on grounds of illness or approaching examinations. But Ahunbayev was insistent. In the end, Ruzi found a solution. Although he was single, he begged another friend of his father's, 'Please tell Ahunbayev that I have a fiancée and that our families have agreed to our marriage and I cannot turn my back on her.' His helper did what was asked of him and the matter was closed.[2]

Kerim Gaybullayev, another family friend from Margilan, was the editor of and one of the writers for *Yash Leninji* (*Young Leninist*), a Tashkent newspaper. He showed great affection and friendship towards Ruzi and gave him a job on the newspaper. So Ruzi divided his days between classes, journalism and the Committee of Oktabryr (October) County in Tashkent. In the evenings, he went to chemistry courses at the Teacher Training Institute. Because he was a Party member, he was able to learn about what was happening in the country and in the rest of the world, while his work as a reporter enabled him to learn about local events.[3]

Every day, information arrived at the paper that someone had been arrested. False stories were published about how the enemies of the people had committed crimes against the Party and the regime. As a reporter on *Young Leninist*, Ruzi certainly knew that at night the NKVD, the Soviet secret police, were arresting many intellectuals. But it was impossible to report objective news about these arrests. They had to be described in exactly the form put out by the Party's press office. Even a hint of criticism would be a death warrant for both the writer and the editor of the paper.[4]

The Teahouse

One activity which Ruzi particularly enjoyed during his Tashkent years was meeting up with his friends in a teahouse and eating Uzbek pilaf with them which had been prepared for the occasion.[5] Teahouses in Central Asia are called *gephanes*, which means roughly 'promise houses'. In Uzbekistan they are the home of a tradition of repartee called *askiye*, in which two or more people compete in talking about a topic, either agreed in advance or picked at random. The word *askiye* is a mangled form of the plural of the Arabic word for 'clever'—*zeki*—and means 'adept in the use of words, knowledgeable and sharp-witted'. Proficient *askiye* players are expected to come up with quips and instant appropriate replies, picking up on any humour, irony and metaphor in their opponent's words. An *askiye* player must try to find a double meaning in every utterance and give a reply which responds to both meanings. For example, if every grain of the Uzbek pilaf was truly perfect, someone might say, 'The food has gone down well.' The rival might immediately respond, 'Where has the food sat down? Has one of the cooking pots got up and gone somewhere else?' The conversation would then continue amid laughter. On such nights, numerous poems are recited and music is played.

Mamurjon Uzakov, the former butcher's apprentice whom Ruzi's father had taken into the household many years before, was now one of Uzbekistan's most famous singers. He loved Ruzi like a little brother. Some evenings he would come to the teahouse and perform Turkestani Uzbek music. He might sing some of the countless songs which Abdulkadir Meragi composed and performed in the palace of Shahrukh, the successor of Timur in the fifteenth century, followed by works of other Uzbek musicians down to the present day.[6] Such nights were deeply emotional and romantic.[7]

Abdulhamit Cholpan, the most popular poet in Turkestan in the early 1930s, had just been arrested and his poems were being read in the teahouses. In the mid-1930s, arrests and killings had begun of poets who had formerly belonged to the Jadid movement and were now members of the Communist Party, on the pretext that they were enemies of the people. Reading out the works of a poet who had been arrested could lead in turn to the arrest of the reader. But after a few glasses of vodka during evenings in the teahouses, the anger in everyone's heart started to gush out.

On such evenings, bitter events were recounted. Tales were told of intellectuals who had been sent when young to be educated in Germany, with money scraped painfully together in the hope that they would acquire new knowledge and return to help their country advance and grow rich. Going to Berlin, one of the most developed capital cities in Europe, from a tiny town in the colonial lands of Central Asia, from a culture which still had the characteristics of a medieval agricultural society, they had been plunged into the midst of modern Western civilisation. There they had completed their undergraduate degrees and gone on to take doctorates. Finally, declaring that their countries needed electricity, they had come back to Tashkent.[8]

In 1923 there had been sixty students from Turkestan studying in Germany, both boys and girls. Eleven of them had been sent there by the Turkestan Soviet Socialist Republic and forty-nine by the People's Republic of Bukhara.[9] Sadly, the story of these young people who carried the heavy burden of being the hope of their country did not finish as well as it had begun. Most became heroes of a great tragedy. Towards the end of the 1920s, the authorities' view of these students began to alter and some who had returned home for the summer holidays were refused permission to go back to Germany. The others completed their education abroad, despite a variety of problems, material hardships and the loss of their scholarships. Most of them then returned to their countries.

Abdulvahap Muradi was the first to return home. He came back to Uzbekistan with his German wife, Marta, and their two children and started to teach in an agricultural school. In November 1929 Munevver Kari and thirty-eight other leading figures of the Turkestan Jadid movement were arrested. Almost all of them received jail terms. Muradi was imprisoned in the Tashkent Prison for a time. Later a Turkestani refugee in Afghanistan called Ferganali Nasrullah would say that he had last seen him in the Solovki exiles' camp.[10]

Some of those who had gone to Germany did not return. They would play an important part in Ruzi's later life outside the Soviet Union and would work with him during his years in Germany and the United States.

Conflicts of Ideas

The situation in the country was oppressive, grave and alarming. In 1933 Ruzi had entered the Technical School after successfully passing a difficult exam. But the following year, the school moved to Samarkand and Ruzi did not wish to go there. He enrolled instead in the Tashkent Pedagogy Institute. At the same time he was attending courses organised by the Komsomol Central Committee.

One of the best features of the Soviet system at this time was the importance it attached to art, even though every branch of art was used for propaganda. In Tashkent there were various theatres and musical groups.[11] Ruzi never missed a concert or play. He had friends among the Uzbek dancing girls who performed in the musicals and among the actors in the theatres. He would often meet up with them and go to their homes, and would watch the girls with admiration as they danced, or grow emotional at the soulful Uzbek songs.

Ruzi had at this time three close friends, people with whom he got on well, shared all their griefs and exchanged views with them on politics. They even discussed anti-revolutionary ideas. The oldest of these friends was Usman Aliyev, who was twenty-seven years old in 1934. The second was Munevverhan Tashojayev, who was twenty-five, and the third was Sultan Aliyev, who was twenty-three and had been educated in Russian schools and trained as a journalist. Sultan was a writer on the newspaper which was published twice a month at the Margilan Silk Factory. He lived by himself in a house close to the factory. When Ruzi was in Margilan, they would often meet at Sultan's home and have long discussions.[12]

In the summer months, Ruzi would return to the family home in Margilan. He never stayed idle there. He tutored children in biology, chemistry and mathematics, and he took care never to miss a meeting of the members of the Komsomol Committee in Margilan.

At the beginning of March 1934, the intellectuals of Margilan held their annual general conference. The meeting was chaired by a member of the town's Communist Party Central Committee called Gaforov, and those attending included the wife of Chairman Pukin of the Margilan State Political Affairs Organisation (the secret police); Munevverhan Tashojayev, the headmaster of the Margilan Lycée; the deputy headmaster, Usman Aliyev; and, youngest of all, Ruzi. Ruzi's confidant, Sultan Aliyev, was also a member, but on this occasion he was away working in another town. During the meeting, a fierce debate broke out.[13]

The Sixteenth Congress of the Communist Party of the Soviet Union in 1930 had resolved that socialism should be introduced into every part of the social order throughout the entire country. Ever since then, this resolution had been frequently repeated. At the meeting in Margilan, Ruzi's friend Usman posed a question: 'According to the teachings of Marx and Lenin, socialism in human history is a stage which has to follow the capitalist period. But Uzbekistan and other Central Asian countries have never lived through a period of capitalism. So how are we going to make the transition from feudalism to socialism?' The question caught the interest of the meeting and an intense discussion followed.

Ruzi had encountered this question in the works of Atajan Hashim, who had been educated in Moscow and Leningrad and had a profound knowledge of Marxism-Leninism. He and two other of his friends now supported Usman in arguing that socialism could only be established after capitalism, using examples from the writings of Marx and Lenin. Mrs Pukin fiercely protested at this. 'No,' she said, 'it is possible to move from feudalism to socialism without a capitalist society being established. Yes, it is possible because the peoples of Central Asia have the heroic and conscious Russian proletariat at their side. The peoples of Central Asia will go straight from feudalism to socialism with the help and leadership of the Russian proletariat.' The meeting ended with the disagreement unresolved.[14]

The Approach of the Terror

The 1930s were years of disaster for Central Asia, just as they were for the whole of the USSR. After Lenin's death in 1924, Stalin succeeded him as head of the Communist Party and moved to concentrate all powers in his own hands. This exacerbated conflicts over the nature of the new regime within the senior echelons of the party and beyond. Wartime Communism, the New Economic Policy which followed it, and the introduction of industrialisation and collectivisation provoked not only disputes among Party members but also strong reactions from ordinary people, leading to revolts in many places. Stalin brutally repressed all opposition, whether from within the regime or outside it. The overwhelming majority of former Bolshevik leaders were either neutralised or liquidated on the grounds that they were bourgeois agents and enemies of the people. Those who remained would be accused of offences like assassination or conspiracy with Western powers in the Moscow Trials of 1936–8.[15]

On 1 December 1934, Ruzi was back in the teahouse with his friends, preparing the ingredients they had bought for an Uzbek pilaf. They were deep in conversation, finding some relief from the oppressive political atmosphere of the country, but when it was time for the news, they all turned their attention to the radio. The presenter excitedly announced that Sergei Mironovich Kirov, a member of the Politburo (the supreme policy-making body of the Soviet Communist Party) and first secretary of the Leningrad Provincial Party,[16] had been murdered. This was completely unexpected news, but no other details were given. Everyone in the teahouse was astonished. Ruzi had closely read all the articles published about Kirov after the Seventeenth Congress of the Communist Party. He was a very talented speaker, a leader who was popular with Soviet intellectuals, and regarded as a potential successor to Stalin. The next day official statements by the Communist Party's Central Committee were published in *Pravda* and other papers, declaring that Kirov had been murdered by 'the enemies of the working class'.[17]

Research has now established that Kirov was probably killed on the direct orders of Stalin himself, but the assassination was used by Stalin as a pretext to eliminate all his opponents and to launch an era of terror and extermination in the Soviet Union.[18] The day after Kirov's murder, Stalin had the Soviet government approve new decisions about political proceedings, investigations and court affairs in the Soviet republics. On 2 December 1934, the following resolution was published in *Pravda*, bearing the signatures of the chairman of the Central Executive Committee of the Soviet Union, Mikhail Kalinin, and its secretary, Avel Safronovich Enukidze:

1. Investigation of suspects will be completed within ten days.
2. Suspects will be informed of the accusations against them at a session.
3. Their trial will begin forthwith.
4. There will be no permission for complaints or protests.
5. Sentences passed will be carried out immediately.[19]

After the murder of Kirov, thousands of people were arrested across the Soviet Union by the NKVD, although Ruzi and his friends, like the rest of the population in general, had no idea of the extent of these actions. Those detained included Grigory Zinoviev, one of the leading personalities of the 1917 October Revolution; Lev Kamenev, deputy prime minister in the Soviet government; and twelve other Party leaders. In 1936 they were tried by a court presided over by Vasily Ulrich, chairman of the USSR's Military Supreme Court, while the case against them was made by Andrei Vyshinsky, the USSR's chief prosecutor. It was announced that all the accused had confessed to being counter-revolutionaries and enemies of the people. Death sentences were passed and instantly carried out.[20]

The Stalinist dictatorship had descended like a nightmare on the entire Soviet Union. Following the trial, Emintay Muminov, the Margilan correspondent of *Young Leninist*, wrote an article about the intellectuals' meeting two years earlier in the Margilan Komsomol Centre at which the progress of socialism had been so fiercely debated. He launched a full-scale attack on Ruzi and his friends, accusing Munevverhan Tashojayev and Usman Aliyev of being 'brought up amid a bourgeois mentality and opposed to socialism' and denouncing them all as enemies of the people. The response in Margilan was swift, and passionate debates and exchanges of views took place. The outcome was that Ruzi and his two friends were thrown out of the Komsomol.

Sultan Aliyev escaped that fate because he had missed the meeting, although he was actually the most opinionated of the three, and had he been present he would undoubtedly have argued with the wife of Chairman Pukin and been expelled too. Munevverhan and Usman lost their jobs. Ruzi knew that he was in great danger too.[21] The Great Purge was now under way and it was quite routine for people to lose those dearest to them in a single night.

Ruzi's friend Munevverhan was a typical Uzbek youngster, quite short and stocky, black-haired and fair-skinned. His eyes were a mixture of green and brown, and the shape of his face was very regular. He was five years older than Ruzi. They felt great mutual respect and friendship. As two young intellectuals, they had often discussed the colonial system that existed in their country and the state of the economy, and exhausted themselves talking about the future. One of their favourite activities was to go for walks and talk together in the orchards far outside Margilan. Munevverhan's father had died long before. His mother was the head of the family and had given him an education, but only with great difficulty.[22] Their house was well maintained and spacious, set in a wonderful green garden.

Munevverhan and Ruzi had to rejoin the Komsomol at all costs, otherwise they stood no chance of getting a job, and so they wrote a petition to the Margilan Town Committee asking to be readmitted. They said that they were faithful to the principles of the Communist Party and offered their apologies if they had made a mistaken interpretation while defending the views of Marx and Lenin. It was a sort of self-criticism. The committee replied unfavourably and told them that they had been expelled a second time from the organisation. The decision taken in Margilan was endorsed by the Uzbekistan Central Committee in Tashkent. Ruzi and Munevverhan knew that Moscow was now the only place where the problem could be resolved, and so Ruzi set out for Moscow.[23]

This was the first time in his life that Ruzi had set foot in the town where the Russian tsars had lived. He made his way to the office of the Central Organisation for the Soviet Union, to which the organisations of the individual Soviet republics were attached, and handed his and Munevverhan's petition to officials of the Central Committee. The officials interviewed Ruzi, asking questions about Marxism-Leninism.

The result was that the petition was accepted and the two of them were once again members of the Komsomol.

Ruzi was overjoyed. He had solved not only his own problem but also Munevverhan's. He stayed for a week in the city and for the first time in his life he watched a performance at the Bolshoi Theatre. This excursion made his already considerable love for the arts grow further.[24]

Usman Aliyev had said that he would solve his problem in a different way. He visited various contacts in Tashkent, seeing senior Party and state officials, and was eventually appointed headmaster of a lycée in the rayon (county) of Kattakorgan in the province of Samarkand. He had not made any effort to get his Komsomol membership restored.

In May 1936, an article appeared in *Margilan Truth*, a local newspaper, headlined 'Usman Aliyev and His Tyro Supporters'. The article claimed that that during his student years, Usman had been a member of a secret anti-Communist society of patriotic Uzbek youths opposed to the Soviets. He was said to have poisoned the minds of youths like Ruzi, Munevverhan and Sultan Aliyev with pan-Turkist, pan-Islamic, anti-Communist and nationalist ideas. After working for eight months at Kattakorgan, Usman returned to Margilan to see his wife and one-year-old baby. The night he arrived, his house was raided by NKVD agents and he was taken to an unknown destination. Ruzi and his friends heard no further news about either Usman or his baby daughter, until years later they learned that he had been sent to a concentration camp in Siberia.[25]

They had been a group of four close-knit young friends. They had talked among themselves about political wrongs, unjust arrests, the transformation of Tsarist colonialism into Soviet colonialism, food shortages, and the future of their country, but they had never entertained any idea of setting up a secret organisation.

A short time after the arrest of Usman Aliyev, Sultan said to Ruzi one evening, 'Ruzi, they are closing in on me. My father was Madaminbek,[26] a hero in the fight against the Soviets and the Red Army. I am his son—so the NKVD suspects me and is following me. I think it would be a good idea to disappear for a while.' The next day, Sultan moved to Tajikistan and lived there for two years. Later, when the Soviet government issued a ruling to the effect that children were not responsible for the crimes committed by their parents, he returned to Margilan, shortly after Ruzi had been drafted into the army. He became the chief secretary of *Margilan Truth*. After he had worked there for a short time, he too was called up to serve in the army. Thereafter Sultan and Ruzi kept in touch with each other by letter until the Second World War began and they lost contact. When, after an interval of fifty-two years, Ruzi was finally able to return to his homeland, he came across some connections of Sultan Aliyev and asked them what had happened to him, but they had no information. Had Ruzi's good-hearted, good-looking and intellectual friend lost his life at Stalingrad? Or in the Far East? He was never to learn.

Another of Ruzi's friends, his mentor Kerim Gaybullayev, the editor of *Young Leninist*, would suffer a fate similar to that of many intellectuals. One night towards the end of the 1930s, NKVD agents raided his home. (As with all totalitarian systems, the Soviet intelligence services chose to operate at night, in order both to conceal their murders and to provoke greater fear. Ruzi would later observe the Gestapo using identical methods in Nazi Germany.) Gaybullayev was arrested and interrogated under torture for many days. Eventually he was sent under guard to Moscow, where he was accused of belonging to secret organisations set up by the former prime minister of Uzbekistan, Feyzullah Hojayev, and the first secretary of the Communist Party of Uzbekistan, Akmal Ikramov. He was charged with being a bourgeois agent and an enemy of the people. He denied the accusations and was murdered in prison. His family was told that he had died there from an illness; he had, indeed, been ill as a result of the severe torture he had undergone.[27]

The Terror in Uzbekistan

In February 1937, Stalin made a speech to the Central Committee of the Soviet Communist Party in which he declared that the time had come to purge the Party and the state of Trotskyists, nationalists, enemies of the people and groups opposed to the working class.[28] Arrests followed all over the Soviet Union, including of course in Uzbekistan.

In May that year a ten-day festival of Uzbek art took place in Moscow. Uzbekistan's most famous artists and performers went to take part in it, but no sooner had they arrived than NKVD agents expelled some of them from the city on the grounds that after the October

Revolution they had been involved in the armed struggle against the Soviets in Turkestan. Those treated in this way included the musician Yusufjan Shakirov, the singer Hafiz Jorahan Sultanov and his two most important musical assistants. When the musicians got back to Tashkent, NKVD agents arrested the husband of Uzbekistan's most famous national dancer, Mukarram Turgunbayeva, at the railway station. He was accused of being a member of a secret organisation set up by Uzbek patriots three years earlier to work against the Soviet Union and charged with selling its anti-Soviet and anti-Communist magazine, *Kalamush (Mole)*. Turgunbayeva's right to work as a teacher was revoked and she was exiled to Siberia. Two years later she found a way to get back to Uzbekistan, and returned there, sick and wounded. Her friends in Tashkent took care of her and later she was given a post as an adviser in a musical theatre called Mukimi.[29]

In June, at the Seventh Congress of the Communist Party of Uzbekistan in Tashkent, Feyzullah Hojayev was accused of being a religious reactionary who adhered to Islamic customs. The Komsomol's first secretary, Israil Artukov, described how Hojayev had buried his brother Ibad with Islamic funeral rites, inscribing a star and crescent and an Arabic formula on his gravestone and giving, as was the custom, a gold watch as a present to the imam who had washed his brother's body. Then the chairman of the Uzbek NKVD declared that Hojayev was a traitor to the Party, the Revolution and the country and an enemy of the people. Hojayev had been prime minister and foreign minister of the People's Republic of Bukhara, but now no one could say a word in his defence. He was not re-elected as a member of the Central Committee, and he was dismissed from the presidency of the Soviet Council of People's Commissars.[30]

After these actions had been taken against him, Hojayev went to Moscow, intending to talk to Stalin. As soon as he arrived, he phoned Mikhail Kalinin, the nominal Soviet head of state, to seek his assistance. Kalinin told him to relax in his hotel and said that he would try to arrange an interview with Stalin as soon as possible. Three days passed, but the interview never took place. During the third night, Hojayev was arrested by the NKVD.[31]

On 1 September 1937 an article appeared in *Pravda*, written by a former NKVD agent called Alexandrovsky now working as a journalist in Tashkent, which accused Uzbekistan's first secretary, Akmal Ikramov, of being an enemy of the people and of sheltering nationalists. On 3 September a second article claimed that Ikramov had protected nationalist writers including Osman Nasir, Abdulhamid Cholpan, Aybek (Musa Tash Muhammedoghlu) and many others. Three days later there was a further article, proclaiming that Ikramov was one of the greatest enemies of the Soviet Union and the Communist Party. A day or two after this, Ikramov was summoned to Moscow. He hoped that he would be able to talk directly to Stalin. Ikramov had been a recipient of the Lenin Medal and for years he had been praised to the skies as Stalin's most successful pupil in Central Asia, but now his star was waning. He was not received by Stalin and had to return to Tashkent. On 25 September 1937, the Central Committee in Moscow held an extraordinary meeting at which he was fiercely criticised and then expelled. As soon as news of this decision reached Tashkent, Ikramov was arrested by an NKVD officer in the offices of the Uzbekistan Central Committee. Colleagues of his who were in the building ran away, and were pursued and arrested by NKVD agents. There was total uproar. The secretary of the Kokand City Communist Party was apprehended while trying to escape dressed as a woman. Almazov, the secretary-general of the Margilan Communist Party, was arrested at the town's Garchakov railway station.

Akmal Ikramov was the son of a well-known Muslim cleric in Tashkent; Feyzullah Hojayev came from one of the leading families in all Central Asia. Both were sentenced to death after a show trial in Moscow from 2 to 13 March 1938, along with other former Party dignitaries such as Nikolai Bukharin and Alexei Rykov. Their personal wealth was confiscated and the death sentences were carried out immediately.[32]

Ruzi was twenty-one years old at the time. He followed the trials of Hojayev and Ikramov closely in the Soviet newspapers each day. Even decades later, he could not get out of his mind a question posed to Bukharin by the Soviet chief prosecutor, Vyshinsky, and the answer it had received. The question and answer demonstrated the degree to which the Moscow Trials were faked. Vyshinsky asked Bukharin, 'You travelled three times to Tashkent in order to rest. But your real purpose was not to have a holiday. Feyzullah Hojayev and Akmal Ikramov had secret anti-Soviet organisations and you knew about them. Did you try to unite both these organisations?' Bukharin's reply was an abject confession: 'Akmal Ikramov had an organisation called National Unity and Feyzullah Hojayev had one called National Independence. These two young men did not trust each other and so they had set up two separate organisations. I talked to them and was successful in getting them to unite.'

Ruzi and his friends were astonished when they heard of this confession. Until the National Autonomous Area of Turkestan established in Kokand in 1917 was overthrown by the Red Army, there had been only one group fighting against the Soviets in Central Asia, the organisation called National Unity. After the overthrow of the national government and the massacre carried out by the Soviets at Kokand, it changed its name to National Independence. Mustafa Shokay had personally announced this at the time. 'The National Autonomous Area of Turkestan has been destroyed by the Soviet army and so the meaning of autonomy has also disappeared. We have now only one aim: National Independence, complete independence.'[33] The Moscow court had mixed some genuine details into a contrived scenario in order to condemn the accused men to death.

Before Ikramov and Hojayev went into court in Moscow, they were placed on open trial in two towns, Margilan and Yengiyol, in Uzbekistan. Ruzi followed the proceedings closely, attending every session of the trial in Margilan.[34] Many of the town's leading Party figures had been in the dock there: the local secretary-general, Almazov; the chairman of the Executive Committee, Haydar Aliyev; the deputy secretary of the Margilan Communist Party, Tormozov; and the deputy general manager of the Margilan Textiles Factory and chairman of the collective farm, Yagajpalvan. The last of these was a tall, handsome man with the figure of an athlete. He had won the wrestling championship for Central Asia and received a gold medal. He was thus a popular hero. The chief prosecutor of the Soviet Republic of Uzbekistan led the case against them. His indictment was read out over the first two days. He launched a violent attack against the defendants: they were enemies of the people, pan-Turkists, pan-Islamists and bourgeois agents. On the third day, the prosecutor cross-examined the Party secretary, Almazov, asking him what had been his aim, and that of the secret organisation he founded. In a calm voice, Almazov replied by criticising the Soviet system. He concluded by saying that they had aimed at independence, peace and prosperity. Prosperity could never be achieved through despotism and a market economy should be established in the country.[35]

The court ordered the execution of four of the accused, while Tormazov, the one Russian among them, was sentenced to ten years' hard labour. All their property was confiscated. A crowd several thousand strong gathered in support of their heroes, crying: 'May they go to heaven in the next world! Amen!' The courthouse was surrounded by armed NKVD personnel and soldiers brought in from the provincial capital, and the four condemned men were put into a prison vehicle, driven to the capital and executed by firing squad just before dawn. Their families were not even allowed to take their bodies.[36]

Farewell to His Father

The year 1939 turned out to be one in which Ruzi lost many people in his life. He began to ask himself whether some day he too would be taken away at night by NKVD agents, sentenced to death in front of a mock court and then liquidated. What would be his fate?

In May that year he learnt that his father, who still lived in Margilan, had suffered a serious heart attack. The news made him extremely worried and he returned home without delay.[37] The summer heat was just beginning and the town was at the height of its spring beauty.

The doctors were doing all they could for Jamshid, but the medical resources of those days were limited. They wanted him to continue being treated in hospital, but he insisted on going home. He felt he needed the tender care which Tajinissa would give him and the warm and loving atmosphere he would find there.[38] Around the same time Ruzi moved back to Margilan and found a job as the head of the cultural section of a large transport company, besides taking on some teaching. He thus had the chance to have long conversations with his father at the family home. Jamshid Ata gave him advice which he would never lose sight of in later life and, as if trying to engrave his words on his son's brain, he linked each precept to an Uzbek proverb. One of these, intended to show the importance of both patriotism and hard work, ran: 'The happiness of a homeland is a throne for those who work hard.' Then he would say that it was necessary to be friendly to everyone and to like people without making distinctions. With this he recited: 'Receiving one person as a guest is better than a thousand journeys to Mecca.' A discourse about the truth would end with: 'A liar is not a human being; telling lies is not something for people who would be glorious.' 'If someone bows their head in front of you,' he would say, 'then bow yours too until it touches the ground. If someone raises up his head arrogantly and proudly in front of you, then raise your own head up until it touches the sky.' His father was trying to attach these Uzbek sayings to Ruzi's ears as firmly as earrings.

Jamshid had been educated according to the Sufi morality of Central Asia and he advised his son to be manly, brave and generous, to keep his word and be truthful. Once he enquired, 'My son, do you want me to tell you what the highest morality is?' He continued, 'If your principle of life is doing good to others at every opportunity, forget your good action the moment you have done it. If you don't, it will cease to be good. But if someone else does something good to you, don't forget it as long as you live, and try to do something good for them every time you get an opportunity. Those who forget good actions done to them are disloyal. Zahir-ud-Din Muhammad Babur says, "There is no good in a disloyal person. And there is no loyalty in a worthless person."'[39]

On the eleventh night after he had arrived back in Margilan, Ruzi's mother told him, 'I am preparing *mantı* for dinner this evening.[40] We will eat it together, and then after dinner your father wants to have a conversation with you about something.' Tajinissa was an excellent cook of all the traditional Uzbek dishes and the *mantı* was magnificent, but Jamshid ate only two pieces, observing his son's hearty appetite with pleasure. When the dinner was over, he began, 'Ruzi, my dear boy, we came into this world as Muslims and, please God, we shall go to him as Muslims.' He went on: 'This world is like an inn with two doors. We go in through one and out through the other. We do not know how long we are going to stay here. It is God who assigns that. But each of us takes this world on trust. No one can know what is going to happen tomorrow. I know that these times we are now in are extremely delicate and difficult. When I die, do not feel any anxiety but carry out all the observances of our religion, put me in my grave wrapped in my shroud, and do so reading the Koran and following the Islamic rituals. Do not hesitate. Allah will be your helper.'

Ruzi was overcome by emotion and asked his father why he was talking like that. 'I hope you are going to live for many more years and we shall have lots more pleasant days together,' he said. Jamshid looked Ruzi tenderly in the face and smiled. 'Let's hope it will be as you say, my son.' That day Ruzi realised that his father had truly lost his strength and that his death was not far off. The twenty-two years of his own life passed before his eyes like a film strip. His brother, Yoldash Kari, came into his mind. Back in January 1924 he had been a member of the official Uzbek delegation from Tashkent which had gone to Moscow for Lenin's funeral. On his return he had brought his little brother Ruzi a toy pistol. At that moment, all Ruzi's memories of his father and his elder brother suddenly came alive.[41]

At half past seven in the morning after they had that last evening meal together, Jamshid died. Ruzi carried out his father's will exactly as he had specified. The funeral *namaz*[42] was performed in Margilan's Kalenderhane Mosque and then the Koran was recited and Jamshid was buried according to Islamic practice.[43]

Islamic custom also specifies that two weeks after the burial ceremony, a dinner should be given for relatives, friends and neighbours, the Koran should be recited and the *Fatiha* prayer read out for the soul of the deceased person. The day before this ceremony was to take place in Jamshid's home, his friend Ibrahim Ahunbayev, the headmaster of the Margilan High School and one of the town's best-known Communists, unexpectedly turned up at the house. As soon as he had finished the glass of tea that he was offered, Ahunbayev said, 'Ruzi, according to what I hear from your sister, Shemsihan, you are going to have a traditional religious ceremony here tomorrow to mourn your father's death. If you will listen to me, don't attend this ceremony. Let the women of the family handle it. I will come here early tomorrow morning and take you off to the centre of Fergana and we can spend the day there together.'

The next day, Ruzi's maternal uncle hosted the ceremony, while Ruzi and Ahunbayev went off to Fergana together. The following day he learned from his sister that the president of the women's branch of the local Komsomol Committee had passed the entire day in the teahouse next door to their home, together with a young man. They had been stationed there in order to see who took part in the ceremony.

Not long afterwards, an article about Ruzi appeared in the *Margilan* newspaper. It claimed that Ruzi was religious and old-fashioned and that he had been influenced by his reactionary mother, who was attached to religious traditions.[44] Ruzi thought that a new investigation into him was about to be launched, but what he expected did not come about. In the years after the Revolution, many intellectuals who had belonged to the Jadid movement joined the Communist Party in order to try to serve their country. Most of them had lost their lives in the arrests and liquidations which followed the murder of Kirov, but there were still some left in the senior echelons of the Party. Ahunbayev was one of these, and by preventing Ruzi from attending the ceremony for his father he had saved his life.[45]

Within three months of his father's death, Ruzi was called up to serve in the army.[46]

3

RUZI IN THE RED ARMY

Off to War

In August 1939 Jamshid's death still felt very recent and Ruzi was now the mainstay of the family. His mother and sister both looked at him with tearful eyes. His mother would put her arms round him, sit him down beside her, and say, 'We have only just buried your father. No good has come to us from this godless Soviet state. They slaughtered your fine elder brother. What fault did he have apart from loving his own country? And now they are going to make you into a Red Army soldier and put a gun into your hand and perhaps they will pour out orders to you to shoot your own people. My son, never do anything wrong. Never forget that you are a child of these lands. I am going to beg God every day to keep you alive and ensure that one day you return to your country safe and sound. You are Ruzi, the son of Jamshid Bey. So go, my son, do what you know to be right and what you believe.' Ruzi tried to console his mother, telling her that she should not be upset or worry about him. The next day he presented himself at the Margilan Red Army Command.[1]

He passed a tough medical inspection which established that there was no physical reason debarring him from military service. So now he was a soldier of the Red Army. Five months' compulsory training followed in the Red Army camps in Margilan—marching, physical exercise and then firing drills. The smell of war was in the air. The officer and NCOs training the new soldiers frequently reminded them that they should learn everything properly, because in war even a small mistake can cost you your life. 'The battlefield is very different from the training field,' they would say.[2]

On 23 August 1939, Joachim von Ribbentrop, the Nazi German foreign minister, and Vyacheslav Molotov, the Soviet foreign minister, signed a non-aggression pact guaranteeing that if Germany went to war with Poland and the Allies, the Soviet Union would remain neutral, and that should the USSR regain the lands lost in the First World War, Germany would not oppose this.[3] On 1 September the armies of Nazi Germany, equipped with the most advanced and lethal weaponry of the time, attacked Poland. Thus the Second World War began.

On 2 January 1940, the railway station at Margilan resembled a scene from Armageddon. Ruzi's basic training had finished the previous day. Now hundreds of young soldiers from Margilan, Tashlak, Fergana and other towns, youths whose moustaches had only recently started to sprout, were at the station waiting to be taken to different lands thousands of kilometres away. Their relatives had come to the station to say goodbye to their sons and brothers, knowing that it might be the last time they would see them.[4]

Ruzi's eyes strained to see his mother and sister and his other relatives. He could see them searching for him too. One of his male relatives managed to push his way through the crowd and pass Ruzi a package. 'Take it, your mother sent it. You can eat it on the way.' It contained *samsa* (a dry pasty), *kazı* (a sausage made from horsemeat), shelled walnuts, almonds, raisins and other provisions. Ruzi's eyes met his mother's. Though he was some distance from her, he could see that she was crying, but she smiled and waved, trying to give her son courage and hide her tears from him. Ruzi waved back. From that day onwards he would frequently see his mother—but only in dreams.

When Ruzi returned to Margilan in 1992, his sister Shemsihan told him that right up until her death in September 1968, his mother would pray for him every day, and that, although she had not had any news of him for years, she believed that her son was alive, happy and successful.[5]

Odessa

The train whistled as it slowly came into the station. Most of its carriages were wagons used for transporting livestock and so had windows high up at the corners. They were each equipped with makeshift wooden bunks. Soldiers were put into the wagons in groups of thirty. Thus began a twelve-day journey through the steppes of Central Asia. The doors were locked from the outside and only opened at mealtimes. After water and food was handed out, five or ten minutes' leave was given to have a breath of air outside and go to the toilet. Then the soldiers were locked up again inside the wagons.[6]

Along the way, some of the soldiers grumbled and asked why they were locked in. Were they prisoners or animals? One of Ruzi's group, a Russian who was still only a boy, cried out, 'Man, the people travelling with us are mostly Uzbeks and Muslims. They are more dangerous than either prisoners or animals. That's why they are locking us in.' Another Russian youth got up and turned to the one who had spoken. 'Don't be impudent. Shut your mouth, or I'll break the filthy thing for you. We are all passengers going on the same journey and we will all share the same fate.' Ruzi was moved by the young Russian's words and went up to him and embraced him. 'Don't be sorry,' he said. 'We have a saying: There is man and there is the semblance of a man; a donkey is better than him.' Ruzi's remarks lightened the atmosphere and there were snorts of laughter in the wagon.[7]

In harsh circumstances people sometimes manage to overcome things that would usually seem impossible. During that long journey, one of the Russian youths put together a musical instrument rather like a balalaika while one of the Uzbeks constructed another stringed instrument resembling a dutar or saz. Songs were sung in Uzbek and Russian and the boys danced their national dances.[8]

At the end of the twelfth day, the train stopped at Torvarniy Station in Odessa, where some of the soldiers, including Ruzi, disembarked. They had not been able to wash for twelve days and there had been no toilets in the wagons, so that anyone who was caught short had to relieve himself inside. The soldiers stank so badly that they almost fainted at their own smell. The next day they were taken to the local Turkish baths. They were each given a haircut and issued with underwear, clothes and shoes. The clothes might have been worn before, but they were clean and ironed.[9]

A captain interviewed the soldiers one by one to establish their level of education and abilities. At school Ruzi's special interests had been in mathematics, physics and chemistry. The army officials chose him along with a Russian youth from Fergana to study defence against chemical weapons. For three weeks, they had full-time courses in a building beside the Odessa Artillery School. Ruzi followed the lessons with interest. At the end of the third week they got permission to go into the city escorted by a senior soldier, and soon after that they were allowed to go into town by themselves. But now their real military service began. There were adventures lying in wait for Ruzi in Odessa.[10]

Before long Ruzi met a lot of his fellow countrymen in Odessa, most of whom had been in the army for more than two years. All the Uzbeks would gather in the coffee houses and chat, quenching their longing for home. Some of the Uzbek soldiers in the Red Army had come from villages or collective farms. They were luckless young men who did not speak Russian and their situation was not good. Russian soldiers constantly bullied them and insulted them, calling them Asians or 'black heads' or *Natsmen* (members of a national minority). The Uzbeks also complained that when food packets arrived from home, they were immediately stolen.[11]

Ruzi's time in Odessa went by under the intense psychological stress of being undecided and uncertain about his future. Odessa itself was like a mosaic of the nations living in the territories colonised by the Soviets. Some people saw Hitler as offering the hope of freedom from the Stalinist regime. There were also Crimean Tatars and Ukrainian nationalists trying to establish relations with the officers of the army that they thought would one day arrive as victors. Even the Odessa Greeks, both those who had been rich merchants before the Revolution and those then working on the docks, felt sympathy for the Germans. From the point of view of the city's Jews, however, life would be intolerable in the event of a German occupation.[12]

One day Ruzi was strolling in the harbour at Odessa, sunk in deep thought about his own future, when a crazy idea suddenly entered his head. 'Why not enrol as a deckhand on one of the Turkish vessels moored here and then go to Turkey?' Turkey, his sister country, lay across the Black Sea on its southern shore. His steps took him toward a freighter flying the Turkish flag which had been loading cargo at the dock for several days. His years at the Nogay School came into his mind. Nogay had sometimes made the children march like soldiers, and as they did so he would sing out, 'Left, right, left, right; just let the fellow called Lenin die; just let the fellow called Lenin die, and Atatürk save us.' He smiled sadly as he remembered how his brother had died in front of a firing squad.[13]

So Ruzi went on board, introduced himself to the ship's captain and started to explain straight away that he was from Turkestan and wanted to go to Turkey. The captain seemed a little afraid and anxious, but he told Ruzi that the ship would be coming back to Odessa from Istanbul in a month's time and, if Ruzi could get hold of the right documents, he would take him.

Ruzi knew this would be impossible, and he sank back once more into despair. He thought of his mother, his sister, his friends and the pretty Uzbek girls he knew, and of his homeland, which was now part of the dark world of the Soviet regime. As someone from a family whose other son had been executed as an enemy of the regime, it would seem that no bright future awaited him in Tashkent.[14]

Tamara Hanım

Ruzi had been passionate ever since childhood about dancing and music. In Uzbekistan, and particularly in Tashkent, he had many friendships and affairs of the heart with singers, actors and folk dancers. All these things were missing from his new life. So when he heard that a group of performers from Uzbekistan would be visiting Odessa, he looked forward to the event with great enthusiasm. Who was coming? Would there be anyone he knew?[15]

In mid-May 1940 Tamara Hanım and her company arrived in Odessa and gave a magnificent concert in the city's largest concert hall. There was standing room only.[16] Tamara's lithe dancing and her songs enchanted the audience, most of whom were youngsters like Ruzi from Uzbekistan or the other Central Asian republics. The final applause lasted for many minutes.

Tamara Hanım was an Uzbek Armenian, born in a district of Fergana province not far from Margilan. She began dancing and singing when she was still very young, before taking lessons in classical Uzbek music from one of the masters of the time, Yusufjan Kızık Shakarjanov. In 1919 she joined the Hamza Hakimzade musical group, then worked in the Tashkent State Theatre, followed by a period of training at the State Institute for Theatrical Arts in Moscow. A magnificent ballerina, she became extremely successful as a performer of Uzbek national dances, as well as a talented actor and leading classical singer.[17] In 1956 she would receive the title of State Artist of the Soviet Union.

Ruzi already knew her from the old days in Uzbekistan, when she had taken part in musical evenings organised by his father at their home. After the concert, he managed to visit her backstage. She greeted him as lovingly as she would have done a brother or son or a lover she had not seen for many years. Ruzi felt as if he was back home, being embraced by his mother or his sister. Tamara introduced him to the other members of the company, including beautiful Uzbek singers and dancing girls. The next day was a holiday, when Ruzi could go into town without a senior soldier at his side. So in Odessa he met up with the young artistes, showed them around the town and took them to coffee houses, and they passed a splendid day together.[18]

Ruzi also learnt that one of the officers on duty in the concert hall the previous evening was a Tatar called Samet who had been born in Fergana. He introduced himself to Captain Samet and they got to know each other.[19] Samet had a wretched life story. He had been orphaned when very young and brought up in the Russian boarding school in Fergana. The Russian units there had adopted him as their mascot, and thereafter, wherever the brigade went, Samet would go too. In time he became an officer, and when he met Ruzi he was the commander of a motorised infantry company. He was married to a Russian woman but they had no children.

In the first days of the war, Samet's unit clashed with German units in Bessarabia and became trapped behind enemy lines. A Russian artilleryman unwittingly aimed a salvo at the Germans, and Samet and a large number of soldiers from his company lost their lives.[20]

The War Begins

In 1941 Hitler launched Operation Barbarossa, a surprise attack aimed at occupying the Soviet Union. Twenty-two months had passed since

Molotov and Ribbentrop had signed their non-aggression pact. German *Blitzkrieg* forces had already occupied Yugoslavia and Greece, while Romania and Bulgaria, then neutral, came under German control. And so on 22 June 1941 the armies of Nazi Germany, with 3,000 tanks, 1,500 aircraft and a million soldiers, reached the frontiers of the Soviet Union. After taking Leningrad, Smolensk and Kiev, the plan was to advance on Moscow and seize the Soviet capital.[21]

Thus began one of the bloodiest conflicts in human history. Hitler believed it would last between three and six months.[22] In fact it would continue until the end of 1945 and claim tens of millions of lives.[23] During the early days of the campaign, the reckoning for the Red Army was one of almost total destruction, with the loss of thousands of tanks, guns and aircraft. The German armies moved rapidly across Soviet territory. By the end of September they had achieved most of their goals, though they had failed to capture Leningrad and Stalingrad.[24] The Soviet dead, wounded and prisoners totalled more than five million.[25] The world waited for Hitler's prediction to come true.

In response to the German attack, the Red Army withdrew to Moscow, using scorched-earth tactics similar to those of Tsar Alexander's armies when they had faced Napoleon. Thousands of Red Army officers who had been arrested in the 1930s and held in prisons or labour camps since then, awaiting the day they would be killed, were released and reappointed to posts in the army. Although Stalin had now learnt that Japan was going to come into the war on the side of Germany, he took the decision to move units of the Red Army stationed in the East, who were still fresh and not worn down by combat, to the West. On 27 November, the vanguard units of the German 1st Tank Division ran into fierce resistance from the Red Army just thirty kilometres from Moscow. The sound of the German artillery could be heard in the Kremlin. Finally the Soviet army halted the Germans before they could reach Moscow.[26]

A month before Operation Barbarossa began, Ruzi had been one of thousands of Red Army soldiers who carried out a major exercise. Units from Odessa, Kiev and other provinces were under the command of the Marshal of the Soviet Union, Semyon Mikhailovich Budyonny, and the first secretary of the Ukrainian Communist Party,

Nikita Khrushchev. Budyonny had been commander of the Red Army cavalry in the civil war.

Ruzi was struck by the fact that the officers in charge of the exercise had known the numbers and names of the German divisions and regiments. He thought to himself that this showed that the Soviet intelligence services had not been idle and that serious preparations for war were being made. A railway line ran beside their barracks, and increasing numbers of trains loaded with military supplies passed by heading west, later returning empty. Ruzi and his fellow soldiers could feel that war was approaching, but they never talked about it among themselves.[27]

At dawn the day after the outbreak of hostilities, Ruzi and his friends woke to the sound of bugles. Distant gunfire could be heard even in the place where they were stationed. The soldiers were sent to Bessarabia, along with weapons and ammunition. As they went, they passed close by two military airports which had been badly bombed by German planes. The aircraft had been completely destroyed. Everything was in flames.[28]

Sub-lieutenant Ruzi

Ruzi was no longer just an ordinary soldier. He was now an officer. Having completed his course in Odessa and passed a further examination, he was given the rank of sub-lieutenant. Just before the war broke out, he was appointed to the intelligence unit of the motorised infantry division. The regiment consisted of three battalions, one a tank division and the other two for armoured vehicles and motorcycles. Ruzi was put in command of a squad in the armoured vehicle battalion. He had three armoured cars under his command, each of them with a driver and a gunner. Above them were the commander and his assistant.

Ruzi's squad began gathering intelligence, working at night because during the hours of daylight the roads were full of retreating Red Army soldiers. One day, Ruzi broke the usual routine by going out of the barracks to collect intelligence during the day. He ran into a group of fifteen or twenty retreating soldiers. They were in a desperate condition and some of them were wounded. Among them he recognised Tashpolat, his friend from Margilan, and called out to him. Tashpolat failed to recognise him in his officer's uniform. As Ruzi ran towards him, Tashpolat gave him a military salute. 'At your command, sir!' he said. Ruzi suppressed a laugh. 'You wretch, Tashpolat, don't you recognise me? What's wrong with you?' Finally Tashpolat realised who he was and they embraced joyfully. Ruzi asked the NCO in charge of Tashpolat's group to let them rest for a few hours. The NCO agreed and Ruzi, and Tashpolat had a long conversation.

Tashpolat had been appointed to a division on the frontier. When the Germans attacked there had been very bloody clashes. Almost everyone in his division had been wiped out. 'Thank God you are alive,' Ruzi said to his friend. Tashpolat had seen almost everything imaginable while still little more than a child. In the 1920s, when the system had allowed people a little freedom and his father had made good money, his family started to have Uzbek pilaf every day; in the 1930s their father's wealth was confiscated and their troubles started again. Tashpolat, the former rich kid, had been drafted into the army as the son of a destitute kulak,[29] and had been sent straight to the front without proper training. He had seen his friends torn to shreds by artillery and tank fire. Now he was marching towards a future about which he knew nothing.

When the time came for them to part, they wished each other health and long life. 'We'll meet again in Margilan,' they said. And indeed they would. For both of them long years of troubles and bloodshed, sadness and joy, good luck and bad lay ahead, but the two friends would meet again on Ruzi's return to his homeland. By then he and Tashpolat would be nearly seventy-five years old.[30]

The Soviet government had decided to send nearly 500,000 of its citizens from Bessarabia into the interior of the USSR. The roads filled up with old women and men, children and babies, and the wounded. The majority of those escaping were Jewish. Ruzi did not yet understand the significance of their flight. The crowds were frequently bombed by German fighter planes and the chaos got even worse.[31]

After ten days on the Bessarabian border, Ruzi's unit was sent to the front. They stayed there for ten days under intense fire from German artillery and tanks and bombs from the air. The worst harm was done by the German mortars. Everywhere Soviet soldiers were trying to retreat, although to do so without authorisation was regarded as desertion and the punishment was to be shot dead on the spot. Ruzi thought that they would be withdrawn to Odessa, but instead they began to retreat towards Ukraine, while trying to fire back at the Germans. Losses steadily increased. The lives of soldiers, and particularly those who like Ruzi came from a colony, had no value in this war. Stalin was determined to win, no matter what the cost. The Soviet army had been issued with orders to leave nothing whole and standing behind it.[32] They withdrew to Ukraine, fighting and destroying as they went.

In Ukraine Ruzi was wounded in his stomach and his palate by the shrapnel from a German mortar bomb. Two medical orderlies dressed and bandaged his wounds, then told him to wait for transport to hospital. But although hours passed, no one came. Ruzi was losing blood. As dusk began to fall, two Uzbek soldiers from a retreating Soviet unit noticed him as they passed him by and felt sorry for him. They were about twenty-two or twenty-three years old, good-hearted farm boys. Both of them had worked on *kolkhozes* until they were called up by the army. They took Ruzi by the arms and began walking with him in search of help. This made Ruzi alarmed for their sake. Leaving their unit for any reason, even to assist a wounded man, counted as desertion. That meant that the two soldiers might face a firing squad. After they had walked for a few hours, Ruzi told the soldiers to leave him. The young men would not agree. A house now appeared on the horizon, and they told him that they would take him there. They reached it after another painful two hours' journey up the mountainside.[33]

The door of the house was opened by a Ukrainian man in his fifties wearing clean clothes. Ruzi was almost unconscious. With a final effort he thanked the young soldiers and advised them to hurry back to their unit. He was too tired and weak even to get their addresses, and they ran off without looking back. As he watched them go, Ruzi wondered whether these two young men, still in the prime of life, would ever return to their own country and their families. Or would they take their leave of life in the endless territories of Russia and Ukraine? He looked after them one last time and prayed, 'Dear God, please protect them and let them get back to their loved ones.'[34]

Dreams

The Ukrainian couple who lived in the mountaintop village house took tender care of Ruzi. They washed his wounds with plenty of *samagon*,[35] then dressed them with bandages which had been boiled clean. They gave him clean underclothes and put him to rest in a comfortable bed in their cellar. Ruzi drank a tea which they had made from various herbs. Then his tired and wounded body could hold out no longer. As soon as he had drunk the tea, he fell into a deep sleep.[36]

At one point during his sleep, Ruzi seemed to open his eyes in a dream which was to affect him powerfully. His mother had left Margilan and come to Ukraine to see her son. She was going around the military units and barracks trying to find him. The soldiers told her that he was in a Ukrainian village, and so she arrived at the house where her son was. But there was a wall of glass between them. Each of them could see the other and they called out loudly, but the glass was so thick that neither could make the other hear. His mother was wearing a silk yashmak. Her face was shining like a light and she was smiling at Ruzi. Even though they could not talk, each could make the other understand by signs. His mother seemed to be saying, 'Hold my hands, my son,' and she reached out to him. Ruzi held out his hands as if to grasp hers, but, despite all their efforts, they were unable to touch, kept apart by the glass wall between them. His mother's eyes began to well with tears. Finally she made a sign to bid farewell to her son, and left.[37]

Ruzi opened his eyes. He was in a fierce sweat. As he was still stupefied from sleep and affected by his wounds, it took a while before he understood where he was. He realised that what had just happened was only a dream—but he very seldom had dreams.[38] He felt sad, as if something had been branded on his heart.

One day before the war, when his father was ill in Margilan, Ruzi had had another of his rare dreams. In Uzbekistan there were fascinating funfairs. Clowns would perform their tricks and tightrope walkers would engage in their dangerous acts. Appetising sweetmeats and *mantı* would be on sale and the finest cooks would offer delicious Uzbek pilaf to their customers. Champion players of the *askiye* game would bandy words with each other, making their listeners roar with laughter.

In his dream, Ruzi found himself in just such a fair. A cord had been tied to the top of a pole about twenty-five metres high and then tightly fixed to the ground about fifty metres away to make a tightrope. His father, Jamshid Ata, was very slowly walking up the rope while holding a balancing stick in his hand. Jamshid went a certain distance, rested, and then started to walk upwards again. When he rested a second time, he suddenly lost his balance and fell down. Ruzi rushed into the crowd to look for his father but he could not find him. He began crying and shouting out, 'Father!' Still weeping, he awoke from the dream. Two days later, his father passed away. [39]

The dream about his mother reminded Ruzi of that earlier one and he inevitably reflected on what had happened two days after it. He put his own interpretation on this latest dream. 'It means that from now on, as long as I live, I shall not see my mother again,' he told himself. In 1992, when Ruzi finally set foot in his homeland again, he would only be able to visit the grave in which she had been buried twenty-four years earlier. [40]

Perhaps it was the effect of the tea that his Ukrainian hosts had given him, but Ruzi awoke after sleeping for fifteen or sixteen hours. When he got up, his uniform and underclothes had been washed, dried and ironed. The owner of the house told him that he should not put his uniform back on. The Red Army had withdrawn completely from the area and it was now under the control of German soldiers. 'This is safer,' he said, and gave Ruzi a set of farmer's clothes. Ruzi washed and shaved. His hosts again washed his wounds with *samagon* and bandaged them. [41]

After the dressing of his wounds, a fine breakfast awaited him. During the meal, Ruzi told them briefly about himself. His hosts listened with interest. From the questions that he asked and the way he spoke, Ruzi drew the conclusion that the owner of the house was an educated man, someone who was cultured and civilised.

His wounds quickly showed signs of healing and Ruzi began to get his strength back. He started to do some of the housework, delighting his hosts, who had no children of their own. They were as kind to him as if he were their adopted child. [42]

Four days went by and then one evening the owner of the house returned full of joy and happiness. He told Ruzi that a national government had been established in the Ukraine, and so that day was a holiday for him. These words gave him away as a Ukrainian patriot. Ruzi congratulated him and then said, 'If only we in Central Asia could set up our own independent government.' This was the first sentence in an uncensored conversation between Ruzi and his host, one that was free of fear and totally sincere. His host began to give Ruzi details of the area. One by one, he advised him on how he should go outside, the times when it would be safe to do so and when it would be dangerous, where he could go and which places he should avoid. A further week went by. Ruzi and his hosts were becoming friends.[43]

Towards the end of the 1920s several hundred Uzbek families who had been denounced as kulaks and had their lands confiscated but who were familiar with cotton growing had been moved from the Fergana valley and settled in Ukraine. The climate there was unsuitable for cotton farming, but although the venture was unsuccessful, they continued living in Ukraine.[44] One day the owner of the house told Ruzi that there was a village of these Uzbeks nearby. He explained that they were good people and that the Ukrainians and Uzbeks lived on friendly terms. During their conversation, he made a note of where and when Ruzi had been born. One evening two weeks later, he came home and told his wife that he wanted to talk to Ruzi alone. When his wife left the room, he told Ruzi that he had gone to the Uzbek village and talked to some of its old people. He had told them that he needed a document to show that the Uzbek youth helping him in his house was a child of one of the families there. The document was prepared and signed by members of the village's council of elders.[45]

With this document Ruzi could now leave the house without any anxiety. Ruzi thanked the owner of the house with all his heart. He was able to go out, to chat and make friends with Ukrainian girls, to go to the village markets and joke with the farmers there. He began to feel that he was a free person. However, one evening the owner came home looking dejected. Ruzi asked why he was so sad. The man told him that the Germans had dissolved the Ukrainian national government and arrested its members.[46]

A Hard Decision

The question of nationalities was one of the Soviet state's most difficult problems, just as it had been under the tsars. Lenin discussed it in many of his articles; Stalin too was closely concerned with it. Before the October Revolution, Lenin and his friends had denounced the Tsarist empire as the greatest prison of peoples anywhere in the world and promised independence for the non-Russian populations.[47] After the Revolution these people living in the Soviet Union realised that they had been deceived, and so they went into the Second World War with high hopes that the Nazis would bring down the Soviet Union and help them to establish their own national states. When the Germans began to occupy territories in Eastern Europe and even got close to Moscow, however, it was clear that the outcome would not be like that at all.[48]

The German army of occupation in Ukraine established auxiliary units composed of young Ukrainian men.[49] These soldiers did not wear an official uniform and carried weapons captured from defeated units of the Red Army. Their duties were to take over as a gendarmerie in their own areas, to protect railway lines, stations, and depots of food and clothing, and to ensure law and order.

The owner of the house Ruzi was staying in told him that he should sign up with an auxiliary unit for his own security. Taking the document which the council of village elders had given him, Ruzi went along and applied to join. His application was immediately accepted and Ruzi began carrying out his new duties in his unit.[50]

Four months went by. Towards the end of October 1941, the weather in Ukraine began to be freezing cold. The sergeant-major in charge of Ruzi's unit summoned him to his office in the headquarters. Sergeant-Major Baumann was from the lake district near Linz in Austria, a grave and serious man of fifty-five or sixty. During the First World War he had been captured by the Russians and held for years as a prisoner of war. During that time he had learned to speak perfect Russian.[51]

'You ordered me to come here. Here I am,' Ruzi said. Baumann welcomed him, asked him how he was and told him to sit down. He explained that the German High Command had begun to establish military units in the Ukraine made up of Muslim Turks from Turkestan, Tatar-Bashkurt and Azerbaijan. Muslim soldiers of the Red Army who had been taken prisoner or had gone over to the German side were being accepted into these legions as volunteers. Private soldiers and officers in the legions would enjoy equal legal status and rights with German private soldiers and officers, and the officers of these new units would come from the Turkic peoples Baumann had already mentioned. But the number of officers would be very small. Ruzi was an intelligent and well-educated Uzbek and so they would like him to become a member of the Turkestan Legion, but the sergeant added, 'We are only able to send you if you want to go of your own free will. If you prefer to stay here in the auxiliary units, the decision is yours. Think it over carefully. You don't have to give a decision immediately. Consider it for a few days and then let me know.'[52]

This proposal made Ruzi's head spin. He thought about it for days and nights, unable to sleep. What was he to do? If he joined the Turkestan Legion and the war did not end in victory for Germany, he would never be able to return to his home country and he would never again see his mother or his sister, or anyone else who was close to him. If he did not join the legion and the Germans lost the war, the day would come when he would fall into the hands of the Soviet authorities and be shot as a deserter. Both paths were risky and dangerous. But the second option had a clear and terrifying end to it. He had no other alternative. Ruzi informed Sergeant Baumann that he would join the Turkestan Legion.[53]

4

SOLDIERS AND PRISONERS OF WAR

The young men from Turkestan called up to fight for the Soviet Union were sent to the front without much preparation. Very few of them managed to retreat with the Red Army in the opening stages of the conflict, and hundreds of thousands were taken prisoner by the Germans. Mustafa Shokay, the Turkestani nationalist leader, wrote from Germany to his wife, Mariya, in Paris, describing the background of some of these captives: 'The prisoners of war from Turkestan were taken into the ranks of the Red Army very shortly before the war began. There are those among them who had been called up only a few weeks before that date and others who had been taken into the army anything up to two years earlier. About 90 per cent of them do not know how to use a rifle. A large proportion of the Red Army's soldiers from Turkestan served in background duties such as being grooms or cooks. A good many of them can be heard saying, "How can we be regarded as soldiers? We haven't even had a rifle in our hands once in a year and a half."'[1]

A group of Turkestani prisoners of war recounted their experiences as follows: 'We were a group of fifteen friends in a class of students at the Pedagogy Institute. On 26 June [i.e. four days after the war had begun] the director entered the class and told us to get into a line and wait for orders from the military administration. An hour later they took us directly to the railroad station, put us into the carriages, and then brought us in an unknown direction for drilling. We had no idea where we were being taken. In the city of Samara they gave us over-coats and rifles. When we arrived at Kharkov, they took the rifles back. A few days later they put us back on the train and took us to a forested area. There they drilled us as soldiers for three days. On the fourth day, we learnt that our commander had run away and that we were sur-rounded by the Germans. So we gathered together as a few hundred Turkestanis, including those who had joined us on the way, and jointly decided to surrender to the Germans.'[2]

In the Red Army, these soldiers from Central Asia had endured bully-ing, insults and hunger, being regarded as second-class human beings. But now something even more painful and terrible was awaiting them. In the Nazi racial ideology, Turkestanis were considered lower than Slavs and were subject to a mass extermination operation.[3] The situation of the prisoners of war was heartrending. Mustafa Shokay wrote to his wife: 'I can't bear any more of it. Yesterday I saved thirty-five people from being executed by firing squad. They had put them into a hole. It is now October. They were wearing summer clothes, and thus were half-naked, and trying to dig out a refuge from the rain and cold with their bare hands. Bread was being thrown at them in the way it is thrown to dogs. These men [i.e. the Nazis] are worse than animals. You can guess how inwardly exhausted I feel. I can't endure it. I want to die.'[4]

A Crimean Tatar, Jengiz Daghji, wrote in his memoirs: 'I was taken prisoner around noon on 9 August 1941. In the first week of November, thousands of prisoners were taken away to the Uman camp at Kirovograd. I don't know exactly how many we were, but there were thousands of us. We were hungry and mostly half naked. There were armed German soldiers on our right and left. We were caught in snow and sleet. Only 3,000 arrived out of 10,000. Those whose strength failed them and fell behind the mass of us were shot dead with bullets. Their corpses were left in the mud which in many places was up to our heels and in some above our knees.[5] The number of those dying in the camp rose from day to day. I never knew whether the prisoner lying beside me was alive or dead. Every day new corpses were added to the heap lying on the other side of the latrines.'[6]

Tens of thousands of Turkestanis lost their lives because of the appall-ing conditions in these camps.[7] One prisoner of war recalled, 'When we arrived at the camp, there were 32,000 of our countrymen there. The number of us fell by half in just one month. When January 1942 arrived, only 2,000 of the original 32,000 were still alive.'[8]

The German and Turkic Peoples

During the First World War, several thousand Turkestanis, Azerbaijanis, Tatars from Crimea and Kazan, Bashkirs and Muslims from the northern Caucasus serving in the Tsarist armies had been taken prisoner by the Germans. Some of these prisoners applied to the German High Command from the Wünsdorf camp near Berlin where they were being held, stating that they wished to fight in the army of Germany's ally, Ottoman Turkey. The High Command of the Ottoman empire was informed of this application and had them brought in May 1916 to Turkey, where they were formed into a unit known as the Asia Corps. After a short period of training in Turkey, they had been sent to the front in Iraq. There the Asia Corps fought heroically against the British and achieved major successes.[9]

Hüsrev Gerede, the Turkish ambassador in Berlin during the Second World War, was aware of this history and of the harsh conditions now prevailing in the prisoner-of-war camps, and had heard from Turkestani friends about the region's problems. The Turkish General Staff were also kept informed. Gerede arranged a meeting with the undersecretary of the German Foreign Ministry, Ernst Heinrich Freiherr von Weizsäcker.[10] Many years later, Gerede described the proceedings in his memoirs. 'I advised them to take advantage of these prisoners of war—making it clear that it was purely my own personal idea and entirely private. I have since read in a volume of German secret documents published by the Americans, that the Undersecretary informed Ribbentrop in detail of our discussion. When I read this work, I recalled that I had indicated that the peoples of the Caucasus could be united in a buffer state and an independent Turkestani state could be set up east of the Caspian Sea.' Gerede gave Weizsäcker names of refugees in Europe who he believed could be useful. One of them was Mustafa Shokay.[11]

In the years immediately after the Communist seizure of power in Central Asia, some of the intellectuals in Turkestan who until then had been struggling to establish an independent, democratic national state fled abroad to countries such as Germany, France and Turkey. They were later joined by young Turkestanis who had been sent to be educated in Germany and remained there, unlike their contemporaries who had returned home only to be arrested, accused of being counter-revolutionaries and executed.

Mustafa Shokay, the head of the national government set up in Kokand in 1918, had emigrated to France in the early 1920s. There he spearheaded the work among the diaspora for his country to regain its independence, publishing the magazine *Yash Turkestan* (*Young Turkestan*). After war broke out, the painful situation of the hundreds of thousands of Turkestani prisoners of war consumed his attention.[12]

At the outbreak of the war, the German Foreign Ministry had contacted Shokay in Paris to ask for his cooperation. Their delegate was Veli Kayyum Han, who had been one of those sent from Bukhara to study in Germany in 1921. Encouraged by Gerhard von Mende, professor of Russian history at the university of Berlin, he had done a doctorate on Turkestan and was now working as a journalist and writing reports for Berlin on Central Asia.[13] Shokay was a firm believer in democracy and detested Nazism, so he rejected the proposal. At that time, Germany had not yet attacked the Soviet Union and the question of prisoners of war had not arisen.

On 22 June 1941, the day Operation Barbarossa began, Mustafa Shokay was arrested and taken to a camp, where he was held for a week. Through the efforts of Professor Mende he was released and taken to Berlin. There he saw some of the first prisoners of war to arrive from Turkestan. After lengthy soul-searching and examination of his conscience, Shokay concluded that he had no alternative but to cooperate with the Germans if the prisoners of war were to be released. He thanked the German authorities for allowing him to make contact with the prisoners of war and launched an intensive programme of work, with Veli Kayyum Han as his assistant.

In July the German Ministry of the East took the decision to establish a Prisoners of War Commission.[14] Shokay had begun further investigations of the conditions in the camps and was appalled by the sights which met his eyes. Through Veli Kayyum Han, he sent this report to German officials: 'You Germans regard yourselves as the most civilised and cultured nation in Europe. If your culture is expressed through the things which I am seeing, then I would wish that you too could suffer the same disaster and be destroyed in the same way as the prisoners are. You are doing in the twentieth century even worse things than Jenghiz Khan did in the thirteenth. You have no right to claim that you are a civilised and cultured nation.'[15]

Others were also concerned about the situation in the camps. The Orientalist and political scientist Professor Mende, who had played a role in Shokay's release, was a Baltic German. He had been born in 1904 in Riga and had been brought up by his uncle after his father was murdered by Communists. His uncle's wife came from a Tatar-Bashkir family who had been taken prisoner by the Germans in the First World War. It was thanks to her that Mende's interest in the Turkic peoples had first been awakened. After the October Revolution, Mende and his family moved to Germany. At university he had read Oriental studies and political science and gone on to study the Turkic peoples of the USSR. His book *The National Struggle of the Turks of Russia* (*Der nationale Kampf der Ruslandtürken*) had been published in Germany in 1936 and was one of the most important works on the subject. While still professor of Russian in Berlin, he was engaged in compulsory military duties under Alfred Rosenberg in the Ministry of the East, as head of the Foreign Peoples section. He was thus well aware of what was happening in the camps.[16] Mende made great efforts to draw the subject to the attention of the ministry in which he worked. In the long term, his hope was that if the Soviet Union broke up, independent states of Tataristan, Azerbaijan and Turkestan would be established on its former territories. In the short term, if prisoners of war from Turkestan were able to fight alongside the German army, their misery in the camps would end.

When the First World War ended with the defeat of the Ottoman empire, Enver Pasha, the Ottoman minister of war and deputy chief commander, left Istanbul and went to Germany. His brother, Nuri Pasha,[17] who had been commander of the Caucasian Islamic Armies, followed him. In 1922 Enver Pasha was killed by Red Army soldiers in Turkestan while fighting for independence.[18]

Nuri Killigil Pasha stayed in Germany until 1938, when he returned to Istanbul. There he remained concerned with the problem of the East. For a time he served as an army commander in Azerbaijan, then returned to Germany, with the knowledge of the Turkish General Staff. In September 1941 he began contacting people in Berlin and had meetings with Ernst von Weizsäcker and Ernst Woermann, head of the Political Division.[19] The pasha outlined his thoughts to Woermann about the regions of the Soviet Union in which Turkic peoples were living and advised him to make use of the Caucasian, Central Asian and Tatar-Bashkir prisoners who were currently imprisoned in the camps.

Woermann was impressed by his argument and sent a report to the ministry making several proposals. These lines in it are particularly relevant: 'Prisoners of Turkic ethnic origin and also all Muslim POWs should be sifted out and gathered in a special camp resembling that established during the First World War near Wünsdorf. A study should then be made of whether a special war unit can be set up drawing on these prisoners. According to information received from the POW Section of the OKW [the German High Command], the Reich Minister for the Occupied Eastern Territories, Dr Rosenberg, has communicated such a request to the OKW. As soon as they are less busy, they intend to begin classifying Russian POWs according to their ethnic and racial origins. Nuri Pasha wants to play a personal role in this activity. He believes that as soon as camps are established, he could participate in the work of selecting human materials and organising them. He thinks that this could be done with the implicit consent of the Turkish Government.'[20]

Relations Between Turkey and Germany

Two other important visitors from Turkey arrived in Berlin around this time. They were Lieutenant-General Ali Fuat Erden, the commander of the Military Academies, and Major-General Hüseyin Hüsnü Emir Erkilet.[21] Turkey had remained neutral so far, but their mission was to hold meetings with the German High Command and to visit the Eastern Front and Crimea. They also wanted to know Germany's postwar plans for the territories inhabited by the Turkic peoples of the USSR.[22] A diplomat from the German Foreign Ministry, Otto Werner von Hentig, accompanied them on their travels, and at German army headquarters they were received by Hitler himself. Briefings were made and maps pored over. The Turkish generals argued strongly in favour of the idea of establishing military units made up of prisoners of war to fight against the Soviets.[23]

Sentimentality is no basis for government policy. No matter how much the people of Turkey had in common with the soldiers of the Turkestan Legion in terms of culture, religion and ethnic background, the Turkish state's approach was always founded on its own interests. If the colonised populations were going to fight for independence, they would need support. But such help never comes without strings and in relations of this sort there are no moral principles, only considerations of mutual advantage. Countries which aid independence movements are much stronger than the organisations which they support and frequently treat them quite ruthlessly. The group receiving the support generally is like a toy in the hands of those extending it; however much they try to act independently, they are helpless, condemned to be made use of. During the years of the war, Turkish–German relations in regard to the Turkic groups living inside the borders of the Soviet Union and to the national committees and legions show that interests of state were placed above all else. Turkey's attitude displayed marked variations according to how the war was going.

In the early years of the war the Germans occupied all the countries of Eastern Europe as well as the Crimea and parts of north Caucasia, and during Operation Barbarossa they reached as far as the gates of Moscow. Turkey was thus closely concerned with the future of the non-Russian peoples and their territories should the Soviet Union lose the war. Turkish officialdom clung very close to Germany's ambassador in Turkey, Franz von Papen, exchanging information and advice. Long before his visit to Germany, General Erden had spoken to Papen about the need to establish Turkish buffer states in the regions in the Caucasus where Turks lived, a point that had also been made by the Turkish ambassador, Gerede, to Ernst von Weizsäcker in the German Foreign Ministry. As soon as General Erden returned from Germany, the delegation he headed organised a meeting in Ankara. According to information supplied by Papen, the meeting was attended by the president of the Republic, İsmet İnönü; the foreign minister (who would soon succeed as prime minister), Şükrü Saraçoğlu; the chief of General Staff, General Fevzi Çakmak; and General Erden himself. The establishment of national committees and legions and the policy to be followed in the event of a collapse of the Soviet Union were discussed, and the general gave a detailed briefing to President İnönü about his discussions in

Germany. The meeting lasted six hours, a sign of the great importance which the president attached to the subject. [24]

Şükrü Saraçoğlu was certain that Germany would win the war. On 5 August 1942 he told the Turkish Grand National Assembly: 'My friends, we are Turks, we are Turkists, and we will always remain Turkists. However much Turkism is a question of blood, it is also at least to the same degree a question of conscience and culture. We are not Turkists who are dwindling and shrinking, we are Turkists who are growing and causing others to grow and we will always strive towards this direction.' [25] The Turkish government continued to send delegations to Germany advising the establishment of national committees and legions.

After the new prime minister had a meeting with Ambassador Papen, the latter sent the following dispatch to Berlin: 'I paid my first visit to the newly appointed Mr Saraçoğlu today. During our discussion about the general situation in Turkey, I asked him to tell me about his general views on the Russian problem. The prime minister immediately replied that he wanted to answer as both a prime minister and a Turk. As a Turk, he strongly wanted to see Russia destroyed. That would be a development of which the Turkish people had dreamed for hundreds of years. No Turks could think differently from what he did on this point. The new prime minister did not know the decision of the Führer about the form that the minority areas would take in the future. The great majority of the population of these areas came from the Turkish race and so it was legitimate for Turkey to feel close concern about the way the problem would be resolved. He reminded me that on one occasion, acting in conformity with instructions from the Führer, I had said to his president that Turkey could act as a strong fortress in the south-east of the new Europe and that, linked to this, the Turkish element in Russianised territories should be noted. It was true that the intellectuals there—if they existed—had either surrendered to Bolshevism or been murdered by it. As a consequence of this, if some of the young people of these countries were sent to German universities and most of them to Turkish ones, then in the future this new generation would guarantee effective cooperation between these two factors. [26]

'Germany had summoned a substantial number of emigrants from these countries to the empire in order to be able to obtain their views and to benefit from their services. If the Russians were totally defeated in the near future, we would see that these countries with non-Russian minorities expected liberty and reconstruction from us. We should not have allowed these hopes to be in vain. Otherwise these minorities would also cause us to be disappointed. Up to this point he had spoken as a Turk. Speaking as prime minister, he said that it was his duty not to give the smallest grounds for anything that might serve as a pretext for a massacre of Russia's Turkish minorities. I thanked the prime minister for his remarks and asked him how we could ensure the economic development of areas captured and Turkey's cooperation in administering them, and also in what way we could take Turkey's interests into account. Saraçoğlu said that if it was necessary he was ready to discuss practical problems with me in secret or to empower a third person to do so. From these remarks, as far as I understood, the prime minister is closely following developments in Russia and especially in the Caucasus with lively interest and wants to be in close contact with me on the subject.'[27]

The form of administrative structure and government that the Germans were envisaging for the Turkic peoples, should the Soviet Union collapse, was actually no different from that of the Soviets. Papen wrote in his dispatch: 'We must try to find persons who can be local representatives of a visible administration in each of the countries in the Caucasus and beyond the Caspian. Alongside the selected leader, there should be a responsible German administrator and he will be the person responsible for taking the decisions. Underneath this section there should be the required number of authorities and administrators with local elements having an important share. The legions that already exist composed of minority nationalities will provide a perfect core for armed forces to be set up in various regions around them. Visible armed forces and police organisations must be represented by local people in places where this is possible.'[28]

The national committees and legions believed that they were fighting together with the German armies for the independence of their countries and that after the war they would live in a free homeland which was no longer a Soviet colony. But Papen, a former German chancellor, was talking at this very time about establishing puppet governments in these countries, totally controlled by the Germans. In the

Soviet Union, too, these republics were independent on paper. Indeed, on paper, they even had the right to secede.[29] These nominal republics were run by their own Communist parties—but these local parties were dependent on the Communist Party of the Soviet Union, based in Moscow, and their cadres. Their first secretary would be a local person and the second secretary a Russian. However, the first secretary would perform protocol responsibilities while the country was in fact run by the second secretary. The system which the Germans contemplated creating in these republics after the war was scarcely different.

During the early years of the war, the Germans felt so sure of themselves that Foreign Minister Ribbentrop wrote to Papen that Turkish interests conflicted with German ones in the territories where the Turkic populations lived, and so Turkish assistance on these issues would be of no benefit. He instructed Papen not to discuss the matter further with Turkish officials.[30] Crimean Tatars, Kazan Tatars, Bashkirs, Azerbaijanis and Turkestanis would all sacrifice their lives fighting against the Red Army with German weapons in their hands, while the Germans were drawing up their plans to thwart any Turkish influence in these territories and to turn them into colonies.

Towards the end of 1941 the German High Command formally decided to establish legions chosen from volunteers in the prison camps. The idea had been accepted without opposition,[31] firstly because the manpower was needed, and secondly because the lands of the Turkic peoples lay beyond the frontiers of the planned expansion of the German Nazi state.[32]

The Turkestan Legion would consist of Turkestani Uzbeks, Turkmens, Kazakhs, Karakalpaks and Tajiks. There was also to be a Caucasus Muslims Legion, made up of Azerbaijanis, Dagestanis, Ingush, Lezgis and Chechens, as well as Armenian, Georgian, Volga Tatar and North Caucasian legions.[33] The task of setting them up was assigned to General Oskar von Niedermayer,[34] commander of the 162nd Infantry Division and a well-known expert on the Middle East and Central Asia. He was head of the General Defence Studies Institute at Friedrich Wilhelm University in Berlin and spoke Russian, Farsi and Turkish.[35] The fact that General Niedermayer had been given the command was no coincidence, but a necessary consequence of the German policy of *Drang nach Osten*, 'the drive eastwards'. The Army Group South, stationed in Ukraine, was entrusted with the work.[36] The auxiliary units, in one of which Ruzi had enlisted, were also attached to this southern command.

While Turkey had encouraged the formation of the Turkestan Legion and sought cooperation with Germany in establishing new states in the Caucasus, Azerbaijan, Crimea, Tataristan, Bashkiristan and Turkestan, it abandoned the policy as soon as it became clear that Germany would lose the war. A tragic aspect of this is that when 195 officers and soldiers who had fought in the legions sought asylum in Turkey, they were delivered to the Soviets by the Turkish authorities at the frontier post at Tıhmıs. According to reports, as soon as they were on the other side of the Turkish–Soviet border, they were gunned down in sight of those who had handed them over.[37]

Legionnaire Ruzi

While he was employed first at the front and then in the auxiliary unit in occupied Ukraine, Ruzi of course had not the least idea about these developments. On 14 December 1941 he was sent to the town of Proskurov, where the legion was being got ready, accompanied by a German soldier who spoke Russian.[38]

The headquarters of the legion and its barracks were four or five kilometres away from the town. They consisted of a two-storey building left standing by the Red Army when it withdrew from the region, several single-storey houses, a large garage and a wide square. There Ruzi met a Volga German soldier who was twenty-five years old and spoke good Russian. They had long conversations, telling each other their life stories. The young soldier had been drafted into the Red Army too, but when the fighting began he had run away and joined the Germans. Because he was actually German, they had immediately accepted him as a soldier. He took Ruzi to the canteen, had him eat his fill, and then gave him a room in one of the buildings belonging to the legion.[39]

Early the next morning a German translator arrived and said, 'Come on, get up; we're off. The captain wants to talk to you.' The captain greeted Ruzi with smiles and asked him endless questions about his military knowledge and his life. Ruzi answered as far as he knew how. After an hour and a half of conversation, the captain thanked Ruzi. He said that intelligent people were needed to train soldiers in the camp and so he was going to put Ruzi in command of a company. 'Now go and pick a bright orderly for yourself,' he said. Ruzi selected a nineteen-year-old lad, an Uzbek villager from Kokand, who never left his side until long afterwards.[40]

Later Ruzi was shown to a large building where Uzbek youths who had been brought from the prisoner-of-war camps were being held. Ruzi was overjoyed to see people from his own country. They introduced themselves and talked. It was there that he learnt for the first time how appalling conditions were in the camps. He reflected that God had protected him several times over: first from dying, then from being taken prisoner, and then from suffering what the prisoners had endured. He had got away with only two war wounds.[41]

The prisoners suffered agonies in the camps and lost most of their comrades, living every day with the danger of death. Ruzi would understand this best from a story which a friend told him many years later. His friend had been wounded and taken prisoner about ten days after the war began. He and his companions had been taken to a large camp and a few days later a group of officers, whom he later learned were from the SS, examined them and started putting them into different groups. He did not understand what was happening. But almost all of the 150 or 160 prisoners who were picked the first day were Turkic Muslims. They were taken outside the camp, each forced to dig a hole, and then immediately shot dead.

Ruzi's friend went on: 'The next day it was our turn. I understood that if they picked me, I would be killed. So I asked the officer in charge through a Russian interpreter if I could perform two *rakat* of my *namaz* prayers. At first they did not understand what this meant, but when he said it was an act of religious worship, they agreed. While I was performing the *namaz*, they watched me curiously. When I had finished, the officer asked me what nationality I was. I told him I was a Muslim Turk. "So you're not a Jew?" he asked. "No," I said. The officer then asked why, if I was not a Jew, I was circumcised, and I told him that all Muslims were circumcised. The officer, the German beside him and the translator conferred for a few minutes. Then, without saying anything, he struck my shoulders with a lash and indicated that I should join the prisoners standing at the front. After that they stopped picking out prisoners. This was the moment at which we understood that the

Germans were implementing a policy of exterminating the Jews, and that to identify Jews they examined the prisoners to see which ones were circumcised. If we had known that the first day, scores of people killed because they were supposed to be Jews might have been saved.'[42]

Similar stories were told by some of the young men in Ruzi's camp. The Jews of Central Asia were known as 'Bukhara Jews'. The Bukhara Jewish community is believed to date back to the first Jewish diaspora and to have numbered more than 150,000 during the years of the Second World War. They had lived in peace with the Uzbeks and Tajiks for more than 2,500 years, following their own customs, engaged in trade and crafts. They spoke a dialect drawn from the Uzbek and Tajik languages, containing many words of Hebrew origin.

Ruzi had read various books and articles on Nazism and had not been able to make sense of the Nazi theory of a super-race. He had been brought up to believe that there were definitely some superior human beings, but this had nothing to do with race or ethnic affiliation. In his view, the superior human being was the one who was most moral, most consistent, manly, generous and pure. It was impossible for him to accept the idea of a hierarchy of Aryans and lower races. In Hitler's ranking, the Germans were the most perfect members of the Aryan race. Asians, including Turks, composed the lower races,[43] while the worst and lowest were the Jews. They were the cause of all the disasters that had befallen humanity in the course of history and so they had to be exterminated.[44]

In the prison camps, Jews would be identified and then shot on the spot, standing in front of pits they had themselves dug. The young men from Turkestan in the camp did whatever they could to help their Jewish fellow countrymen. They managed to save some of them by saying that they were Bukhara Tajiks, but this was highly risky. Should someone else say that the person concerned was not after all Tajik but Jewish, then execution by firing squad was inevitable.

A friend of Ruzi's, Hussan Ikram Han, told the following story. 'It was our second week as prisoners. One evening one of my friends, Mustafa Mehmetzade from Azerbaijan, came up to me. He had an expression of great fear on his face. "Hussann, Hussan, move at once, the Germans are calling for you," he said in great agitation. There were some soldiers by the door of the camp's administration block. We were confronted by two German officers, two private soldiers, a translator and seven young men who were standing stripped to their underpants and with their faces to the wall. One of the officers turned me and asked me who they were. "I don't know," I said. "They must be Jews," he said. I replied, "Let me talk to them." They turned their faces towards me. "Where are you from and who are you?" I asked. One of them replied in a low voice and with trembling lips, speaking Uzbek with a Bukhara Jewish accent, that they were Tajiks. I turned to the officer. "They are Tajiks," I said. I can't tell a lie, my body was drenched in sweat. If my deception were found out, I would be killed on the spot. The officer asked how I could know that they were Tajiks. "They speak Uzbek with a very good Tajik accent," I said. "Bukhara Jews couldn't speak Uzbek like that. Everything about them makes it obvious that they are Tajiks." The officer turned to the young Jew and asked him if he knew any Russian. "*Nyemnoshka* [a little]," he replied. Mehmetzade confirmed what I had said. The officer pointed his pistol at each Jew one by one and said, "Tell the truth. What's your name?" Each Jew replied with the first Muslim name that came into his mind. The officer explained something to one of the soldiers and sent him upstairs.

'The minutes seemed like lifetimes as they passed and then finally a tall plump lieutenant came downstairs. The officer who had been interrogating us told him briefly what had been said. The lieutenant came up to me and shoved the barrel of his pistol hard against my chest. "You tell me the truth or you know what is going to happen to you," he said. I realised at that moment that to retract my lie would mean that I was going to die. In a loud voice and syllable by syllable, I said, "I am certainly telling the truth. These men are Tajiks." He left me alone. Then he stuck his revolver against Mehmetzade's breast. He repeated to him the question he had just asked me. Mehmetzade said that I had told the truth and that the men were Tajiks. As he left the place where we were, the lieutenant said something to the officer who had questioned us. "*Jawohl*," he replied and saluted. The interpreter turned to the Jews. "You are free now. Go upstairs and write your names and surnames correctly." He told us that we should take them into our group. As he went upstairs himself, the interpreter said to them in a low voice, "Write down your Tajik names and don't forget them."

'After they had written down their names and we were going back to the sheds, I gave them a very stern warning. "There are more than three hundred Turkestani and Caucasian prisoners of war in this camp. They know who you are. Do not tell anyone in the barracks what you have just experienced. Don't go around in a group." Then I thanked God that we had been able to save these people without having anything happen to us.'[45]

Ruzi had been raised to believe that to save the life of one human being is to save the life of humanity, and to kill one human being is equal to killing the whole of humanity. He felt very happy when his friends told him how they had helped these people and he was proud of them.[46] Ruzi simply could not come to terms with the atrocities being visited on the Jews. His heart was full of feelings of warmth and friendship towards them. During his years in Uzbekistan, he had had young Jewish friends of whom he was very fond. The Uzbek poet Gulam Gafur, who was executed by the Bolsheviks in the 1930s on the grounds that he was an enemy of the Revolution, had written a poem about the Jews which had etched itself on Ruzi's memory in his early youth.

> Jewish—a mighty and a beautiful name,
> But everywhere meeting pain and troubles.
> Pain and disasters rain down on us,
> This nation which raises the greatest minds.[47]

The Legionary Camps

On 1 November 1941 there were about three million former Red Army soldiers being held as prisoners of war. Of these as many as 800,000 were Muslims.[48] Alfred Rosenberg, the Reichsminister for the Occupied Eastern Territories, declared in a speech that out of 100,000 prisoners of war from the Soviet republics of Central Asia, only 6,000 had survived.[49]

Most of the youngsters whom Ruzi got to know in the legion's training camp were Uzbeks, Turkmens and Tajiks. They told him that the other buildings were also full of young men from Turkestan, and Ruzi managed to talk to many of them too. Some said they had been rescued from the unbearable life of the prisoner-of-war camp by Mustafa Shokay and Veli Kayyum Han.

Ruzi had learned about Mustafa Shokay from his elder brother, and hearing his name again made him feel easier. During his early days in the legion, in December 1941, some Uzbek youths told Ruzi how they had met Shokay. 'We were in the Częstochowa camp in November 1941. Most of us were ill, suffering from dysentery, typhoid and similar infectious diseases, and we lived in the middle of an army of fleas. There was no medicine and no doctors. Then one day they told us that one of the great men of Turkestan, Mustafa Shokay, the prime minister of the National Government set up in 1918, would be paying us a visit. We were in a wretched state. They gathered us together in the camp's central square. Shokay addressed us. After telling us how sorry he was for us, he said that he was making great efforts to ensure that these evil days would soon be behind us and gave us the good news that we would be liberated. After he had spoken, he shook hands with us. A good many of us hugged him. And indeed a few days later we were taken out of the hellhole of the camp and brought to this legion camp where we are treated as human beings.'[50]

The prisoners in the camp did not know what had become of Mustafa Shokay since then. Alihan Kantemir, a North Caucasian who worked with Shokay on the Prisoners of War Commission, later described what happened. 'Towards the end of November 1941 we visited the *Ostministerium* [Ministry of the East] with Mustafa Bey [Shokay]. We learnt from von Mende, who was always helpful to us, that large numbers of Turkestanis and Caucasians and others had been brought to the camps at Częstochowa and so it was necessary for the national commission to go there immediately. Mustafa Bey then turned to me and said, "Let's go. I really wondered about this camp. Let's take a look at it, then rest because we are really tired." The following day we set off by train for Częstochowa.'[51]

Shokay and his companions had been told that, as infectious diseases like typhoid and dysentery were rife in the camps, they would have to be careful. 'Despite the warnings, Mustafa Bey did not bother about the dangers of disease and began receiving his fellow Turkestanis. The flea-ridden prisoners crowded around Mustafa Bey, scratching themselves as they did so, while he made a fiery speech. Faced with this situation, I got up from my seat several times and tried to warn him, but though I told him to be careful, he took no notice. We boarded the evening train for Berlin and set off for the capital. A short while after the train had started, Mustafa Bey began to complain of a headache and of a rising fever and began asking for water. On the morning of 22 December 1941 we arrived at Spandau Station in Berlin. Mustafa Bey's illness had got much worse and was getting serious. So Veli Kayyum Han immediately had him admitted to hospital. Five days later, on 27 December 1941, Mustafa Bey died. Veli Kayyum Han told me the dreadful news over the telephone, sobbing with tears.'[52]

So while Ruzi and the new friends he had met in the legion were talking hopefully about the future and speaking about him with love and admiration, Mustafa Shokay was already dead.

5

RUZI AND THE LEGIONS' WAR AGAINST SOVIET RUSSIA

Training at Proskurov and Ruzi Meets the NTUC

Before military training began in the legion camp at Proskurov, the soldiers were divided into nine companies of around 200 men each. As the weather was fine, the German officers in charge of the camp gathered the soldiers together in the square and began to explain their duties as legionnaires. Everything they said was translated first into Russian and then from Russian into Uzbek.

At the end of the first week in the camp, military training started. The legion members wore German uniform and had a tough course of instruction, lasting at least seven hours a day. German officers carried out the training without ever stopping and listening. The lads from Turkestan generally enjoyed taking part.

A month passed without a single Turkestani leader visiting the camp. No one knew any more about the establishment of the legions than the very superficial details they had been given. It would be some months until they obtained detailed information about how the legions and the national committees had come into being and who had been the mover behind them.

Ruzi was put in command of the first company, whose work was fortification and which consisted of soldiers who had been trained in that area in the Red Army. He had his own room and was assisted by the orderly he had chosen. When the first month of training was over, weapons that had been left behind by the Red Army during its retreat were distributed to the legionnaires.[1] Then came target practice. Those who scored highest were given prizes. At the end of this first month, the legionnaires were paid their salaries.[2] From then on they were allowed to go into town on leave at weekends. During his period at the Proskurov camp, Ruzi trained more than 5,000 young Turkestanis.[3]

There were no special cadres at Proskurov engaged in educating the soldiers about ideology, but among the legionnaires there were a number of highly competent intellectuals who had studied history, law, economics and other subjects in the universities and high schools of the Central Asian republics. They now began to give their fellow soldiers lessons in the history of Turkestan, the recent colonial policies of Moscow, and the cruelty and murders for which the Soviets were responsible.[4] Ruzi later recalled: 'After a while educational materials began to arrive at our camp from Berlin. In the bulletins we learned that the first Turkestan Legion had been established before our one at Proskurov in a former Polish Army barracks building in the town of Legionowo near Warsaw.[5] When the educational materials reached us, intellectual activities intensified. There were more lessons and courses about the national independence of Turkestan and establishing unity between the different states of Turkestan.'

Ruzi tried to find ways of contacting the National Turkestan Unity Committee (NTUC) in Berlin and was eventually able to send a letter to its members via the Muslim chaplain in the camp. This was his first formal link with the committee. The NTUC had come into being without encountering any opposition. October 1942 is regarded as the official date of the committee's foundation, but it was already active in 1941 when Mustafa Shokay and Veli Kayyum Han were entrusted with the problem of Turkestani prisoners of war.

Shokay had been the head of the Turkestan national independence movement, and when he died late that year Kayyum Han became its de facto leader. Alfred Rosenberg, the Reichsminister for the Occupied Eastern Territories, had been against the idea of national committees early in the war, since the Nazis were opposed to the existence of rival governments in the territories they occupied. But since Germany needed Turkestani soldiers and had no plans to occupy Central Asia, the NTUC was able to establish itself as a sort of Turkestani government in exile. Apart from Kayyum Han, virtually all of its twenty-one members had grown up in the Soviet Union and had come to Germany either as prisoners of war or voluntarily in their youth.[6]

From August 1942 Shokay's magazine *Young Turkestan* continued to appear as the publication of the NTUC, under the name of *Milli Turkestan* (*National Turkestan*). Kayyum Han, as the NTUC's acting chairman, had assistants each of whom specialised in a particular area—defence, education, health, prisoners of war, and so on. The deputy chairman responsible for defence matters was forbidden by the German High Command to interfere in the legions' military activities. His duty was to liaise with the legions and send them educational materials. For the committee, their real task was to prepare for what would happen after the war, training the soldiers fighting in the legions and making them aware of the problem of Turkestan, instilling in them the idea of an independent nation, and—as a government in exile—trying to establish relations with other states.[7]

In practice, therefore, the NTUC worked as a kind of national government and, when the possibility that Germany might lose the war started to grow, its position in Berlin got stronger. Germany needed soldiers from Turkestan—it now had more than 100,000—and the German arms industry equally needed the workers from Turkestan it employed, numbering more than 200,000.[8] Consequently the Nazis were forced to forget their claims of racial superiority over the Turkestanis, and the committee was able to carry out its work with greater independence.

Coincidences

Training in the Proskurov camp went on at full speed and with great intensity through January, February and March 1942. In April a passing-out ceremony was held in the camp's square for all the soldiers from the nine companies. The camp commandant made a speech in which he thanked the Turkestani soldiers, praised their disciplined demeanour and said the time had come for them to make war for Turkestan against a common enemy. He bade farewell to these friends with whom, he said, he shared a common fate, and then dispatched the units to various parts of the Eastern Front.[9] Ruzi and the two Turkestani company commanders were ordered to remain in the camp.

The commandant later summoned Ruzi and his two soldiers to his room. After praising their work throughout the training period, he said that new soldiers would be coming to Proskurov soon and these men would be entrusted to them too. The very next day, 2,000 more volunteers from the prisoner-of-war camp arrived. They looked dreadful, resembling skeletons that had just jumped out of their graves. They had been disinfected and cleansed of fleas before they set off on the long train journey. Ruzi felt a pang of grief at the emaciated condition of his fellow countrymen in their ragged clothes but looked at them with affection. They were given haircuts and baths, then divided into nine companies. And thus, over two days, 2,000 former conscripts of the Red Army were turned into 2,000 German soldiers.[10]

The new recruits rapidly adjusted to camp life. Quite soon the skeletal beings filled out into healthy soldiers. Potatoes were the main item of food available in the camp, but the Turkestanis could not do without their Uzbek pilaf, and it was frequently prepared in the kitchens. In terms of flavour it could not match what they were used to eating at home, but the pilaf days were feast days for the soldiers. Even the German officers enjoyed it.

Ruzi was sure he had seen two of the new soldiers before. Eventually he remembered. One was Ergesh Shermet and the other was a man named Polathanov, who had been headmaster of the village of Ingigche near Margilan.[11] One day during the summer of 1936, Ruzi had been cooking a pilaf in a vineyard with his friend Munevverhan Tashojayev, who was then the headmaster of a primary school. They had just opened their bottles of vodka when they were joined by two other young men, whom Munevverhan introduced to Ruzi. Munevverhan and Polathanov had just been on the same law course in Moscow. Ergesh Shermet was a mutual friend of theirs who had stopped off to see them on his way to his birthplace, the small town of Bulakbashi in the province of Andijan. They spent a long and pleasant day together, talking and singing. Munevverhan could not stop teasing Ergesh. 'Your nickname is "Log", isn't it?' he would say. Ruzi asked why, and Munevverhan replied, 'Well, he is like a log: very hard to get on with.'[12]

Towards the end of the 1930s, the chief prosecutor of Uzbekistan was arrested by the NKVD and executed by firing squad after a brief trial. Ergesh Shermet, by then a young associate professor of law, was appointed in his place. Six months later he was removed from this post and made associate professor again, this time in the law faculty of Sheyhantahur in Tashkent. In 1941 he was drafted into the Red Army and sent to the front, then taken prisoner by the Germans. Ruzi learned all this after they renewed their acquaintance in the camp at Proskurov. They would become close friends.

Throughout 1942 volunteers arrived at the camp at intervals of three or four months, each new batch exactly the same as its predecessors, consisting of walking skeletons in torn clothes, sad-faced. Ruzi did all he could to comfort them and tried to help them to fit into their new surroundings. The majority were assigned to the 162nd Turkish Infantry Division, under General Oskar Ritter von Niedermayer.

In 1912 Niedermayer had been sent by the German army to Iran and India to learn about the local peoples' beliefs and traditions. Germany intended to employ him against the British in India and Afghanistan in the same way that the British had used T.E. Lawrence among the Arabs in the fight against the Ottoman empire. On this mission Niedermayer was the first European to travel the full length of the Dead Sea. He mastered the languages of the area and became as familiar with Islam as if he had been a Muslim student of theology. Just before the outbreak of the First World War, he returned to Berlin, and the German military command immediately sent him to Afghanistan and India on a new special mission, accompanied by a small team.[13] In September 1915 he reached Kabul. There he failed to convince Emir Habibullah Khan to ally Afghanistan with the Central Powers— Germany, Austria-Hungary and the Ottoman empire—against the British and Russians. From there Niedermayer and his colleagues made a dangerous journey across part of Russia and managed to arrive in Ottoman territory on 1 September 1916. Niedermayer was then sent to command German military units in the Middle East. In March 1918 he returned to Berlin.

Between the world wars, Niedermayer earned a doctorate *summa cum laude* at the University of Munich and, after writing an outstanding thesis about Russia, was made a professor. In 1932 he was employed in the office of the German military attaché in Moscow, and the following year he was appointed to the chair of military, geographical and political sciences in Berlin University. On 27 June 1937, he took up a new post in the Institute for Military Strategy and Doctrines, which fell directly under Hitler. He worked alongside Field Marshal Wilhelm Keitel, the commander-in-chief of the German armies, until 25 May 1941, when he was appointed to the command of the 162nd Turkish Infantry.

The career of General Niedermayer was a classic example of the real aim of Western Orientalism: to learn the languages, religion, history, geography and culture of the Muslim countries perfectly, in order to colonise, reshape and govern them. It supports the argument of Edward Said, that while there are Orientalists who have produced valuable work on languages, history and culture, even the best did so essentially in the service of Western colonialism.[14] Niedermayer's identity was primarily academic, not military, but his task was to send hundreds of thousands of Muslims to their deaths in the interests of the German state.

For the young soldiers from Turkestan who had endured hardships and insults in the ranks of the Red Army and then faced death, disease and hunger as prisoners of war, Proskurov was almost like a holiday camp. But it offered no relief for their homesickness, something that gnawed at their hearts. It was impossible for them to write to their mothers and fathers or lovers. Instead their families and loved ones had to be the comrades with whom they trained, shoulder to shoulder. Ruzi knew that their days in the camp would soon come to an end and their life on the front would begin. He prepared himself psychologically for this moment.

In February 1943 the German High Command took a decision to transfer groups of twenty soldiers each from the Turkestan, Tatar-Bashkurt and Azerbaijan legions to the German base in the town of Rovna in the Ukraine. Ruzi was given the task of selecting the sixty soldiers, and he was able to make sure that Ergesh and Polathanov were included. They were first sent to Potsdam on a ten-day theoretical training course. The day after their arrival was a Sunday and there were no classes. Ruzi, Ergesh and Polathanov went together to the NTUC offices in an apartment close to the centre of Berlin, where other national unity committees and governments in exile were based. The door was opened by someone they knew well, Genje Resul.

Genje Resul was good company, humorous and witty. He spoke Russian fluently. Uzbekistan's first president, Yoldash Ahunbayev, came from Margilan and had taken him under his wing. At the age of only twenty-four he had been made chairman of the Margilan Communist Party's Executive Committee. Thereafter he had become president of the town's Institute of Cotton Production, after which he had moved to Samarkand and been made deputy chairman of the Provincial Communist Party Executive Committee—in other words, deputy provincial governor. But Genje was extremely fun-loving, and after he took a second wife and continued to philander he was removed from his post. He was then made head of a primary school in Ingigche. In 1938 he was arrested by the NKVD, given a public trial lasting five days and sentenced to ten years' hard labour. Extraordinarily, six days later he was set free and made head of the Andijan Teaching Institute.[15]

Ruzi had last seen him in Andijan during the festivities marking the opening of a canal. Genje was astonished at seeing his fellow country-men so unexpectedly. He embraced them all with great joy and invited them in. He then introduced Ruzi and his companions to Dr Said Maruf Kerimi, the general secretary of the NTUC, and to Ahmedjan Umarov, president of its educational propaganda branch. Before he was called up for the army, Umarov had been one of the most powerful members of the Samarkand Provincial Communist Party's Central Committee. He and Ergesh Shermet knew each other well. Meeting these old acquaintances eased their homesickness somewhat. They joked with Genje and he told them stories, while Kerimi and Umarov talked about the problems of their country.[16]

Dr Maruf Kerimi was an intelligent and highly cultivated person. He came from Tashkent and belonged to one of that city's most respected families. He must have been pleased by his discussions with Ruzi and his friends, for he said he would ask Alfred Rosenberg, the Reichsminister for the Occupied Eastern Territories, for permission for Ruzi and Ergesh to stay in Berlin and work for the national committee. Ruzi explained that as deputy commander of a unit he ought to go back to the legion, while his friend Associate Professor Shermet was a private soldier, so the application should be made to Rosenberg on his behalf.[17]

Sociable as always, Genje Resul invited them out to a restaurant near the committee's offices. They ate, drank and laughed their heads off.

During the dinner, Genje told them about the power struggle going on between Baymirza Hayit, Veli Kayyum Han's assistant, and Maruf Kerimi, the committee's general secretary. Both were making an all-out effort to become the number two. After the dinner was over, Ergesh and Ruzi talked over the information they had been given and decided that they would stay out of the power struggle.[18]

Many years later, when Ruzi was in the US embassy in Ankara, he learned that Genje Resul was in Turkey and met him at his villa in Bahçelievler's Third Street. Genje explained how he had managed to stay alive. When the Germans lost the war, he had gone into hiding. He had previously married a Dutch woman, with whom he had a son, and had also met a large number of Turkish students in Germany. With their help, he obtained a document from the Turkish consulate in Munich which stated that he was a Turkish national and a citizen. Turkey was at this stage trying its best to help the Turkestan legionnaires, but doing so as secretly as possible in order not to upset the Soviets. Stalin had demanded Turkey's provinces of Kars and Ardahan, close to the Soviet frontier, and was also seeking rights to establish bases on the Straits.

Genje's application to go to Turkey was accepted. He and his wife and toddler son made the journey in a manner which suited his adventurous character: not by bus or train, but on a motorcycle. He found out that there were many people from Turkestan in Adana, and so they settled in Ceyhan in the heart of the Çukurova, Turkey's cotton-growing district. There he taught the villagers modern methods of growing cotton. Genje did not live to see the break-up of the Soviet Union and the establishment of Uzbekistan as an independent country, but apart from his yearning for his homeland he lived a happy life and ended his days in Turkey.[19]

Challenges for the NTUC

The NTUC was well organised. German officialdom approved of this, and so it helped win a good reputation for the organisation. The committee had a substantial budget which had been approved by the Nazi Ministry for the Occupied Eastern Territories. For every soldier fighting in the legions, the committee was paid one Reichsmark (RM) a month, three RM for NCOs and between five and fifteen RM for officers according to their rank. The NTUC was thus freed from dependency on the German government. It attached great importance to its publications and educational activities. Along with *National Turkestan*, which appeared once every two weeks, it also published a weekly magazine for the troops called *New Turkestan* and a periodical called *National Literature. National Turkestan* started off with a print run of 15,000 copies, but its circulation eventually rose to more than 80,000.[20]

Meanwhile, the committee was trying to resist SS policies and planning that went against the interests of Turkestan. In 1941 it had to contend with an SS officer called Andreas Meyer-Mader, an adventurer who worked with Shokay and Kayyum Han on the Prisoners of War commission. Meyer-Mader was the commander of the first Turkestani units of the German army, established in October 1941 under the supervision of the German armed forces' Special Intelligence Unit. He had taken part in the commissions set up for the Turkestani prisoners of war and in the process of selecting them for the German military. Meyer-Mader collected a group of wild Tatar, Azerbaijani, Turkestani, Uzbek and Kirghiz youngsters around him and hoped to become the 'T.E. Lawrence of Central Asia'. His idea was that the legions would go to Central Asia and start a guerrilla war against the Red Army. The Turkestani intellectuals on the committee were seriously concerned about how this project would turn out and objected strongly. Together with some of his legionnaires, Meyer-Mader attempted to assassinate Veli Kayyum Han. Two Turkestanis who took part in the plot were hanged. At the beginning of 1944, Meyer-Mader together with his unit was accepted into the SS.[21] After his involvement in the assassination plot was discovered, he applied to SS Central Command, asking to be tried by a military court in the hope of being cleared. This was refused and he was executed by firing squad.[22]

On the sixth day of the course that Ruzi and his friends attended in Potsdam, Veli Kayyum Han arrived to give a talk, along with Dr Selimi, a mathematician who had been a lecturer at the State University of Central Asia. Kayyum Han outlined the cultural and political history of Turkestan up to the nineteenth century, and then explained how Russian armies had begun to occupy the country from the 1830s onwards. He described Tsarist policies of Russification and Christianisation and told them how Turkestan had been turned into a colony, before going on to speak about the October Revolution and the Soviet period.

Some of those close to Kayyum Han's inner circle argued that the Nazi system was the most perfect form of government and that Turkestan should have a leader who would be totally obeyed, just as Hitler was in Germany; this leader could only be Kayyum Han. After the lecture, Ruzi spoke to Dr Selimi and learnt that he held that view. Polathanov objected: 'We have witnessed the dictatorship of Stalin in the Soviet Union, and his murders. And here we see Hitler being a *Führer*. We lived through painful times in the prisoner-of-war camps and we can all see what is going on here now. If one day, please God, our country does become independent, let's hope there will be nobody there like Stalin or Hitler. Turkestan should be run by a democratic government of the kind which the Jadid movement envisaged.' Ruzi, Ergesh and their friends all supported Polathanov, and Selimi was forced to be silent.[23]

After they had completed the course, Ruzi and Polathanov returned to the camp at Proskurov. The committee's application to the Ministry for the Occupied Eastern Territories on behalf of Ergesh Shermet had been approved, and he was allowed to work for the NTUC. He would later be made head of the Turkestan section of the German Ministry of Propaganda's radio station.[24]

Polathanov completed his training and was sent to the front. Ruzi never saw him again. Towards the end of the war, a wounded soldier returning from the front told Ruzi that he had seen him in East Prussia. After the war, Polathanov was not among the soldiers of the legions remaining in the West, which left two possibilities. Either he had died during the Red Army's advance or he had been taken prisoner and ended his life in a camp in Siberia. When Ruzi eventually returned to his homeland, he was unable to learn anything that suggested Polathanov had survived.

Young Turkestanis were constantly arriving at Proskurov. But Ruzi's own time in the camp was now drawing to an end. Towards the end of 1943 he and his company were sent to the Ukrainian province of Poltava to join the 423rd Sapper Regiment.[25]

Poltava and Kharkov

Ruzi behaved kindly towards the people of the town which his unit was defending, and they liked him. When instructions came from the commandant's office to obtain provisions from the town for the soldiers, Ruzi often made an excuse not to do so, saying that the town had come under attack from partisans and people's eggs and chickens had been stolen. Though this was not actually the case, he managed as a result to spare the inhabitants from giving up their food on several occasions.[26]

The inhabitants of the town at that time were old people, women and children. Its men and boys old enough to bear arms were either fighting in the German army, in the mountains with the partisans, or serving in the Red Army. Ruzi would never forget the things that he lived through on Christmas Eve 1943. For Catholic Ukrainians the Christmas season was especially important. The celebrations began on 23 December and continued for several days, reaching a peak on the evening of the 24th. The commandant had invited Ruzi to the Christmas celebrations that the Ukrainians were holding in the town's guesthouse. Tables were laid with every kind of dish, prepared by the local women. Girls were singing and dancing. The peasants were charging their glasses with home-made *samagon*, making short speeches and then downing their glasses in a single gulp.[27]

Ruzi sat down at a table with the old men of the town. While chatting to them, he was also looking at the girls, who were dancing with each other because—apart from himself—there were no young men present. He had never forgotten the Ukrainian family who had treated his wounds and saved his life at the start of the war. This experience made him feel a particular fondness for Ukrainian people. One of the pretty girls now came up to him and said jokingly, 'Of course a German officer who believes that the Germans are a master race is not going to condescend to dance with Ukrainian ladies like us. So he knows what we should do. We'll dance girl to girl just like this.'[28]

Ruzi had not joined in the drinking so far that evening, but now he called his orderly over and, giving him his pistol, told him, 'Keep your eyes wide open and make sure that you don't touch a single drop of vodka.' Then he filled his own glass, raised it, wished everyone in the room a happy Christmas, and then drained it in a single draught. After this, the girls started to come up to Ruzi to offer him vodka they had made themselves. He would drink with them and then they would dance. The festivities went on until daylight. During the night Ruzi drank so much that he got alcohol poisoning. The old men and women of the town massaged him with snow and made him drink a potion they had prepared from mountain herbs, but it took a good two days before he was restored to health.[29]

The Red Army had not been idle during its retreat to Moscow and had mined all the major and minor forest roads. Ruzi's company had the job of clearing the mines. The work took approximately four weeks. As soon as it was finished, the order came to go to the front at Kharkov.[30] Ruzi and his soldiers from Turkestan took up a defensive position outside the city together with other German units. He was now the commander of a company of 300 soldiers and a few junior officers in the army of Marshal Manstein, commander of the Southern Forces, consisting of hundreds of thousands of men.[31]

The Red Army had suffered huge losses during 1942, both of men and of supplies. The year 1943 therefore was one of preparation for the Soviet forces. Stalin and most of his generals favoured a direct attack on the Germans. But two Soviet generals, Zhukov and Vasilevsky, opposed this plan, arguing that they should wait for the Germans to attack, halt them and then counter-attack. At the beginning of July 1943 they got their way: the Germans attacked the Red Army's lines on two fronts, but were halted in both the north and the south after fierce battles.[32] Zhukov and Vasilevsky had got what they wanted. Red Army units now launched a return offensive at Voronezh and on the steppe close to Kharkov.

The middle of 1943 was a turning point for both the Germans and the Russians. On 17 July, Hitler ordered the German units to withdraw to the positions they had held before the attack. On 21 August Manstein gave orders to evacuate Kharkov.[33] No one knows how many Turkestani soldiers and officers were in the ranks of the Red Army at this date. But well over 100,000 Turkestani soldiers attached to the legions were then fighting with great courage and dedication against the Red Army on the Eastern Front.

Ruzi did all he could to ensure that losses in his company were as low as possible. He had lost fourteen of the Turkestani soldiers he loved dearly and twenty-one had been wounded. Most of those who died drew their last breath in his arms. Though the cause of the Nazis was unjust, the legionnaires thought that they were fighting to rescue their country from captivity and colonisation. Consequently they believed that God was with them and that if they died, they would go to heaven as martyrs. Throughout his subsequent life, Ruzi would always remember the smiles on the faces of his soldiers at the moment of death.

Ruzi himself was wounded by shrapnel in his stomach and his face. But for his helmet strap, the small piece of shrapnel which hit his face would have killed him. Wounded men were treated first in field hospitals close to the military units. Those whose conditions were serious were then sent to hospitals in nearby towns. Ruzi was taken to a hospital in one of the small towns near Kharkov, where he stayed for a few weeks. As soon as he came out of hospital, he was sent back to the Proskurov legion. New Turkestani soldiers had arrived from the camp to fill the places of those who died. They began a further month's training near the village of Barysaw (then Borisov) in Byelorussia.[34]

The sapper company which Ruzi commanded was given the task of building defensive bastions on the banks of the River Berezina. Nine of his soldiers and a corporal were removed from his command and sent to a different unit. Ruzi later learnt that the whole group, whom he had personally trained and looked on as younger brothers, had been lured into a trap and taken prisoner by the Russians. As former Soviet soldiers, they were shot on the spot as deserters.[35]

6

THE TIDE TURNS AGAINST GERMANY

Officer Training

At the start of 1944 Ruzi was wounded again, during an attack by the Red Army near the town of Berezina. Once again he was hit in two places, his stomach and his foot, but this time the injuries were more serious and he lay in the German military hospital in Warsaw for more than three weeks. A panel of military doctors then gave him a general medical check-up. His recent and past injuries led them to conclude that he would not be fit for any further active service at the front.[1]

There existed at this period a General Command for Voluntary Units attached to the Supreme High Command of the German army. Ruzi was placed at the disposal of this command, which was headed by a three-star German general, General Ernst-August Köstring. Ruzi met General Köstring and told him that his health had improved and that he wanted to work with him. The general talked with him for nearly two hours, asking a variety of questions, including how Ruzi and other soldiers would react if the Turkestan Legion was placed under the command of Andrei Vlasov, the former Red Army general who was now working for Germany. Ruzi said that such a decision would be extremely wrong. The Turkestanis' aim in fighting with the Germans against the Red Army was to win independence for their country. But Vlasov dreamed of a great Russia, with himself as dictator, which would include all the territories then part of the Soviet Union. Ruzi's reaction must have influenced Köstring, for he was later a member of the group which opposed placing the legions under Vlasov's control.[2]

General Köstring wanted Ruzi to take up a post in a school which had been established in the small town of Bitsch (or Bitche) in Alsace-Lorraine to train the officer corps needed for the foreign legions. Ruzi accepted and was appointed as an inspector and teacher. The school was close to the Franco-German border, near the Maginot Line of defensive fortifications erected by the French. Selected legionnaires were given a month's intensive education here and then faced an examination. Those who passed it graduated from the school as officers or NCOs depending on the training they had received. They then hurried to the front. Those who failed were thrown out of the army and assessed for the civilian services. Unsuccessful candidates were in a pitiable position. Ruzi opposed the promotion of anyone who was incompetent or unfit, regardless of background. He had served on the bloodiest fronts in the war and had seen with his own eyes how a small mistake could cost the lives of many people. He gave low marks to nine candidates and prevented them from becoming officers. He later learnt that certain people had complained about him to the committee because of this.[3]

Ruzi was given the job of escorting some of the successful graduates to East Prussia. He handed over the new officers at their headquarters and on his way back he stayed a few days in Berlin. At his hotel, he met his friend Ergesh Shermet and they rejoiced at being together again. They attended a concert given by the Russian Cossacks' Choir, then went out to dinner. During the meal they chatted about the state of the legions, the course of the war, what was going on in the NTUC and relations between the legions and German officialdom. They were uneasy about the attitude of some SS officers to the committee and to the legions.[4] The news from the Eastern Front was worrying. If the Germans were to lose the war, what would happen to the soldiers serving in the legions? What would their own position be?

Next day, Ergesh took Ruzi to a building in the Kurfürstendamm. There Ruzi met Kadir Osman, a history professor at Samarkand State University; Dr Yaşar, a heart specialist at the same university; and a former director of the Central Asia State Bank, the vice president and executive member, Kasım Inayeti. Inayeti was also an excellent Islamic scholar, who had studied in the madrasas of Bukhara before the October Revolution. Because of his deep knowledge of religious matters, he had been appointed head imam of the Turkestan Legion.[5] Veli Kayyum Han also arrived, along with an Uzbek officer and Baymirza Hayit, who had been taught by Kadir Osman. Ruzi had met Hayit for the first time in 1939 in the Teachers' Club in Tashkent, where he stayed when visiting Kerim Gaybullayev, editor of *Young Leninist*. The director of the club, Ikramov, had been a close friend of Ruzi's. They had talked while eating Uzbek pilaf together.[6]

On this occasion Kasım Inayeti and Dr Yaşar had prepared some fine *chuchvere*, a Central Asian dish rather like Turkish *mantı* or ravioli. During the meal, Ruzi had a brief but fierce argument with the Uzbek officer about the candidates he had refused to pass at the training school. The officer berated Ruzi and asked him how he could possibly have held back Turkestanis from being promoted. Ruzi answered him coolly. 'I come from the front, from the midst of blood, fire and death. How could I possibly entrust the lives of hundreds of our sons to youngsters who know nothing about the art of soldiery and lack the ability to defend themselves or their soldiers? They are not fit to be officers. That is why I blocked them. And I am not going to act any differently in the future.' Veli Kayyum Han intervened and stopped the argument.[7]

The most important topic discussed during that lunch in Berlin was the activities of General Vlasov. The members of the NTUC and the Turkestani officers were aware that Heinrich Himmler, the head of the SS, supported Vlasov's proposal to set up a Russian Liberation Army and wanted to place the Turkestan Legion under his command too. These were extremely disturbing developments.[8]

Vlasov and the NTUC

Andrei Andreevich Vlasov had been born in 1901 into a family of Russian peasants. He was one of the sailors who started the October Revolution, and rose rapidly in the ranks of the Red Army. He joined the Russian Communist Party in 1930, and was later sent to China as a military adviser to Chiang Kai-shek. In November 1941, as commander of the 20th Army, he distinguished himself by retaking the strategically important town of Solnechnogorsk near Moscow, which had been in the hands of the Germans. He received the Order of the Red Flag for his service in the battle of Moscow. On 13 December that year, *Pravda* mentioned him and published his photograph as one of the heroes of the siege of Moscow.[9]

In January 1942 Vlasov was promoted to lieutenant-general and in March he was personally received by Stalin. He was put in command of the 2nd Shock Army of the Volkhov Front, with its headquarters at Leningrad. All the supply lines of his army were cut off by the winter conditions and finally, on 12 July 1942, Vlasov was taken prisoner by the Germans. Until his capture, Vlasov had enjoyed a brilliant career and had been devoted to Stalin. Put another way, he had been at the service of the Soviet state and shared the vision of an imperialist Soviet Russia.[10]

At that time, Foreign Armies East (Fremde Heere Ost), an intelligence organisation attached to the German High Command, was working to build up an army of ethnic Russians to fight against the USSR, drawn from the hundreds of thousands of former Red Army soldiers then held as prisoners of war. But despite extraordinary efforts by several Russian émigré groups, who viewed the achievements of anti-Soviet organisations in Western countries and also of the NTUC with considerable jealousy, no discernible results had yet been achieved. A small unit called the Russian People's Liberation Army had, however, been established within the German 2nd Panzer Army, under the command of Kaminski, a former Soviet officer of Polish origin.[11]

This initiative was mentioned to Vlasov during his interrogation after he was taken prisoner. Captain Wilfried Strik-Strikfeldt of the Gehlen intelligence and counter-espionage organisation was keen to win him over as a propaganda coup. Eventually Vlasov agreed to work with the Germans and in April 1943 a decision was taken to set up the Russian Liberation Army (ROA) under his leadership.[12]

As a result of the NTUC's representations, objections were raised by Professor Gerhard von Mende, who was head of the Caucasus division at the Ministry for the Occupied Eastern Territories, Otto Bräutigam, head of the Eastern Department in the German Foreign Ministry,[13] Field Marshal Manstein[14] and other generals. The NTUC set out its opposition to Vlasov's plan in articles published in the *National Turkestan* magazine. One of them read: 'We have no international character. We are not against the BOA's work to win Russian territory. If Vlasov can save his people and his lands from Bolshevism with his own strength and his own Russians, if he really can manage it, that would be a great achievement for his own people. If there are people hiding under the mask of the ROA, and if they are trying to divert the soldiers of Turkestan from their course, indeed if they are trying to get them to discard the crests which say "Allah is with us" which Turkestanis pin to their arms, and put up the ROA crest in its place ... these people are Bolshevik agents.'[15]

In its publications the committee stressed that the legions had been set up to fight for the independence of Turkestan, and that this was the sole reason for cooperating with the Nazis and fighting with them against the Red Army.[16] Giving command of the legions to General Vlasov would mean that the war had lost its entire legitimacy for them, and would have consequences that could not be put right later. On 8 June 1944, Hitler gave instructions that the Vlasov movement could only be used for propaganda purposes. But the NTUC's efforts did not cease.

Between 8 and 10 June 1944, the NTUC held a conference in Vienna. Soldiers from the Turkestan Legion attended along with 537 NTUC delegates. In his opening speech, Veli Kayyum Han declared the congress to be the National Assembly of Turkestan. Thirty-six declarations were presented and resolutions were passed, including decisions not to recognise Vlasov's Russian Liberation Committee,[17] to denounce those joining the Russian Liberation Army as traitors, and to oppose Russian imperialism in all its forms. The congress also stressed that the Soviet policy of splitting Turkestan into different republics could not be condoned and that a single united and democratic Turkestan should be created, with a market economy and religious freedom. The Communist Party would be outlawed in Turkestan. A further resolution decided that the congresses set up by the Kokand and Alash Republics would be regarded as the first and second National Congresses of Turkestan. The 1922 Tashkent Congress of Turkestan Muslims would be treated as the third, and the present conference would be the fourth.[18]

Veli Kayyum Han was re-elected as chairman. The delegates appointed thirteen committee members and seven branch chairmen: Dr Sayid Karimi, Baymirza Hayit, Satar Alambet, A. Zakiy, Ravshan and Ayit Beys, and Ergesh Shermet, whose selection particularly pleased

Ruzi. On top of all that, the congress created a National Assembly with seventy members.[19]

Despite the NTUC's efforts, the problem of Vlasov remained. At a meeting over dinner in Berlin in June 1944 at which Veli Kayyum Han was present, the matter was discussed at great length and possible strategies were identified. The most urgent necessity was to have the Turkestani legionnaires on the Eastern Front sent west. Should the war be lost, the committee wanted to prevent its soldiers from falling prisoner to the Soviets.

On 16 November 1944, Himmler and Vlasov held a long meeting in which two SS officers also took part.[20] It concluded with the decision to set up two divisions as a Russian Liberation Army. Himmler agreed to Vlasov's condition that the legions made up of soldiers of non-Russian nationalities—in other words, the Turkestanis, Azerbaijanis, Tatars and Bashkirs—should also be under his command. The record of the terms of the agreement stated: 'When Russia is freed from Bolshevism, it will be an independent state and the people will determine the form of government. It will have its pre-1939 borders. The Crimea will be an independent region and the Russian Cossacks will be given maximum political independence. The maximum level of cultural autonomy will be given to the non-Russian peoples.'[21] This was stabbing the Turkestan Legion and the NTUC in the back, since they were fighting for the independence of their country. Himmler had accepted that Turkestan would continue to be a Russian colony after the war.

The first outcome of the meeting was the setting up of the Committee for the Liberation of the Russian Peoples, chaired by General Vlasov, for whom this represented a complete victory. The general had been made the representative of all the peoples who had been colonised first by Tsarist Russia and then by the Soviet Union and the commander of hundreds of thousands of troops. On 14 November, Vlasov published his Prague Manifesto, declaring that his committee would take charge of all the national committees and the legionnaires of the Russian Liberation Army. The statement was made public on 18 November 1944 at a showy ceremony in Berlin.[22]

Ruzi and his friends were both worried and saddened by the attempt to place the legions under the command of a Russian general with a 'Greater Russian' mentality. The NTUC, and the other national committees representing the Tatar-Bashkir, Azerbaijani, Armenian, Georgian, Crimean Tartars and North Caucasians, issued a statement in which they rejected Vlasov's manifesto and conveyed three important requests to the German government. 'The claim of Vlasov to represent the non-Russian peoples must be rejected and this view prohibited. The right of the national committees and the non-Russian peoples to establish independent states must be recognised. The political administration of all the units belonging to the legions must be given to national committees remaining within the structure of the German High Command.' The statement also stressed that the national committees could not be held responsible for the negative consequences of placing their units under the command of Vlasov, a clearly implied threat that soldiers might defect to the Red Army.[23]

The SS forced Veli Kayyum Han, as chairman of the NTUC, to meet with Vlasov. Kayyum Han informed Vlasov that he would not work with him. Furthermore, he told the Germans that if they insisted on attaching the legions to Vlasov's command, he would be unable to keep control of them. Himmler's decision was doomed to exist only on paper, and caused the already tense relations between the NTUC and the SS to grow even worse.[24]

The SS gave Vlasov financial support on a large scale. On 17 January 1945, an agreement was signed between the Committee for the Liberation of the Russian Peoples and the German Foreign Ministry giving Vlasov access to almost unlimited funding. But the mountain brought forth a mouse. Despite his huge financial resources and the hundreds of thousands of Russian prisoners of war and workers whom he hoped would join, the numbers of soldiers in Vlasov's two army divisions only amounted to around 10,000.

Resisting Vlasov

On 6 June 1944, Allied forces under the command of General Dwight Eisenhower landed five divisions in Normandy on the French coast. By the middle of July, more than a million Allied soldiers reached the shores of western Europe, and by September they had advanced deep into France.[25]

The German High Command decided to transfer the officer training school where Ruzi worked to another city. Ruzi was sent back to

Berlin, where General Köstring informed him that the NTUC had applied for him to be their liaison officer with the High Command. Eventually this was agreed, but Ruzi would only learn later the real reason why the NTUC had asked for him. The committee was of the opinion that officers and soldiers serving in the legions needed to be enlightened about General Vlasov. Ruzi's first duty in this connection was to visit the Turkestanis stationed in East Prussia, to talk to soldiers, NCOs, officers and Muslim chaplains and raise opposition to Vlasov.[26]

Ruzi was much loved by the legionnaires and by his fellow officers. He had instructed thousands of young Turkestanis in the Proskurov training camp and earned their affection. He had put his own life in danger countless times to save his men. A disciplined soldier, he did not look down on anyone.

Ruzi visited the units in East Prussia first and held a series of meetings. He frequently met soldiers whom he knew from his home country and spent time with them, trying to relieve their homesickness and their longing for their families. The soldiers fighting in the legions had endured a terrible time in the ranks of the Red Army, so it was not difficult to explain matters to them. Within three weeks he had collected more than one thousand signatures from leading figures in the legions objecting to Vlasov's plans. He returned to Berlin and handed over the signatures to the committee, describing the situation at the front as he did so. Three weeks later he left on a second tour, this time together with his friend Ergesh Shermet, who was working for the German Propaganda Ministry. This time his task was to visit legions which had been withdrawn from the Eastern Front and were stationed in Königsberg in East Prussia. Again he obtained more than a thousand signatures. The significance of this was that everyone who signed did so on behalf of all the soldiers in his unit. In other words, all the legionnaires declared themselves to be against the Vlasov movement.[27]

The NTUC required financial resources to publicise Turkestani opposition to the Russian Liberation Army. Ruzi and Ergesh asked the legionnaires for help, assisted by the legions' Muslim chaplains. An account was opened in the name of the committee at the Dresdner Bank and very soon there was more money than required to carry out the work. Vlasov had the large budget he had been given by Himmler, and the Dresdner bank also proposed extending a large loan to him.[28]

But as a result of the work done by Ruzi and Ergesh, the legionnaires had even more funds than Vlasov did.

During these tours one of the most interesting people that Ruzi met was Gulam Alim, a former NCO in the Red Army who had crossed the lines to the German side in order to fight in the Turkestan Legion. He had displayed great bravery on the Eastern Front and been awarded the highest medals for heroism.[29] At the time when the disagreements between the NTUC and the SS were at their height, he had seen that the legions needed to make some concession to prevent Himmler growing even more hostile, and so he had gone along with a decision to include his regiment in the structure of the SS, even though personally he opposed it. When Baymirza Hayit visited him on behalf of the NTUC, Gulam Alim had told him openly that it would be quite impossible to submit to being commanded by General Vlasov.[30] Hayit had replied that he would try to get the decision rescinded.[31] Hayit did indeed talk to General Berger of the SS in Berlin, but Himmler would not go back on the agreement he had made with Vlasov.

Gulam Alim

Gulam Alim had been born in Andijan, one of the most beautiful towns of the Fergana valley, and he and Ruzi considered themselves as virtually fellow townsmen. He had prepared a fine dinner for Ruzi: Uzbek pilaf, *samsa*, salad, beer and schnapps. Several of the youngsters from the battalion who had the best singing voices were present, some with their sazes. They were singing melancholy Uzbek songs. One of them sang the poem 'My Andijan' by the homesick Emperor Babur, which he had set to music in the Oriental *rast* tonality.

> My Andijan, my heart is ruined by love of you. What should I do?
> Longing for you has filled my eyes with tears. What should I do?
> My body stoops. What should I say?
> My soul is full of pain. What should I say?

During the dinner, Gulam opened his heart to Ruzi, who was a few years older than him. He told him what he had lived through in recent years; he spoke of the intrigues directed against the NTUC and the Turkestan legions by Himmler and other leading SS officers, and of what he had done in response. 'Do you realise, my brother Ruzi, if you don't have a strong state of your own, and if another country has occupied your lands and the world's great powers are competing to get hold of your country, then however well intentioned you are, you will never escape being used?' he said. 'When I was fighting in the uniform of the Red Army against the Germans, I was fighting for an army which was present in our country as an occupier and a colonist. I fought regretfully, feeling I was condemned, and without believing in what I was doing. Now we are on this side, we say that we are fighting for our country and its independence and so we fight on. From our point of view the situation is actually as follows. The Germans are fighting to enlarge their own territory, fighting other nations to occupy their lands. We have taken our place in their ranks because they need us. They think pragmatically and tell themselves that they should use us. We know that, of course, and despite it we join their ranks, because we have no alternative. More than a hundred thousand of our young men are fighting with their weapons in their hands against the Red Army. These youngsters were condemned to die in the prisoner-of-war camps. What would have happened if the NTUC had left them there? All of them would have died there in the midst of filth, like dogs with mange. Now they are fighting for a sacred cause. So we say, perhaps if the Germans win the war, if the Red Army is defeated, then our country will be rid of its occupiers. But I don't believe we are going to be able to achieve this goal. I am a soldier, my brother Ruzi. The Germans are losing the war. What have we done? While the Germans believed that they were using us, we tried to use them.'

Himmler sent a telegram to Gulam around this time telling him that he must submit to Vlasov's orders, but he told the NTUC that he had refused. Ruzi asked Gulam what he would do if the SS continued to insist. Gulam was silent for a long time. Finally he replied, with his eyes fixed on Ruzi's, 'Carry on fighting the war, but follow a path we believe in, no matter what the conditions may be.'[32]

Gulam told Ruzi about the plans which the SS officers General Gottlob Berger and Reiner Olzscha had for the Turkestan Legion—projects which were incompatible with the interests of the Turkestanis, aimed at using them mercilessly—and the divisive actions of Andreas Meyer-Mader. The SS had decided that the 450th Turkish Regiment should become an SS battalion, and later a brigade, under Meyer-

Mader, who would take it into Central Asia and start a guerrilla war there against the Red Army.[33] The NTUC opposed this idea vehemently. At this point the outcome of the war was unclear, and if the Red Army was not defeated, then spreading the war into Central Asia could lead to be one of the worst disasters in the history of Turkestan. Memories were still fresh of the atrocities committed by the Red Army and the NKVD. This time Stalin could carry out a genocide.

Gulam also described how the SS sought to exploit differences between the Turkestanis. In his unit, Uzbeks, Kazakhs, Kirghiz, Turkmens and Tajiks fought side by side like brothers and chose their deputies from different clans. 'Moscow declared war on the Jadid movement in Turkestan in order to stop the emergence of a nation conscious of its identity, and instead set up Soviet republics which turned clans into nations and made dialects into national languages. I detect signs in the SS headquarters that the Germans will behave in the same way towards us in their future projects,' he said.[34] He revealed that it was he who had caught the two would-be assassins, Suleimanov and Abdullayev, who were going to carry out Meyer-Mader's plot to kill Veli Kayyum Han in March 1944. Both were tried by a military tribunal and hanged. Gulam had argued that Meyer-Mader himself should face the same justice, but the SS had refused. Subsequently it was announced that he had died during an attack by the Russians. 'But I know that he was killed by the SS,' Gulam said.[35]

In the months that followed, Gulam Alim became increasingly reluctant to take orders from General Vlasov. He no longer felt it was legitimate to fight alongside the Germans, since Himmler and Vlasov had destined Turkestan to become a colony of a new Russian state.[36] On 24 December 1944 Gulam invited all the Russian SS officers in his regiment to dinner. Midnight approached and the SS officers were tipsy. Upon orders from Gulam, Turkestan Legion soldiers arrested all those who had served as officers in the prisoner-of-war and concentration camps. He identified sixteen of them who had treated prisoners like animals, killed for fun when they felt like it and murdered innumerable Jews without mercy. He told his soldiers that the sixteen officers he had picked out were butchers without consciences and that their punishment must be death. The officers were forced to kneel on the ground, just as they had made the Jews do in the camps, and then each was killed with a bullet in the back of the head.[37]

Gulam Alim then withdrew with his unit to a forest area near Myjava in Slovakia, about a hundred kilometres north-east of Vienna. Here he made contact with anti-Fascist Slovak partisan groups and, together with them, began to organise attacks and sabotage operations on German units in the area. A beautiful Slovak girl became his lover—but she was in fact a Russian agent in contact with the NKVD. She told the Russians where he was, and one evening he was captured by Red Army soldiers.

The Red Army court martial decided that Gulam Alim's desertion from the German army and his work for the anti-Fascist partisans were extenuating circumstances, and consequently he was given a life sentence of hard labour in a Siberian concentration camp, instead of being executed.[38] Yet the conditions in these camps could in effect be a death sentence in themselves.[39]

Gulam Alim's detention in Siberia was, however, not the end for him. In 1956 Nikita Khrushchev, as first secretary of the Soviet Union, publicly condemned the purges of the Stalinist period. Suddenly it was accepted that the victims of show trials from the 1930s onwards had been treated unjustly, and those who were still alive in prisons and camps began to be released. One spring day in 1961 Gulam arrived home in Andijan, the town which Babur never stopped praising in his poems. The harsh conditions of Siberia had wrecked his body and permanently damaged his health. But despite that he lived another decade in his home town before he died there.[40]

The Legionnaires on the Western Front

A day after his meeting with Gulam Alim, Ruzi left his unit. He spent two weeks visiting the legion camps, sometimes with Ergesh Shermet and sometimes by himself, collecting signatures against Vlasov, fundraising for the NTUC and setting up communications.

The Soviet army was now advancing westwards and the Turkestan legions were preparing for a defensive war. Trenches were being dug, refuges prepared and bridges were blown up. Ruzi observed that morale was good despite the situation. The men joked among themselves, told each other stories, played games and shared meals. Their most popular topic of discussion was how to avoid falling into the hands of the Red Army.

During the early years of the war, the soldiers of the legions had been treated with contempt by Nazi officers and by Germans in general, brainwashed by Hitler's theories of a master race. Heygendorff, the commander of the 162nd Turkestan Infantry,[41] once asked a young soldier returning to camp why he had not used up the remainder of his leave. The soldier replied that he had been travelling on a tram when an SS officer told the driver, 'I won't board a tram that has got this animal aboard. Get him off it,' and off it he had been thrown. Unable to tolerate this and other insults he received on the streets, the young man returned to his unit.[42] Nazi ideologists declared that it was necessary to prevent members of 'inferior' Asian races from marrying German women.[43] Yet despite these humiliations, and even when it became clear that Germany had virtually no chance of winning the war, only very few of the legionnaires from Turkestan, Tatar-Bashkurt, Azerbaijan and the Northern Caucasus defected to the Red Army. Some who did so were thought to have been agents planted in the legions by Soviet military intelligence. Others were Orthodox Christians who had formerly been Red Army soldiers.[44]

For some time the NTUC and the officers in the legions had concentrated on having Turkestani units moved westwards, away from the Eastern Front. By early 1945, to a substantial degree they had succeeded in doing this. The largest, the 162nd Infantry Division, which had done sterling service against the Red Army on the Eastern Front, was now stationed in Italy, near Lake Como, preparing for a fierce defence against the advancing American and British forces.

Ruzi travelled by train from Berlin to Italy. He knew all about the 162nd Infantry Division, but this was the first time he had actually visited it.[45] His mission was to discuss the Vlasov problem and postwar strategy with officers and NCOs on behalf of the NTUC.

Before he set out for Italy, Ruzi had been briefed about Heygendorff by colleagues who knew him.[46] The general was popular with his men and was strongly opposed to placing them under the command of General Vlasov. He had a good understanding of Soviet history and politics and had been the first deputy German military attaché in Moscow before the war. Everyone at the NTUC in Berlin had been delighted when he was made commander of the 162nd.

Heygendorff greeted Ruzi warmly, despite the difference in their ranks, and held a long conversation with him. Ruzi was curious about

Niedermayer's arrest; all he knew was that the former commander of the 162nd had criticised Hitler's policies. He asked the general what Niedermayer had said, and what he himself thought about it.

'Provided this conversation remains between us,' replied the general, 'I will give you an honest answer. You were in Ukraine when you joined the legions. You know how we Germans were received when we went in there. The people of Ukraine celebrated their release from the oppression of Moscow and set up their own national government. The Crimean Tatars too thought that we had liberated them. But what did we do? On the grounds that these territories were *Lebensraum* needed by Germany, we dissolved the Ukrainian national government and arrested its members. Not only did we not recognise the independence of Crimea, we declared it a German colony and holiday resort. The German army stayed in the Crimea for two and a half years, and for five or six months in the Kalmuck Steppes and the Northern Caucasus. During that time, all those places were under military administration.[47] Alfred Rosenberg said that those territories had been directly annexed by Germany and that a new German colonial system would be set up there. Crimea, Northern Caucasus and the Kalmuck Steppes were all going to be run by German governors-general. Indeed, in Berlin there was talk of transferring the Crimean Tatars somewhere else and settling Germans from the South Tyrol and Palestine in their place. These people had hailed German soldiers as liberators when they first set foot there. But a year later they could see that Nazi rule was not much different from Stalin's, and they united against the occupying forces. Ahmet Ozenbeshli, the leader of the Crimean National Party and the symbol of resistance against the Soviets, declared that the Nazis were no different from the Bolsheviks, and because of this he was arrested. And so we made enemies for ourselves.[48]

'Today we hear that Stalin has removed the Crimean Tatars from their country and exiled them to other parts of the Soviet Union. He has punished them for welcoming us with flowers. He pretends not to see that they now loathe us. One reason is that Russia wants to make the Crimea its own territory, and the other is those few months at the start of the war when they trusted us. Mammad Amin Rasulzade, the president of the independent Azerbaijani Democratic Republic which was set up in 1918, offered to cooperate with us on condition that we agreed to the independence of his country. We refused even to make a formal declaration. The nationalities problem is undoubtedly one of the most important that the Soviet Union faces, and we have done nothing that would satisfy people by providing them with a solution.

'You, Ruzi, are fighting alongside us. But for what? So that your country may one day be free and return to being an independent republic. General Niedermayer knows the East very well. He is well informed about the great states and civilisations of your ancestors. He knows your beliefs and your traditions. Could people like him or myself possibly believe the Nazi rubbish about the Aryan race?[49] General Niedermayer placed his knowledge and his experience in the service of the German state. But Hitler was in no mood to understand this. The general knew very well that victory would never be won in this fashion, but Hitler accused him of being pro-Russian, of protecting Russian interests. The truth will surely come out one day. But I hope that it will not be a very bitter day for us all.'[50]

Ruzi looked with respect and affection at the general, who had opened his heart to him. He told him that he felt uncomfortable after his conversation with Gulam Alim and the events he had described.

'Which of us doesn't feel uncomfortable, Ruzi?' Heygendorff asked. 'You should take care to stay alive; do your best to save yourself.' They talked further about the progress of the war and the future of the soldiers in the legion. They dwelt on what could be done to ensure that, if the war was lost, they would not fall into the hands of the Soviets.

Fethalibeyli

Half the soldiers of the 162nd Infantry Division spent their time at Lake Como preparing defences by day, and half by night, each working while the others were resting. Ruzi went out by day and by night to talk to them, always with two German soldiers at his side. He collected signatures and asked the men about their cares and difficulties.[51]

On one of these days Ruzi ran into Abdurrahman Fethalibeyli Dudenginski, the chairman of the Azerbaijani National Committee, whom he already knew from Berlin. Thousands of kilometres from their home countries, the two friends embraced each other on the shores of the lake. Fethalibeyli had been born in the small town of Duden in

Nakhchivan in 1908, making him nine years older than Ruzi. They had almost a brotherly relationship, affectionate and respectful.[52]

Fethalibeyli enquired what Ruzi was looking for and told him about his own work. He too was opposed to Vlasov and was convinced that only a dreamer could now believe the Germans would win the war. The pressing problem for them was to save the lives of the soldiers in the legions. Fethalibeyli told Ruzi that he had gone to Rome to ask Mohammad Amin al-Husayni, the grand mufti of Jerusalem, for his assistance in ensuring that Azerbaijani soldiers did not fall into the hands of the Soviets. On the way to Rome he had wanted to visit his wife, Leyla, and his son, Ali, whom he had managed to evacuate from Soviet territory to a small town in northern Italy, but he had been unable to travel there and so had come to Lake Como instead to visit the legionnaires of the 162nd Division.

Ruzi knew this was a rare chance for him to talk freely with the Azerbaijani leader. He told him about his own past, his family and Margilan, and asked about Fethalibeyli's life story.[53]

Fethalibeyli belonged to a respected and well-known family with links to the Safavid dynasty, former rulers of Iran. He had chosen to become a soldier and studied at the Tiflis Officers Academy. Early in the 1930s he had gone to Leningrad and there joined the Communist Party. In 1936 he passed the examinations to enter the Frunze Military Academy. But during the years of Stalin's terror he had been expelled from the military on the grounds that he was a counter-revolutionary and a bourgeois nationalist. In 1937 he had married Leyla and their son had been born. Like other officers who had been expelled from the Red Army, Fethalibeyli was summoned back when the Second World War began and had his rank restored. He had been sent to the Finnish Front, received the Red Star medal and in 1941 he was promoted to the rank of major, but in September that year he was taken prisoner by the Germans.

In the prisoner-of-war camp, he began reflecting on ways of extricating himself from the wretched conditions there. So he wrote a long letter to the German High Command, proposing that an Azerbaijani legion should be set up and that he should be given a position in it. This chimed with what the German authorities were hearing around the same time from figures such as Nuri Killigil Pasha and the ambassador

Hüsrev Gerede. Fethalibeyli was taken into the German army and given a post on the Caucasus Front. He displayed exceptional ability and in 1943 he was appointed to the Azerbaijan Liaison Office, which later became the Azerbaijan National Committee. On 6 November 1943 the Azerbaijan National Congress met in Berlin and he was unanimously elected chairman of its National Committee.

A short-lived Azerbaijani Republic had been set up in 1918 following the October Revolution. It was led by Mammad Amin Rasulzade, but he was arrested and sentenced to death after the country was occupied by the Red Army in April 1920 and proclaimed the Soviet Republic of Azerbaijan. Thanks to his earlier acquaintance with Stalin, however, his sentence was commuted to exile. Rasulzade was to spend the rest of his life in Germany, Poland and Turkey, until his death on 6 March 1955.

Ruzi asked Fethalibeyli if it was true that he had differences of opinion with Rasulzade. Fethalibeyli replied that Rasulzade was the natural leader of the Azerbaijani independence movement, that there were no disagreements between them, and that it was only on the strength of Rasulzade's endorsement that he himself was at the head of the movement's military wing. Fethalibeyli was cooperating with the Germans in order to keep tens of thousands of Azerbaijanis alive who would otherwise die in camps, and because Azerbaijan needed an army to fight for its independence. Rasulzade thought that if the Germans did win the war, they would immediately have to grant Azerbaijan its independence, and he was right to think so. But the Germans would under no circumstances openly proclaim this. Fethalibeyli claimed that the Germans wanted to be the only ones in control of Azerbaijan's oil after the war.[54]

Ruzi asked after a good friend of his, Fuad Emircan, who had been working with Fethalibeyli. Fuad was the son of a minister in the 1918 government in Azerbaijan. He had been educated at Galatasaray Lycée in Istanbul and then studied in France. When the war began, he had come to Berlin and had met Fethalibeyli in the camps. Fethalibeyli said that Fuad had disliked the attitude of the Nazis, and so had returned to Paris.

At the end of a long conversation, Ruzi and Fethalibeyli said farewell, exchanging good wishes for the future.

7

ESCAPING FROM THE JAWS OF DEFEAT

Return to Berlin

After eleven hectic days with the 162nd Brigade in northern Italy, Ruzi returned to Berlin by train. There had been no attacks from the air during his time there, but the units were on a state of alert, expecting Allied planes to arrive at any time. At Landshut in Bavaria, the train stopped and several aged-looking carriages were added. Passengers boarded, then the train travelled north through the Bavarian forest for about half an hour. There was a magnificent view from the windows and everything was calm.[1] Then suddenly alarm bells started to ring and the train came to a sharp halt. Allied aeroplanes were attacking. Ruzi and the other passengers abandoned the train and hid in the forest while bombs and bullets rained down.

Eventually the attack came to an end. Four passengers had been killed and another twenty wounded. The train staff prepared to get going again, warning passengers to make haste.[2] Ruzi climbed aboard the nearest carriage. It was furnished luxuriously and tastefully, and there were just four people inside: a beautiful and fashionably dressed blonde woman aged about fifty, a girl of sixteen or seventeen, and another woman, also well dressed and attractive, with a baby in her arms. Ruzi felt awkward and said, 'I didn't know that this carriage was reserved. I had to get on board in a hurry—I do apologise. I will get out at the next station.' The older woman replied that they would be happy for him to travel with them.

Ruzi learned that the older woman, Frau Blaschke, was the wife of a very senior government official in Vienna and that the two younger women were her daughters and the baby her grandchild. The Viennese official, sensing that conditions were becoming dangerous, was trying to send his family to Hamburg. The women were completely unaware of the brutality being practised in the Nazi prison camps and the massacres in the concentration camps. Their pride in their nation was extremely high and they believed that their own race was supreme and that all others were lower. They nonetheless behaved respectfully towards Ruzi, and the younger ones did everything they could to attract his attention.[3]

The train journey lasted two days, with long waits while repairs were made to lines damaged by air attacks. During one halt in the forest the young mother began to open her heart to Ruzi. She had married two years earlier. Her husband, like most young German men, was a soldier. One week after their wedding he had gone back to Ukraine, and soon afterwards he had been killed in an attack by the Red Army. The baby in her arms was a reminder of the short time they had spent together. Since then there had been no more affairs of the heart for her. She longed to love and be loved. Ruzi told her his own story. The young woman was amazed. 'Have you really never been married?' she asked. He explained that he had been drafted into the army at the age of twenty-three and that in his own country this was still considered too young to get married. In any case, with war looming he would not have wanted to marry and then leave a young wife alone.

'You acted correctly,' said the young woman. 'Look at what happened to me. I was twenty-two when I got married and my husband went off and left me behind. If I did not have this baby to remember the marriage by, perhaps I would have long since forgotten it. Well, then, why have you not married a German woman?'

Ruzi replied, 'We are at war. We do not know what will happen tomorrow. I dream of returning to my country when the war is over. I have no idea how a German woman would adapt to life there.'

She answered, 'If people love someone, they can adapt to life anywhere. It looks as if you have found someone you love and who loves you.'[4]

'There is something else which is important,' Ruzi said.

'What is that?' she asked and looked at him with curiosity.

'You know the Nazis' claims about a master race,' Ruzi said. 'The SS have banned marriages between foreign legionnaires and German women.'

The young woman gazed deeply at Ruzi with eyes that were as blue as the sea. She grasped his hand and then suddenly the words poured out of her. 'The cause of all these disasters is *them*, isn't it? I hope they go to hell, both they and their perverted theories. Come on, marry me. We will have beautiful children ... People of mixed blood are beautiful, you know.'

'Let's get back on the train,' said Ruzi. 'It's about to go.' For the rest of the journey, he tried not to bring up the subject again.

When they reached Berlin, Ruzi said goodbye to his fellow passengers, who were going on to Hamburg. Although they invited him to visit, he never met them again.[5]

During that journey, Ruzi realised something very important. A fanatical minority, their ideas shaped by perverted theories, had taken control of the destiny of a nation and brought down an enormous disaster on themselves and on humanity. The same was true in all totalitarian systems. The Bolsheviks had gained control of the October Revolution with slogans about rights, justice, equality, the brotherhood of different peoples and the right of nations to determine their own destiny. Yet Stalin had murdered tens of thousands of people whom he considered dangerous to himself. Millions of middle-class people had been liquidated on the grounds that they were enemies of the state. For the Jews and others suffering under Nazi oppression, the biggest tyrant was Hitler. For those enduring the oppression of Stalin, he was the greatest tyrant. Perhaps systems like this had been the enemy of humanity throughout history.[6]

In the USSR Ruzi had had plenty of Russian friends who were highly moral people and whose hearts were full of love for humanity. And during his years in Germany, he had made friends with Germans who possessed the same qualities. It was not nations and peoples as such who were the sources of oppression but fanatics with a totalitarian mentality who established a system of rule for their country and dominated it. Ruzi had experienced both types of totalitarianism and understood their real nature. He hated both Communism and Nazism.[7]

The Red Army Approaches Berlin

In the fortnight that followed Ruzi's return to Berlin, everything changed completely. The Allies were advancing into the interior of Germany from the south, the west and the east. There was now no point in thinking about Vlasov and his activities. His priority was the future of the Turkestani legionnaires. At the series of meetings in February 1945 known as the Yalta Conference, Churchill, Roosevelt and Stalin decided the shape of the postwar world. On 11 February, they agreed that former Soviet citizens who had left the USSR before 1 January 1939 could remain in the countries where they were currently living, but those who had left at a later date must, if the Soviet Union requested it, be sent back. For Ruzi and the NTUC, the practical import of this was that soldiers who had fought in the national legions would be handed over to the Red Army.[8]

In Berlin in April 1945, it was as if the end of the world had come. The city was bombed every night for hours and the ear-piercing shrieks of the sirens would wake people up and drive them down into bomb shelters. Ambulances carried the injured to hospitals. Ruzi tried to get medical help for wounded legionnaires from the Eastern Front. They had lived for years face to face with death in the midst of blood and gunfire. Now they were on their own. Most were village boys from Turkestan, hardly able to speak Russian when they were drafted into the Red Army, given no proper training, and then sent out to be cannon fodder during the German invasion. They had fallen prisoner, undergone the hell of the camps, and then been sent out to the front again, this time on the other side. They hadn't learned proper German either. Ruzi went around Berlin in a car that the German High Command's Volunteers section had assigned him, and when he ran into one of these soldiers he would do what he could to help him.[9]

Under these conditions, it was impossible for the NTUC to continue its work in Berlin. The committee had rented a beautiful building in the spa town of Marienbad in the Sudetenland,[10] and at the start of April Veli Kayyum Han and Baymirza Hayit, his deputy in charge of military affairs, moved there along with Ergesh Shermet from the propaganda radio station and three or four soldiers from the legion. The NTUC was on good terms with General Werner, the regional military commander, and Major Heipel, who commanded the town's garrison.[11] The committee's building was a kind of sanatorium, and Ruzi was able to send some of the less seriously wounded soldiers to recuperate there.[12]

As a soldier himself, Ruzi had to visit the Volunteer Command headquarters. After reporting there, he would go on to the old NTUC offices, now almost deserted, but still a refuge for Turkestani soldiers who managed to get to Berlin. Ruzi advised them to escape to the south or the west in order to avoid the Red Army.

The German army had now split into Northern Group Command, with its headquarters at Hamburg, and Southern Group Command, based at Salzburg. Ruzi was placed under Southern Group, a decision which pleased him because it included the 162nd Turkish Infantry Division.[13] One day a lieutenant-colonel at the Volunteers headquarters told Ruzi to bring his military ID card with him the next time he came.[14] The following morning Ruzi went early to headquarters and handed over his ID to the lieutenant-colonel. He was expecting to be discharged. Three hours later the officer reappeared and held out Ruzi's ID card. 'Good luck on your new mission,' he said. Ruzi read the following lines:

> The officer to whom this card belongs has been sent on special duty to northern Italy. Every member of the German Armed Forces who sees this document is obliged to give him the fullest possible assistance.
>
> (Signed) Field Marshal Wilhelm Keitel, Commander-in-Chief of the German Armed Forces[15]

He had no idea what his task would be, but he had in his hands a document that would clearly open many doors.

The colonel then told him, 'After you returned from the 162nd Infantry, US and British forces launched a major attack on it and the division sustained heavy losses. Its units are completely scattered and they need to be pulled together and to take up a defensive position. We don't have any officer on active service available who knows the division, speaks their languages and understands their ways. So you have been given the job. You will go to northern Italy, regroup the scattered units and get them reorganised for defensive warfare. If you can, set up a brigade; if not, a regiment. Good luck!'[16]

It was a mission that would normally have been assigned to an experienced general. Ruzi was still an army captain, just twenty-eight years old. He was being asked to rescue the remnants of the 162nd Turkestani Infantry Division, while he was thousands of kilometres away from his own country, in lands belonging to others where he had been cast by fate.

'Well, go, and if the war is lost, however many Turkestani soldiers you do manage to save from the Red Army, you will have saved that number of lives. There is nothing written down in your army card which specifies your mission. You can use Keitel's signature to protect the legionnaires and yourself too.'[17]

Chorabay

At this time Ruzi was living in a district on the western side of Berlin. One day around noon, a young Turkestani called Jizzakli Chorabay, who worked for the propaganda radio station headed by Ergesh Shermet, came all the way from the eastern side of the city to visit him. Because of the constant bombing there was no public transport. Ruzi was rather startled to find that this young man had spent hours sweating on a bicycle to reach him at a time when the Red Army was very close to Berlin and the city was being bombarded night and day.[18]

Chorabay spoke both German and Russian very well. He had defected from the Red Army to the Germans around a year earlier. He had told the Germans that he wanted to fight against Russia in the legions and asked to meet Veli Kayyum Han. He was, he said, going to express his devotion and respect to him and also give him important information.

When he was taken to see Kayyum Han, however, Chorabay told him that he was an NKVD agent who had been specially trained to assassinate him. He said his conscience was uneasy and he had decided not to carry out the murder because he knew that Kayyum Han was a patriot working for Turkestan. He would accept whatever decision Kayyum Han made about him. Kayyum believed what Chorabay told him, took him under his protection and got him a job working for Ergesh Shermet.[19]

After the customary greetings and questions, Chorabay asked Ruzi what his plans for the future were, now that the Russians were so close. Ruzi became suspicious and gave evasive answers, saying he had not thought much about the future and didn't have any kind of plan. He mentioned nothing about his new mission. Chorabay said that he and several friends had decided to remain in Berlin and that they did not expect to face any problems which could not be overcome. He advised Ruzi to stay too. Ruzi told Chorabay that he was pleased with his suggestion and would give it serious thought, and would let him know as soon as he took a decision about it.[20]

Chorabay was in reality an NKVD agent, but there had never been a plan to murder Veli Kayyum Han. The story of the assassination had been made up in order to win Kayyum Han's trust. His real purpose was to glean information for the NKVD about the activities of the committee and the legions.[21] He had come to see Ruzi in order to lure him into the hands of the Soviets. Once again, Ruzi was saved from certain death by his caution and intelligence.

In the years after the war, Ruzi and Baymirza Hayit heard from a friend of theirs by the name of Muminjan, who was studying in Berlin. Muminjan had lodged with a German family there, and he knew that Chorabay had lived with their daughter. He asked the girl if she had any news of Chorabay, and she showed him some letters. Chorabay wrote that for years he had been informing Soviet intelligence about the committee and its work. He had now returned to the Soviet Union, but his treachery had not done him much good, as the NKVD had forced him to live in the town of Jizzakh in Uzbekistan.

Thus Ruzi learned that his suspicions about Chorabay's untrustworthiness had been correct. It also emerged in the years after the war that the NTUC's official photographer had been a Russian agent.[22]

Innsbruck and Bolzano

Before leaving on his new mission to Italy, Ruzi filled a suitcase with his diaries and a collection of important NTUC documents and photographs. He put his spare clothing into a second suitcase and gave both to Tashkentli Maksum, one of his friends, who was going to Italy as interpreter to a group of legionnaires trying to join up with what remained of the 162nd Infantry Division. Maksum was a clever young man who spoke perfect German and excellent Russian. Ruzi warned Maksum not to allow the suitcases out of his sight until he handed them over again in Italy. Then, taking only those things he would need during his own journey, he went to the railway station and left Berlin.

It would be many years before Ruzi next saw Berlin, where he had lived through so many experiences, both painful and happy. As the train pulled out, he gazed back at the city he was leaving behind, sunk in thought. A series of memories passed before his eyes: the restaurants and cafés on the Kurfürstendamm, the cabarets on the Alexanderplatz where he had danced like crazy until dawn, and the brief love affairs.

Ruzi remembered the family of one of his friends, Kasım Inayeti, a Finnish Tatar who was a regimental imam in one of the legions in France. He was also a member of the NTUC and head of its religious affairs section, highly cultivated and venerable, and helpful at every opportunity to those around him. He would frequently invite Ruzi to his home for dinner, and his wife would fill the table with the Uzbek dishes which their guest loved.[23] When the Allies began to advance into France, he had sent his wife and four daughters to Berlin, thinking that they would be safe there, and asked Ruzi to keep an eye on them. The eldest daughter was twenty-two and the youngest eleven. All were angelically pretty, and the eldest extremely beautiful, with blonde hair and deep blue eyes. She was engaged to an officer from Turkestan. One day during an air raid, the mother and three of her daughters went down into the cellar of a neighbouring building, while the eldest girl remained upstairs with her fiancé. A bomb struck the house and killed the four who were sheltering in the cellar. It was fate, or something like it.

Ruzi reflected on human nature. He had seen SS officers who had killed men for pleasure and NKVD officers who had done the same. But he had also seen people sacrifice their own lives to save someone else's, regardless of their religion or nationality.[24]

Air raids were now constant, and so trains travelled only by night. In many places the rails had been torn up. After delays that lasted hours, Ruzi's train eventually arrived at Salzburg, where the German army's Southern Command had its headquarters. Two German officers met him at the station and handed him the documents he would need for his journey to Italy. They also gave him a bag full of Italian lire and Reichsmarks, telling him that his mission was of the utmost importance and that in the course of it he would need a great deal of money.[25]

Ruzi had to wait until 10 p.m. for the next train. The journey between Salzburg and Innsbruck normally lasted two hours, but in April 1945 it took Ruzi an entire day to complete it.[26] Innsbruck resembled a scene from the Last Judgement. The town was full of soldiers who had been withdrawn from Italy but did not know what to do or where to go. The German officers in Salzburg had told Ruzi that it would be impossible to travel by rail or road to Italy. American aircraft were constantly monitoring the roads and any traffic would be targeted and bombed.

Ruzi wasted no time in going to Army Command in Innsbruck. He showed Field Marshal Keitel's signed instruction in his ID card and was immediately admitted to see the commander. Ruzi explained his mission. The commander stressed the dangers of going further south at a time when everyone had withdrawn from the area. But Ruzi was insistent. He wanted to get to the Turkestanis and help them. The commander said that he would give Ruzi a Volkswagen car and a driver in civilian clothes, but he warned him, 'Don't go along the main roads. Travel at night and use the minor roads between the villages.'[27]

Following this advice, Ruzi managed to reach Bolzano in northern Italy. The small town was full of SS officers and their families fleeing from the Allied forces. Ruzi's driver asked permission to return to Innsbruck, and they said goodbye. Ruzi had been on the road for days and he was very tired. He went to a hotel in town, arranged his luggage, took a shower and had a shave. After a short rest, he made for the garrison commandant's office.[28]

The garrison command at Bolzano was a large old building. Its garden was full of German soldiers, among whom Ruzi noticed a group of Turkestanis. Some had been sent to Bolzano from other fronts to join the 162nd Infantry, while others were from the shattered division itself. He was delighted to meet even a small number of his fellow countrymen, particularly when he recognised one of them. This soldier was called Hussan Ikram and he had worked in the Turkestan branch of the German propaganda radio; Ergesh Shermet had introduced them one day. All the Turkestani soldiers were pleased to see Ruzi too. They knew of him as a popular and well-respected officer who had been given wide powers, and they were keen to tell him their stories and have his assistance.

Hussan Ikram explained to Ruzi all that he had gone through in the last few months.[29] At the beginning of March, Baymirza Hayit had called him in and handed him a letter, asking him to take it to a group of Turkestanis at an address in Prague written on the envelope. Hayit told him that the outcome of the war was now clear and the legionnaires would have to be quick-witted. The people to whom he was taking the letter were a group of key soldiers working in the legions. In order to avoid falling into the hands of the Soviets, they should now withdraw southwards and into the interior of Germany. Hayit also mentioned the Yalta Conference and its decision about former Soviet citizens. 'As soon as you have handed over the letter, come straight back to Berlin. We are going to Marienbad and we will send you there too, along with your friends.'

Hussan had stayed four days in Prague. As soon as he got back to Berlin, he called in at the NTUC offices, but the chairman and other members of the committee had already left.[30] A German officer from Volunteer Command was on the premises, with a translator called Luderzin and a few Turkestanis. 'You must join the 162nd Infantry Division in northern Italy. You will set out on a long journey at once,' said the officer, holding out two envelopes. One contained travel documents, the other a letter for the commander of the unit he was to go to. Hussan went to the station to find out the times of the trains. On the way he ran into Jizzakli Chorabay, who worked with him on the radio station.

'Where have you been?' Chorabay asked. 'I've been wanting to give you some good news for days. I've been looking for you in order to rescue you.'

Standing beside Chorabay were two German women whom Hussan did not know and a Turkestani called Rejep Said. They repeated what Chorabay said. Hussan was delighted to think that with his friends' help he would be able to get back to his home country.[31] They parted, agreeing to meet again the next day at the same place and time. Hussan turned up on time for the meeting. He waited an hour and a half but Chorabay did not come. Years later he learned that Chorabay had been an agent of Soviet military intelligence. He had been prevented from coming that day by an air raid. Otherwise he would have led Hussan away and handed him over soon afterwards to the Red Army to be summarily shot. The women had been members of the German Communist Party. His life had been saved by a coincidence.[32]

Hussan decided to return to Prague, where he thought he could meet up with the soldiers to whom he had given Hayit's letter and perhaps travel to Italy with them. A general instruction had been sent out for Turkestani legionnaires to join the 162nd Infantry, no matter what unit they were currently attached to. But when Hussan reached Prague, an old woman who had been the soldiers' servant told him that they had taken a sudden decision to leave the city in order to evade the Red Army. Hussan then embarked on a train journey full of adventure which took him through Vienna, Linz, Salzburg and Innsbruck. In his memoirs he described what happened when he eventually arrived in Bolzano and found the garrison command building.

'A lieutenant looked at my document and said, "You stay here now and rest. We are gathering you people [i.e. those who were under orders to join the 162nd Infantry Division] here. In two or three days' time, cars will go from here to Verona and we can send you with them." And saying that, he took my document. One of the sergeants took me up to the first floor and showed me the beds. "Choose whichever bed you want. There is food downstairs at all times," he said. After he told me that, I felt worried, wondering whether I was going to have to stay there for weeks.[33]

'I got myself washed and went downstairs and wandered around in the courtyard, which was like the quadrangle of a palace. There were perhaps ten Red Cross nurses cooking food in the kitchen. In one room, five or six officers were sitting around a table and talking. Some of the ordinary soldiers who were there had formed a group and were chatting. There was a great deal of activity in the yard.'

One of the soldiers beckoned Hussan over.

'"Sit down and let's talk," he said, and asked me, "Are you going to Verona?"

'"Yes," I replied, and briefly explained my mission.

'"We have had orders to go to Verona too," he said "But you listen to me now. Perhaps before we go to Verona, we'll be going to our own homes. If they haven't already sent you there, you can thank the Lord. By not sending you they've saved you from being taken prisoner or even death."

'"Why are you talking like that?" I asked.

'"The owners of the place we are going to went there ahead of us. The Americans have come to occupy it. The war in Italy is coming to an end. Perhaps they will now give us orders to return to Germany.""[34]

Hussan stayed in the dormitory that night, and the following day started to wander around the streets of Bolzano. The town was seething with soldiers fleeing from the south. He observed that the cafés were full of Italians, and that people were excitedly explaining things to each other and that they seemed extremely merry.

In South Tyrol, ethnic Germans and Italians lived side by side and consequently most Italians spoke at least some German. Trying to find out the cause of all the laughter, Hussan greeted an old Italian with a good-natured face who he thought would not be unfriendly. 'Why are you so cheerful, father? Please explain so that we can share in your happiness, and have fun too.' The old man said that the Americans were rapidly advancing and that they were laughing with joy because they would soon be liberated from German occupation.

Hussan Ikram wandered around Bolzano for two further days. During that time he ran into other Turkestani legionnaires and the fourteen of them stuck together as a group. It was on the second day, as they were waiting in the garden, that he saw Ruzi approaching, walking with firm steps, evidently sure of himself.[35]

Ruzi looked affectionately at these exhausted young men. Like tens of thousands of other Turkestani legionnaires, they were naïve, innocent and helpless. There was no longer a 162nd Infantry Division. The great majority of its soldiers had perished in Allied attacks. Most of the survivors had surrendered to the US army in northern Italy. There was no way Ruzi could form a new unit with the remnants of the shattered 162nd. All that could be done was to save as many lives as possible. But the chain of command had broken down and each soldier was simply trying to save his own skin. If they fell into the hands of Soviet units, they would be killed on the spot. If they surrendered to Allied forces, they would be handed over to the Red Army, as the terms of the Yalta Conference made clear, and then executed.[36]

Ruzi showed Field Marshal Keitel's signature to the garrison commandant's aide-de-camp, and once again he was received straight away. The brigadier greeted Ruzi warmly, asking him what he could do for him. Ruzi explained the reason why he had come. The brigadier replied that it would be quite impossible to create a new military unit out of the destroyed division. He told Ruzi, on condition that it remained between them, that their units of the 162nd Infantry were now being released into the interior of Germany and that Bolzano was full of officers and their families and ordinary soldiers who had come from the south. Then he asked Ruzi what he wanted to do, given the situation. Ruzi told the brigadier about the decision of the Yalta Conference and how the lives of the legions' soldiers were under threat. The brigadier enquired how he could help. Ruzi told him about the fourteen Turkestanis who were at that very moment waiting in the garden. They had been Soviet soldiers before they joined the German army and so were liable to be executed on their return, but if they were given a military discharge they would be considered to be civilians and would have a chance of survival. Ruzi concluded, 'I request you to release these soldiers from military duty and to sign their discharge papers.'[37]

The brigadier looked Ruzi in the face with a mixture of warmth and sadness, then called his aide-de-camp and gave instructions for the discharge papers to be prepared. Ruzi went out and noted the names and ID numbers of the fourteen soldiers, and gave these to the aide-de-camp, who took the list and went back inside the headquarters. Ruzi began to chat with the soldiers. He ordered tea for them, then handed them each some of the money he had been given by the Germans at Salzburg station and told them to buy something to eat. About two hours later, Ruzi was called back into the commandant's room and given the papers releasing the fourteen men from the army. Ruzi thanked the aide-de-camp and said farewell to him.[38]

Ruzi had not told the soldiers what he had been discussing with the brigadier and trying to achieve. He now explained the situation and placed their discharge documents one by one in their hands. The soldiers were overjoyed, as if they had been given an official document allowing them to return home. One of them was an associate professor in the Department of Persian Language and Literature at Samarkand University. This man asked Ruzi, 'Please act as our leader and get us out of here. Let's go to one of the countries to the south. Even if we don't go home immediately, we'll find a way to get to East Turkestan later and that way we will be near to our own country.' His innocence and optimism grieved Ruzi. The young fellow and his friends had no idea of the impossibility of reaching East Turkestan, to the north-west of China, from Italy. He did not tell them that they were naïve and living in a world of dreams.

'I am still a soldier,' Ruzi said. 'I have no discharge papers, and there are things I can accomplish as a soldier. Whatever fate lies ahead for my fellow soldiers, let it be mine as well. I am going to return to Germany. If any of you wants to go back to Germany with me, I will take him along.' But only Hussan Ikram accepted. Ruzi said his farewells to the thirteen others on the spot, for these simple boys supposed that they would be able to go straight home. [39]

Ruzi and Hussan were to spend the last months of the war, and the first years after it, together. For both of them these were exciting days, often full of adventures and terrors but also frequently happy. Their friendship was close though not one of equals. Hussan would write in his memoirs: 'Though Ruzi and I were the same age, I always regarded him as an elder brother, or someone like a commander. I was always astonished by his intelligence, his humanity and his courage.' [40]

After the war, Ruzi always wondered about the fate of those thirteen youngsters. In later years he tried hard to find them or learn what had happened to them, but in vain. Most likely they had fallen into the hands of Red Army soldiers who were searching for legionnaires house by house, street by street, in villages, on mountaintops and by the sides of roads. In the first months after the war, Soviet military police even hunted together with American soldiers. The years went by, but Ruzi never heard anything further of them.

Turkestanis Handed Over to the Soviets

These were the final days of the war. Leaders of the national committees were struggling to get away to other countries. The German authorities did not put up any obstacles and even helped them obtain the necessary documentation. Fethalibeyli, the chairman of the Azerbaijani National Committee, had been smuggled out to Egypt. Alihan Kantemir, the chairman of the Northern Caucasus Committee, and Kedia, the chairman of the Georgia Committee, had gone to Switzerland. However, Veli Kayyum Han, the chairman of the NTUC, wanted to share the fate of his colleagues on the Turkestan committee. He declared that he would stay in Germany and rejected proposals to get him out.[41]

Legionnaires and former Soviet citizens who gave themselves up in European countries occupied by the Allied forces were speedily handed over to the Red Army. Only a very small number of these people were tried in courts martial. One of those court-martialled was General Vlasov, who was taken to Moscow after being captured by the Red Army.[42] On 1 August 1946 he was condemned to death by hanging and the sentence was carried out immediately.[43] Others were given sentences ranging from death to a minimum of twenty years' hard labour in work camps in Siberia. But the great majority were shot dead at the place where they were handed over.

Thousands of soldiers from the 162nd Infantry Division who surrendered to the Americans were taken by boat to the Soviet Union. Some of these threw themselves into the sea off Istanbul and a number of them managed to avoid being taken back on board. But even those who got away were later caught and handed over to the Russians. Their fate was no different from that of the other legionnaires. They were either condemned to death or sent into exile in Siberia.[44]

On 29 May 1945, Veli Kayyum Han, some other members of the NTUC and 120 high-ranking Turkestani military officers were arrested by American soldiers in Marienbad on orders from the supreme Allied commander, General Eisenhower. Along with soldiers from the legion, they were sent in goods wagons by train to Prague and handed over to the Red Army. The NTUC members, with the exception of Kayyum Han, were then released on the basis of immigration documents endorsed by German officials confirming their status as civilians.[45]

In Dachau in southern Germany, around thirty Turkestani officers who had been locked up prior to being transferred to Russian custody set fire to the building and died. They hoped that by sacrificing themselves they would save the lives of their friends who were also waiting to be handed over to the Soviets. Perhaps it was because of this incident that Eisenhower ordered that Kayyum Han, who was awaiting this fate, should be spared. Apart from Baymirza Hayit and a few others, almost all the remaining captives were immediately murdered by the Soviets.[46]

The Yalta Conference in February 1945 had decided that only countries which had declared war on the Axis powers by 1 March that year could take part in the founding sessions of the United Nations Organisation. Turkey therefore officially declared war on Germany, and in June the Turkish government took a decision to hand 195 ethnic Turkish refugees over to the Soviets. This was one of the most shameful events in recent Turkish history. In 1951 Şevket Mocan, deputy for Tekirdağ in the Turkish Grand National Assembly, raised the question of these refugees in the assembly. The minister of justice, Rükneddin Nasuhoğlu, answered that the handover had been carried out according to the rules agreed for military fugitives and on the principle of reciprocity. He added that in 1947 a parliamentary committee had abolished Turkey's internment camp at Yozgat was scrapped and that those of its inmates who wanted to remain in Turkey and were of Turkish descent had been given the right to acquire Turkish citizenship. The minister also noted that two former Red Army officers, Enver Anar (aka Kaziyef) and Kadri Başaran (aka Adem Kardeşbeyli), were among the 195 people who had been returned to the Soviet Union.[47]

Şevket Mocan was not satisfied by the minister's answer. He replied: 'My honourable friends, the events which I have drawn to your attention are not just simple things that happened in the past and are now finished. The damage they caused is a historical responsibility which continues today, which is why it would have been a crime against history not to draw them to the attention of the Grand National Assembly, and I have done so. But these events did not take place in the way that the Justice Minister has just explained. That is the aspect that makes me saddest of all. At no time were these people, as has been stated, soldiers who had been interned. I ask you to pause and think about this for an instant. Were these people soldiers who had been interned or were they political fugitives? When one refers to military fugitives, as far as I know, one is talking about people who either entered our territory because their plane crashed, or who did so in an armed clash and were interned by the military authorities. But when it comes to people who saved their own lives in a disaster and then took refuge within our frontiers, they are exclusively termed political refugees. Among them there are those who, although they had no previous connection with our country, were removed from camps and were being taken to Russia by ship and who then risked their lives by jumping overboard into the Bosporus near Arnavutköy[48] and were rescued by local fishermen and sought asylum in Turkey. These are political refugees, are they not?'

Mocan also referred to the case of two former Red Army officers who were brothers-in-law of a current assembly member: 'Once long ago they were officers in the Russian army but they did not forget their nationality and they did not adopt the new creeds [i.e. Communism] but fled to Germany, where they remained for a long while. Then they came to our country and took refuge with their sister ... But, and this is something deeply shameful, one day they were taken from their home, told that they were being sent to Ankara but actually escorted by Police Commissar Ali Riza to the frontier and offered up as sacrifices on this altar. In the history of this nation, there are many noble examples of us fighting to defend a single fugitive, as we did for King Charles XII of Sweden, but there have till now been no disgraceful or shameful cases of offering up political refugees as sacrifices on an altar.'[49]

Ergesh Shermet sent an official letter on 8 February 1952 to Abdulvahap Oktay, a representative of the Turkish Grand National Assembly, which included the following statements: 'The total number of our countrymen who either crossed over to the Germans in the course of the war or were taken prisoner by them was around 400,000. Around 90,000 to 100,000 of these either died because the Germans let them starve to death in the POW camps, or were killed because they were alleged to be Jewish, Mongolian or Communist, or perished from various diseases. Of those who survived, about 100,000 were taken out of the camps and placed under arms. The remaining 200,000 were used as "eastern workers" on the various fronts. Until the opening of the Western Front, our soldiers fought against the Soviets on the Eastern Front. But after the opening of the Western Front, the National Committee put forward various pretexts and succeeded in having 70,000 to 75,000 soldiers transferred there. Our aim in doing this was to prevent those of our soldiers who were taken prisoner from falling into the hands of the Soviets. Most of these soldiers were deployed in France and Italy. After the war, the work began of handing our people over to the Russian side. We were unable to prevent this and more than 70,000 of our men were forcibly handed over to Russia. After the war we began the work of regrouping those of our countrymen who had managed to conceal themselves in some corner of Germany. We finally managed to locate up to a thousand of them in Europe.'[50]

Another writer makes these striking observations: 'To sum up: around 300,000 Turkestanis fought on the German fronts either as legionnaires or as "eastern workers". A large proportion of these lost their lives on the Eastern or Western Fronts. Almost all of the remainder, apart from around one thousand men, were handed over to the Soviet Union when the war ended. The bill for the four-year-long German–Russian war, as far as the Turkestanis were concerned, was the loss of around 400,000 human lives just on the German side. Losses on the Russian side cannot be known for certain but are probably much larger than this number. Throughout history this is perhaps the first time that Turks have fought for other masters in a war of which they themselves were not one of the masters and they perished on both sides in this struggle which was no concern of theirs. As Sir Olaf Caroe said, "In this game of chess between two emperors, their role was to be a pawn and this was their tragedy."[51]

8

REFUGE IN ROSENHEIM

Lange

The soldier Ruzi and the new civilian Hussan were determined to return to Berlin. They had no shortage of money, but they knew that there was a lack of food in Germany and everything must be obtained with rationing coupons. Ruzi gave Hussan some Italian lire and told him to buy as much food as he could carry. He himself went to see the officer in the garrison who dealt with communications and asked him to get them two places in a vehicle carrying military materials to Germany. The officer told them to be there at 9 p.m. Cars could only travel at night because of the danger of air attack. Ruzi made a note of the number plates of the vehicles and went back to the army guesthouse.[1]

Hussan was waiting for him and showed him his purchases. He had managed to buy plenty of rice, oil, sausage and salami, bread, various canned foods and many other provisions. 'I also bought sixty pairs of nylon stockings,' he added.

'I can understand you buying so much food, but I can't see why on earth you would buy women's stockings,' Ruzi said.

'I bought lots of food, as you can see, without using up all the money you gave me. I saw that nylon stockings were very cheap. Well, we are leaving Italy and I didn't want the lire to go to waste, so I bought the stockings. You may not understand now, but you will very soon see how useful they can be. And then you will say I was right and thank me,' said Hussan.

Ruzi asked him how he was going to carry such a heavy load back to Germany, and Hussan answered: 'What am I waiting for here? I'll carry them on my back. If I get very tired, I'll find people to help me.'

And in the days that followed, those stockings would indeed be very useful. Perhaps they did not save their lives, but they certainly made their time on the road a great deal easier. At each house they stayed in, they gave the women pairs of stockings and thus ensured that they displayed all their skills as cooks. Ruzi and Hussan were entertained like two princes.[2]

Ruzi and Hussan turned up at nine o'clock that evening as they had been told, but the car only arrived an hour later. It took them ten hours to cover a distance which normally should have taken two. The road was full of vehicles carrying soldiers retreating from Italy and their goods, as well as the families of officers. In addition to the traffic, attacks by Allied aircraft slowed progress to a crawl.

At Innsbruck they went to a hotel and rested there for three or four hours. Ruzi suggested to Hussan that since they had nothing to do until midnight, they should make use of the time by looking around the historic city. While they were strolling about, they bumped into Tashkentli Maksum. He was wearing a very smart civilian suit; it had come from Ruzi's suitcase, and it suited him very well. As a joke, Ruzi said, 'Congratulations on your new clothes, Maksum.' But his mind was on the other suitcase, the one full of documents. With some embarrassment, Maksum told them his story. Only three or four members of his group had made it to Italy. They had run into danger on the road and most had scattered. Maksum had barely escaped with his life. Thinking that the documents and pictures in Ruzi's suitcase might be incriminating, he had burnt them, just keeping the clothes for himself.

Ruzi was upset at the loss of his diaries, which he had believed would cast light on an important period in the history of Turkestan, and the papers and photographs. But it was wartime and there was nothing to be said or done. Trying not to let Maksum see how upset he was, he told him he could keep the suit, shirt and shoes as a present.[3]

In Innsbruck they also met some other Turkestani friends. These were Karis Kanatbay, who had been elected as general secretary of the

NTUC in Vienna in 1944; Associate Professor Ahmedjan Umarov, formerly an official in the cultural and propaganda branch of the Samarkand Communist Party; and Salim, an associate professor of mathematics at Tashkent State University.[4] Karis Kanatbay was the leader of the group opposed to Veli Kayyum Han, the NTUC chairman, and his two companions also belonged to it. Ruzi believed that the existence of an opposition within a movement was a sign that it was in good health; he thought Kayyum Han and some of the NTUC members were not as democratic as they should have been. But he had not approved at all of this opposition faction's decision to leave the NTUC and found a new 'Council of Turkestan'—for which they could only find five members—or their decision in April 1945 to join Vlasov's anti-Soviet force.[5] They chatted for a while, but Ruzi did not mention that he and his friend were returning to Germany, or the plans he had for the future.[6]

That night Ruzi and Hussan boarded another military goods vehicle and set out for Rosenheim in upper Bavaria. Because of dense traffic and frequent checkpoints, they only managed to cover forty kilometres and were forced to stay overnight at the small town of Kufstein. At half past seven the following morning, they managed once more to get places in a goods truck in a military convoy and set off along the Munich–Salzburg autobahn in the direction of Rosenheim. Hussan Ikram described this journey in his memoirs: 'As soon as we entered a village called Happing, two kilometres outside Rosenheim, an American airplane appeared in the distance. The driver stopped the truck and yelled, "Get out of the vehicle and hide." Everyone threw themselves to the ground and began running towards the woods. We hid in the trees near to the road. From about 100 to 150 metres, the plane began raining bombs down on to the tarmac road. Then it flew over us and did not come back. A little later we gathered around the truck. It had suffered a direct hit and its engine was now useless. Petrol was leaking out of the tank. Holes had been torn in some of the bags at the back. The Germans in the truck decided to go on to the town on foot and we set off with them. But there were the foodstuffs and the other things we had purchased from the special shops in Italy. The food and our own packs were a bit heavy for us and we began to get tired.'[7]

They had walked about 600 metres carrying their goods when they came to a white-painted house. They decided to ring the bell and ask permission from its owners to rest there for a little while. A man came out. He was tall, rather heavily built, sported a long upturned moustache as thick as a finger, and had a long white beard. He greeted them, told them his name was George Lange, and invited them inside. He was the owner of the house, a retired railway worker.[8] They explained that they were going to the town and asked whether they could leave their things with him until they came back.

'Of course you can leave your things here as long as you like,' he said. 'You look very tired. Come in first and rest for a little while and then go into town.' His proposal delighted Ruzi and Hussan. Meanwhile, two women came into the room, one in her mid-forties and one around thirty, holding the hand of her young son. They were astonished to see these unexpected guests. They gazed at them with curious eyes for a moment and then said, 'Don't be shy. Sit down and rest.' They brought their luggage inside, and the old man who owned the house showed them to the bathroom, saying, 'Take a bath first and get comfortable.'

Ruzi and Hussan enjoyed a shower and a shave and put on clean underwear from their bags. Meanwhile, the women had been preparing breakfast in the dining room. There were five or six slices of bread on the table, jam, sugar and two glassfuls of milk. Hussan told them that they had brought food from Italy. The women stared at him as if afraid that their guests did not like the breakfast they had prepared. Hussan took out salami, cheese, butter and a loaf of bread from his case, real luxuries in Germany at that date. He gave them to the younger of Herr Lange's daughters. 'Please put these on the table too,' he said.[9]

The guests insisted on their hosts joining them for breakfast. At first they politely refused, but soon they sat down at the table. This was a feast for them. After breakfast the women were enchanted when Hussan gave each of them a pair of nylon stockings, explaining that he had purchased them things from the special shops in Italy. He said that he had easily been able to pay for such expensive goods, but he did not mention that the money had been given to him by Ruzi.[10]

Both of Herr Lange's daughters were married. They had heard no news of their husbands for months. At that time, when the Soviet forces entered Germany from the east and the Allies from the south and west, they had no idea of what had happened to them or even whether they were alive or dead. Ruzi tried to console them. 'You have given us a fine breakfast and a warm bed. God never leaves any act of goodness unanswered,' he said.

Ruzi told Herr Lange that he was heading for the military school in Rosenheim. The old man explained how to get there. He added, 'Your business may take a long time. Go and settle your affairs, don't worry. We will let you be our guests here as long as you want.'[11]

Ruzi and Hussan walked the four kilometres from the village of Happing to the military school. The front of the building was crowded with waiting soldiers. As usual, having shown the signed instruction from Field Marshal Keitel in his military pass, Ruzi was quickly taken to the commandant. He explained that he had to go to Berlin and asked for a car. The commandant replied, 'The staff officer of our school is about to give a briefing on the most recent state of affairs. I would like you to attend it too. Then we can talk about your request.'[12]

Ruzi told Hussan to wait outside and went in to the briefing. The officer explained at length that the area around Rosenheim was surrounded by American units and that they were preparing to enter the town. The only possible way to get out through the encirclement was to cross the River Inn. After the meeting, the commandant asked Ruzi, 'In these circumstances, do you still want a car?' Ruzi replied that, as it was no longer possible to go to Berlin, he no longer had any need for one.[13]

Then Ruzi said, 'If you will permit me, I do have a different request to make of you.' The commandant made a favourable response, so Ruzi continued: 'There are legionnaires here who fought shoulder to shoulder with German soldiers throughout the war. If they are captured, it will be the end for them.' He explained about the Yalta agreement and told the commandant that if these soldiers were given discharge papers, then they would count as civilians and might not be handed over to the Soviets. The commandant said that he knew the 162nd Turkestan Infantry Brigade well and had a lot of respect for it. 'Prepare a list of all the people you have in the area and give it to me, and I will sign their discharge papers.'

Ruzi and Hussan made up a list of twenty people. They had of course already obtained discharge documents for Hussan from the garrison commandant at Bolzano. Ruzi warned him not to tell anyone that the people whose names were on the list were not actually there with them. Soon afterwards the commandant gave Ruzi the discharge documents he had signed for all the people named on the list. Ruzi thanked him and they bade each other farewell. Then Ruzi and Hussan set off back to the village of Happing.[14]

Four years is a long time in the life of a young man, and that was how long Ruzi had worn a German uniform. By a strange irony of fate, the day Ruzi took off that uniform for the last time would be 8 May 1945, the day the Allied forces accepted Germany's unconditional surrender.

A New Era

In the centre of Rosenheim, Ruzi and Hussan saw large numbers of people, soldiers and civilians, men and women, rushing around with bags of food. They asked an elderly German woman where people were getting the bags from. She replied that the garrison commander had given orders to distribute the foodstuffs in the army storehouse. So those who went into the depot came out with their arms full.[15]

When they got to the depot they saw that a captain with a light machine gun in his hands was overseeing the food distribution. Ruzi recognised him. He had served as an NCO in Ruzi's section in Ukraine during the fighting around Kharkov. He had been brave, hard-working and good-hearted. He knew Ruzi instantly, and they greeted each other and embraced. In the couple of years since they had last met, he had been promoted. He told Ruzi that if he had discharge documents for several people, he could go into the storehouse and claim the foodstuffs needed for that number.[16]

Most of the stores had already been taken, but Ruzi and Hussan managed to collect five kilos of sugar, a tin of artificial honey, some tea, a can of sunflower oil, laundry soap, half a bag of tobacco and a few other small items. They carried these out with the help of two or three other soldiers, and then Ruzi waited with the goods while Hussan went to the village and told the Lange family what had happened. The old man was almost beside himself with joy. In these final stages of the war, what Ruzi and Hussan were bringing was a virtual treasure for people who seldom saw any food other than potatoes and onions. Hussan and Lange borrowed a wooden wheelbarrow from a neighbour, loaded the goods onto it, and set off for the village.[17]

A small stream called the Mangfall runs between Rosenheim and Happing before joining the River Inn near the town. As the friends approached the stream, they saw that German soldiers were preparing to blow up the bridge over it. Locals were watching with anxiety. Ruzi stopped the wheelbarrow and went over to the soldiers. He showed Field Marshal Keitel's signature to the sergeant-major in charge, who promptly saluted and asked for orders. Ruzi told him that blowing up the bridge would achieve nothing. Rosenheim was now surrounded by the Americans and they would inevitably soon enter the city. The soldiers abandoned their attempts to destroy the bridge, and the delighted crowd thanked Ruzi heartily.[18]

They learned that two American tanks had halted beside a church on the road leading to Happing, so they could no longer go that way. They crossed the bridge which Ruzi had just saved and plunged into the woods. After a long, cold and arduous walk along tiny paths in the rain, they eventually reached Herr Lange's house. The women of the household put the things they had brought down in the cellar. Herr Lange clasped the half-bag of tobacco to his chest, murmuring, 'This is my life, this is my treasure.' It turned out that he was an incorrigible pipe-smoker who had been unable to get hold of decent tobacco for a long time.[19]

The women now showed Ruzi and his friend two small rooms in the cellar that they had prepared for them, inviting them to relax and sleep. On their beds the clothes they had taken off that morning lay washed and ironed. Hussan could not help saying to Ruzi, 'Now do you see why I bought those nylon stockings?' They had another shower and then rested. The women brewed tea from the depot, sweetened with honey, which they drank with pleasure.[20]

Late at night they heard noises outside. Heavily loaded horse-drawn carts were passing by on the road near the house. Herr Lange went outside to investigate. Soon he came back and told them, 'There was a big storehouse of foodstuffs in the woods too, and the commander has ordered it to be handed over to the people. So the villagers who own horses have been there to fill up their carts. They're going home now.' Herr Lange was a little upset that because he had neither a horse nor a cart he would have to miss this opportunity. Ruzi put his uniform back on, stuck his revolver into his belt and went out. He stopped every cart that went by and took a bag of flour from one, a bag of macaroni from another, then sugar, then wine; one bag of whatever there was. The villagers were so used to being given orders by armed German officers that they obeyed him without any trouble. The goods were carried down to the cellar of the house. Herr Lange's daughters were beside themselves with joy. They now owned several months' supply of foods that they had done without in the last few years. Ruzi was so tired that he fell asleep without even waiting for his dinner.[21]

At breakfast the next morning, sitting in front of a well-stocked table, Herr Lange said, 'The two of you have brought us luck. It is obvious the war is soon going to be over. We have not been able to get any news from our sons for the last four months. I pray that they are both still alive. Why not stay with us until they arrive? We will look after you. When they do come, we will decide what we should do and find a way. But don't leave us until they are here.'

Ruzi and Hussan knew that Germany was about to sign an unconditional surrender. What was going to happen—and what would become of them—once the war ended? For now there was nothing they could do but wait. So they decided to accept Herr Lange's proposal and stay for a while.[22]

After breakfast they went down into the town again. They noticed a large building where officers and private soldiers were going in and out. It was a clothing depot where civilian garments were being distributed. Ruzi and Hussan showed the officer on duty the discharge documents that they held for twenty soldiers and asked to be given clothing for their friends, but he replied that clothes were only being handed out to individuals on receipt of a signature. Ruzi told the officer that his friends were busy assisting a group in need of urgent aid and they had delegated him to represent them.

'When they come back from their mission, they can pick up their pay and clothing,' said the officer at first, but eventually he agreed to give them coupons for five people. They showed these to a second officer and collected lots of clothes, which they took back to Herr Lange's house.[23]

During the years of the war many Italians went to work in Germany, particularly in the Ruhr valley. When the war ended, they wanted to return home, but because of the damaged state of the roads they could often only travel by bicycle. Ruzi and Hussan met two Italians doing exactly this, and bought their bicycles in return for some suits from the clothing depot and a sum of money on top. So now they had bicycles and could be mobile.[24]

Hard Times

A very difficult time now began for the legionnaires. Those who had managed to remain free in the interior of Germany were being hunted down. In every town teams of four soldiers, one American, one British, one French and one Russian, rode around in the streets in military vehicles looking for dark-haired people whose features betrayed them as Orientals. It was at this time that Rezzak Baki, Burhaneddin Kasim and Kadir Bek, members of the Turkestan Committee, were arrested by Soviet soldiers and put to death.[25]

While the manhunt was going on in full force, Ruzi and Hussan were in hiding. Hussan recalled the events that followed Germany's unconditional surrender on 8 May: 'Herr Lange told us to stay inside the house while he went to the village to find out what was going on and get some news. He went off and came back at midday. "American and British soldiers have entered Rosenheim and they may be coming to the villages too," he told us.'[26]

Ruzi and Hussan watched from the window of the house's drawing room, never taking their eyes off the road. At about six o'clock on the morning of the third day, Herr Lange told them in great agitation that American soldiers had got out of their jeeps and were coming towards the house, so they should go and hide themselves in the hayloft. The two friends hid themselves in the hay, and Herr Lange's daughter called out to them every half-hour, 'Father hasn't come yet,' which was a code they had agreed on, meaning 'Don't come down'.[27]

A couple of hours later, Herr Lange returned and called for them to come down. He said, 'I was in Helmut's restaurant. Two Americans and a British soldier arrived and ordered beer. There were four elderly Germans in the restaurant. One of the soldiers asked Helmut whether there were any German soldiers in the village. Helmut replied that those from the village who had gone off to the army had not yet returned, and that there were no soldiers in the village at all. So they got into their car and drove around two or three streets and then went off.'[28]

Every day Herr Lange would go outside two or three times and prowl around. On the morning of 12 May, soon after he had left the house, he came back looking fearful. He asked his daughter for a glass of water and then said: 'Last night three American soldiers and a

German interpreter turned up at Helmut's restaurant. They each had a beer and then asked to pay the bill. Helmut said that they were his guests and refused to take any money. Then the soldiers asked for a stronger drink. Helmut said that because of the war, he did not stock any hard liquor. But one of the soldiers went down to the cellar to look for drink and there he saw two fugitive legionnaires, whom they promptly arrested. One of the soldiers said to Helmut, "You lied to us," and began to strike him. But one of the Turkestanis interrupted and said that they had been hiding in the cellar without Helmut's knowledge. One of the American soldiers stayed in the car with the two fugitives, while the other two went with three old people from the village to search their homes.' Herr Lange was extremely anxious. 'They have caught two people. We are going to have to be very careful.'[29]

Ruzi and Hussan then endured a fortnight of fear and anxiety which seemed to them to last for years. They later found out that in those two weeks more than a hundred soldiers of the Turkestan Legion had been captured around Rosenheim, in the villages of Happing, Bad Aibling and Kolbermoor, and then handed over to the Russians.[30]

Towards the middle of May they had a second narrow escape. Hussan recalled: 'One day in the afternoon, Herr Lange came back to the house, terrified and pale with fear. His lips trembled as he spoke to us. He began to tell us how seven or eight soldiers and officers had gone drinking in the Traberhof beer house. An American NCO had paid a dollar and said, "We don't have any more money. What can we do?" Manfred, the owner of the beer house, had replied, "You are our guests, one doesn't accept money from guests," and had handed back the dollar. Then the soldiers left and spread out across the village. "It is likely they will come back in this direction," Herr Lange said. "God protect us—and you too. I am going to look out of the windows. If I sense danger, I will immediately let you know. Meanwhile, go back up into the hayloft."'[31]

After supper that evening, Herr Lange talked about important things that had happened in his life, and the two friends spoke of how they had been drafted into the army after university and the dangers they had seen at the front. They heard noises outside and Herr Lange immediately hurried outside, soon returning to say that soldiers were coming out of the house next door, some 200 metres away. Ruzi and Hussan ran up to the hayloft and hid, each breathing through a straw. Soon afterwards they could hear voices speaking English and German. Hussan sweated and trembled with fear and had difficulty drawing breath through his straw.[32]

A moment later, they heard boots on the stairs. Hussan believed that his end had come and there was no point in hiding any longer. They are going to find us anyhow, he thought to himself, so I might as well hand myself over. Ruzi, lying beside him, must have understood from the thumping of his heart and his shaking what Hussan was thinking, because he whispered, 'For heaven's sake, get a grip, Hussan. Being frightened doesn't do anyone any good. Whatever God has decided is going to happen. Give your heart to God.' And he squeezed Hussan's hand so hard that it hurt.[33]

The soldier who had come up to the hayloft began to look down at the beautiful view around the house. He called down to his friend below and he too came upstairs. In the doorway of the hayloft the two soldiers said something to each other. Then one of them asked, 'Why have they piled this hay here?' There was a pitchfork standing by the wall and Hussan wondered what he would do if the soldiers plunged it into the hay. But the soldiers only stopped to enjoy the view from the hayloft for a few minutes and then went downstairs again.[34]

The sounds of the soldiers' boots on the stairs were like a proclamation of liberty. The two friends stuck their heads out and drew in deep breaths. They sat for a while in silence.

After making Ruzi and Hussan endure their moments of terror in the hayloft, the two soldiers searched everywhere else in the house, including their rooms in the basement, then they went outside and looked in the field of maize and in the high bushes growing between the trees. On finding nobody, they left without saying anything.[35]

The two friends spent most of May hiding in the house. One day in early June when Herr Lange was going to Rosenheim, they begged him to find out what was going on in the town. Was it still being patrolled by American, British, French and Russian soldiers? Herr Lange reported that the town was now very quiet and there was not much military activity on the streets, but that legionnaires who had been caught in neighbouring small towns and villages were being held in the barracks of the officer training school and the stadium. 'I don't know where they are going to take them later,' he said. Ruzi and Hussan were pleased that the town was once again calm but greatly saddened to hear about the captured soldiers, who they were quite certain would be handed over to the Red Army.[36]

One day when they were sure that all was quiet, they asked Herr Lange to go to the nearby small town of Aising and discover what was going on there. Having heard that there were no soldiers on patrol there, they went by side roads to Aising and found the registrar's office there. They presented their discharge papers and said that they lived in Happing and wanted to be officially registered. Once this was done they were entitled to the same food coupons as German citizens and they had the right to work. They had begun to make preparations for the time after the war.[37]

From now on Ruzi and Hussan went regularly to Rosenheim. Only American soldiers were now patrolling the city in their jeeps; the others were nowhere to be seen. They breathed more easily at the absence of Russians. But still, whenever they saw American soldiers, they would turn and glance behind them, pretending to be looking in a shop window.[38]

Baratbay and Nur Mehmet

One day Ruzi and Hussan were walking around Rosenheim when they met two soldiers from the Turkestan Legion. They were overjoyed to learn that there were other Turkestanis who still remained free and had not been handed over to the Soviets. After they introduced themselves, one of the men, whose name was Baratbay, said, 'It's dangerous here. Let's go into that church. No one will disturb us there; in fact it's empty at the moment.' Ruzi and Hussan were astonished. Why go into a church, and what would they do there? The other soldier, Nur Mehmet, told them not to worry. He and his friend were staying there. They went into the church, which was indeed empty, and they swapped stories of what had happened to them in the last month.[39]

Baratbay and Nur Mehmet had been among more than a hundred Turkestanis who had been taken prisoner by the Americans on the border between Czechoslovakia and Austria. They were herded into a barracks building with other members of the national legions. The

Americans treated their detainees well. Two days later a group of Russian soldiers and officers had arrived, but the American officer commanding the barracks refused to let them see the Turkestanis, who took hope from his attitude. However, around the same time, a larger number of captured legionnaires were brought in, and on the fifth day of their captivity around 400 detainees of various nationalities were made to get on board goods wagons, which were then locked from the outside. It was exactly the same as when they had been drafted into the Red Army: put on board goods trains and sent from the towns of Central Asia to Russia. No one knew where they were going,[40] but people were talking about an order that had been given by Stalin declaring that former Red Army soldiers who had fought against the Soviets were traitors to their country and should be shot. Some of the young legionnaires on board assumed that at some point the train would stop and they would be taken off it and executed. Others were more hopeful: 'They may be taking us to labour camps in Siberia,' they said.

After seven hours, the train stopped in Rosenheim. Baratbay, Nur Mehmet and the rest were taken to the stadium, which had been turned into a holding camp. There they were told that when the number of prisoners reached 400 or 500, they were to be handed over to Red Army officers who would take them away by train. In the previous few days, thousands of legionnaires had been brought to the camp and handed over in this way. But there were only rumours about the trains' destination and the fate of those on board.[41]

As Baratbay and Nur Mehmet were being taken from the station to the holding camp, they noticed that the troops escorting them were chatting among themselves and paying little attention to their prisoners. They took this to mean that either the Americans did not consider them as their prisoners or that they knew what was in store for them and so would turn a blind eye if they escaped. 'The soldiers in charge are at the front,' Baratbay said to Nur Mehmet, 'so when they turn a corner, they can't see us. Let's seize our chance then, and run into the town and hide somewhere.' So as soon as they got an opportunity, they ran. When they had gone about 300 metres they had seen this pretty little church and slipped inside. The priest was astonished when he saw them, covered in sweat and gasping for breath. 'Have you come here to worship?' he asked them. They explained the situation and the priest immediately hid them in a small room beside the altar. They waited for hours, but no one came looking for them.[42]

The priest fed them and found them civilian clothes. During services they hid in the little room. Days went by, but still no one came asking after them. This was the first day they had gone outside, when they ran into Ruzi and Hussan. According to the priest, prisoners were still being brought to the camp and handed over to the Russians every two or three days. He thought that this would carry on for several more weeks and that it would be risky for them to remain in the church, so he had told them that he planned to find them a place to stay with friends of his in a village some distance from the town until the danger was over.[43]

Nur Mehmet went to fetch the priest, who lived nearby, and when he joined them he told them about the hardships being faced by the populace, many of whose sons had gone off to war and never returned. 'These farmers are good-hearted,' the priest said. 'They will happily embrace young people like you who can help them.' Ruzi and Hussan thanked him and explained that they were now living in a farmhouse and were very well treated, but that if they got into difficulties they would remember his offer of help. They said their farewells to Baratbay, Nur Mehmet and the priest, and then left the church.'[44]

Sufis do not believe in coincidence; they hold that the will of an individual is just one tiny part of the immense universal will of the Creator. 'There is no such thing as a coincidence, there is only concord,' they say, implying that all experiences in life are preordained in eternity.

In 1963, when Hussan Ikram was living in the United States, he went one day to watch a football match in New Jersey and after the game he ran into Nur Mehmet. They met up a few more times and reminisced about their days in Rosenheim. Almost thirty years later still, when the Soviet Union had broken up, Uzbekistan became an independent republic once more, and Hussan went back to his home town of Namangan, he had a remarkable experience.[45]

During the long time he had been away, new avenues and streets had been built in Namangan; new buildings had gone up, and many things had changed. Hussan began to search for the family home where he had been born and which he had left so many years before. He asked directions of a white-bearded old man who was walking along, leaning on a stick.

The old man gazed a long while into Hussan's face and asked him if he came from abroad.

'Yes, from a very long way away,' he replied.

The old man embraced him and said, with tears in his eyes, 'But what has happened to my son?' Hussan understood that he was looking for a son who, just like him, had gone off to war many years before.[46]

'I had just one son,' the old man said, 'but more than half a century ago they took him away to be a soldier and I never had any news of him again. Officials told me that he had lost his life in the Great Patriotic War. But I didn't believe it. I kept on seeing him in my dreams. I know that he is still alive.'

Hussan asked him his son's name. 'I am called Nur Ahmet and my son's name is Nur Mehmet,' he said. 'Do you know him?' Hussan was overcome by emotion and his eyes grew moist, but then he hesitated. He had seen Nur Mehmet in New Jersey in 1963, and it was possible that since then he had died. So he said nothing. Even if Nur Mehmet was still alive, he would be at least seventy-five years old. 'If he is still alive, then he will definitely revisit his country one day, just like me,' he told himself.

The old man began to tell him that around a thousand Turkestanis had stayed in the West after the war and that those of them that were still alive had begun to return to their country now that the Soviet Union was no more.

'I hope that your son will ring your doorbell too one day, saying, "Dad, I have come back," and hug you,' Hussan said.

'Are you on a visit?' the old man asked. When Hussan replied that he was, he put his arms round him again and wiped away his tears. 'When you go back, please look for my son and tell him that his father has been waiting for him for fifty-two years.'

Nur Ahmet then told Hussan how to find the family home which he had left so long before. He walked on for another kilometre and a half and finally found it.[47]

After they had said goodbye to Baratbay, Nur Mehmet and the kind-hearted priest in Rosenheim, Ruzi and Hussan returned to the house of Herr Lange in Happing. Wanting to let things settle down a bit, they did not visit the town again for a few days. Life gradually began to return to normal. The search for prisoners ended, and the holding camps in the stadium and the garrison command were closed. Some days later, when they went into the town again, they saw that many shops and restaurants had reopened.[48]

9

THE COLD WAR AND THE NEW ESPIONAGE

The Postwar World

After the defeat of Germany, the occupying Allied forces conducted an investigation into whether the NTUC and the Turkestan legionnaires had been involved in the Nazi genocide of the Jews. It was eventually understood that, far from helping the Nazis on this matter, they had saved the lives of many Jewish people. Veli Kayyum Han, the NTUC chairman, was arrested and put on trial for war crimes at the Nuremberg tribunal but was then released, partly through the intervention of the chief of the counter-espionage service in Marienbad, whom Ruzi had got to know through a friend called Mikhail Alchibaya, a member of the Georgian National Committee.[1] It emerged that Kayyum Han had personally saved the lives of two Bukhara Jews by claiming that they were Tajiks and employing them, one as a cook in the kitchen of the NTUC and the other as a chauffeur. He presented evidence that he had had serious disputes with Himmler and the SS organisation. It was also clear that neither Kayyum Han nor any of the committee members or officers of the legion had been a member of the Nazi Party.[2]

According to the Russian prosecutors, Kayyum Han had denied the existence of distinct Uzbek, Kazakh, Kirghiz, Turkmen and Tajik nations in Turkestan. He told them that he still held this view and that the tribal republics were the product of Moscow's colonialist policy of creating a nationality out of a tribe and a national tongue out of a dialect. One of the American judges asked why he had refused to work with General Vlasov. Kayyum Han's answer had a profound effect on the Americans, and he was released the same day, after two years under arrest. 'Vlasov was a traitor because he was fighting against his own nation, the Russian people. I fought for the freedom of my own nation and of Turkestan against the Soviet Union and Bolshevism, which were exploiting my country, not against my own people.'[3]

Although the war had ended, and hopes were high for a lasting peace, the fate of nations remained in the balance. The Americans supposed that the Soviets would need US credit and materials for the reconstruction of their country. They had not grasped that the Soviet planned economy would be capable of repairing the ravages of the war by placing the burden on the backs of the mass of its people. The Soviets, meanwhile, believed that the capitalist world was on the threshold of a pre-revolutionary crisis, and did not anticipate that American capitalism would survive by creating new opportunities for the US economy through Marshall Aid and the opening up of new markets. The Americans also believed that they could use their possession of the atomic bomb to put pressure on the Soviets. In due course the USSR would manufacture its own bomb.[4]

As the Soviet armies advanced westwards during the final months of the war, they occupied Poland, Hungary, Romania, Bulgaria and a third of Germany. Stalin would fight hard not to lose the territories he had obtained at the cost of twenty million human lives. According to the Yalta agreement, these countries were to be independent after the war. However, the Cominform, which replaced the earlier Communist International (Comintern) organisation,[5] was engaged in trying to spread the Communist system to other countries. The Cominform had been set up in order to coordinate the activities of Communist parties outside the Soviet Union. In Poland, Hungary, Romania, Bulgaria, Czechoslovakia and Yugoslavia, the local Communist parties had taken power with the support of the Red Army immediately after the war.

In the course of the war the Soviet Union had occupied Iran and established two puppet republics in the north of the country: the Republic of South Azerbaijan and the Mahabad Kurdish Republic.[6] In

Greece the Soviets gave military and financial support to the Greek Communist Party in its fight against the central government. Moscow also demanded that Turkey hand over the provinces of Kars and Ardahan, which had been ceded by Russia to the Ottoman empire during the First World War, and also sought a naval base on the Bosporus.[7] On 2 November 1945 the United States proposed to the Turkish government that an international conference should review the Montreux Convention, which since 1936 had regulated the passage of vessels through the Turkish Straits. The conference would not discuss the granting of naval bases to the Soviets and would only consider the rights of warships from Black Sea countries to pass freely through the Straits. This appeared to be in accord with Turkey's thinking. But when in 1946 Stalin reinforced Soviet troops in Iranian Azerbaijan and threatened both Iran and Turkey, and then went on to strengthen military forces in Bulgaria which could be deployed against Turkey or Greece, the US attitude towards the Soviets grew tougher. In a letter which Truman wrote but never sent to James F. Byrnes, the US secretary of state, he observed: 'I no longer have any doubts left that Russia wants to invade Turkey and take control of the Bosporus region. If we do not put a stop to what is going on and show them an iron fist, another war will break out. They understand only one language: how many divisions do you have?'

It is not known whether Stalin really did want to attack Turkey. Most probably he was thinking in terms of forcing the country into diplomatic isolation and then compelling its government to accept a treaty that would first have given the USSR bases on the Bosporus and eventually control over the whole country. In order to stand up to Stalin, Turkey needed to find an opposite, balancing force. So long as Turkey lacked a military deterrent, diplomatic initiatives would be useless. The first thing that the government of President İnönü had to do was ensure that the United States and other Western governments would not agree to the Soviet demands. Its second task was to obtain financial assistance from the West to keep the Turkish army mobilised. The third was to set up an alliance with the West that rested on security guarantees, so as to provide long-term protection against the Soviets.[8]

On 12 March 1947, President Truman made a speech to the US Congress in which he said that he stood by those countries whose independence and very existence were being threatened by the Soviet Union. He said the US would assist the Greek central government in the civil war against Soviet-backed Communist guerrillas, and would also help Turkey, which faced Soviet demands for territory and bases. He allocated $300 million in aid to Greece and $100 million to Turkey. Truman then called on the USSR to withdraw from Iran and to disband immediately the republics of South Azerbaijan and Mahabad which had been set up on the Iranian territory the Soviet army had occupied.[9]

The expression 'Cold War' was first used in this context by an American journalist, but it was introduced to the world by Bernard Baruch, an adviser to President Truman, who proclaimed in a speech in 1947 that 'Russia is waging a cold war against us'.[10] The Cold War was a conflict between the superpowers over both sovereignty and ideology, an indirect war of propaganda and psychology as well as a war over frontiers. Its weapons were espionage, terror, sabotage and infiltration.[11]

Intelligence agencies in Russia and the USA

Throughout Russian history the intelligence services have played a key role in the functioning of government. For the Russian tsars, espionage and the secret police were the most fundamental institution of the state.[12] After the Revolution, Lenin set up an Extraordinary Commission, known as the Cheka, to combat enemies of the state and to collect intelligence. In November 1923 the NKVD (People's Commissariat for Internal Affairs) was established and the Cheka, now reorganised as the GPU (State Political Directorate), was attached to this ministry. During the early years of the war, the NKVD and the GPU carried out counter-intelligence and espionage activities. In the 1950s the KGB (State Security Committee), which attached much more importance to intelligence and operations,[13] replaced the NKVD.

In the United States, by contrast, there was no well-established intelligence service. During the Second World War, intelligence activities were carried out through the Office of Strategic Services (OSS) under General William Donovan, by American diplomats and by counter-intelligence services in the army. But the OSS was only a provisional wartime entity. Years later Truman would write to a friend that when he took over the presidency, 'no structure existed through which secret information, obtained in every quarter of the world, could be set out in front of me'.[14] Spurred on by the knowledge that Stalin was convinced the US and Britain had created an alliance aimed specifically at weakening the Soviet Union, in June 1947 President Truman signed the National Security Act into law. The law established a National Security Council attached to the executive office of the president. Shortly after this, the US Central Intelligence Agency (CIA) was created, on 18 September 1947.[15]

Kennan's Long Telegram

During the Cold War one of the United States' most important analysts was the diplomat George Kennan. In 1946, when he was based in Moscow, he sent a famous 8,000-word 'long telegram' to Washington, spelling out his views on the Soviet Union, and in 1947, as head of the newly created Policy Planning Staff in the State Department, he followed it with a detailed assessment presented to a handful of officials in the State Department, the Pentagon and the White House. In Kennan's view, although the American people might not approve of this method, the United States had to fight fire with fire to protect its security.[16] He believed that guerrilla units should be set up to fight against the Soviets in the countries of Eastern Europe and in the non-Russian territories of the USSR, and he emphasised the necessity of establishing secret intelligence networks throughout the world.[17] Kennan believed there were three indispensable props to the strategy that had to be pursued against Stalin in the Cold War. The first was the Marshall Plan, which would give $13.7 billion over five years for the postwar reconstruction of countries aligned with the United States. The second was the Truman doctrine, by which the US guaranteed the protection of countries like Greece and Turkey whose independence and territorial integrity were threatened by the Soviet Union. The third was the operations which the CIA would carry out against the Soviets across the entire world.[18]

In this war it was only natural that refugees who had come from countries which were colonies of the Soviet Union, and who had been fighting for their independence, would side with the United States. The United States for its part would cooperate with them and try to use them in its quest to bring about the collapse of the Soviet system.

Rahimi

After the war Ruzi's friend Hussan Ikram Han was living near Frankfurt with a German family who had saved him from being handed over to the Soviets. The family made and sold tobacco pipes, and Hussan, who was smooth-tongued and likeable, had proved an excellent salesman. On his birthday, he invited Ruzi and various other people he knew in Munich to his birthday party.[19]

Ruzi, Baymirza Hayit, Ergesh Shermet and Kadir Egemkul set off by train from Munich to Frankfurt. They were chatting in their compartment, laughing at Kadir's jokes. At one point Ruzi went out to have a cigarette. A neatly dressed, tall and good-looking German, aged around forty-five, said that he had heard their cheerful voices and laughter and asked where they came from. Ruzi replied that they were Turkestanis. The man asked, 'You are Turkestanis, but are you Uzbeks, Kazakhs, Kirghiz, Turkmens or Tajiks?' Ruzi realised that he had met someone who knew a good deal about Central Asia. The man explained that he had done research on the history of the area and its languages and civilisation, and said he needed some assistance. Ruzi gave him his address in Rosenheim.[20]

A few weeks after Ruzi's return from Hussan's birthday party, this mysterious German arrived in Rosenheim. He told Ruzi some brief details about his past. He had been an army officer, and during the war he had been posted to the Middle East, among the Kurdish tribes in Iran. There he had worked for the military intelligence organisation Foreign Armies East (Fremde Heere Ost). When half of Iran was occupied by the British and the other half by the Soviets, he had begun working against the Soviets with the Kurds. Towards the end of the war he had been captured by the British and then been included in an exchange of prisoners. He explained that German officers were now working with the Americans against the Soviets and that they wanted him to join them. If he accepted, they would to send him to Iran. Ruzi thanked him but apologised, explaining that for family reasons he could not accept the proposal: his new wife, Linda, was pregnant. He gave the man the names of Veli Kayyum Han, Baymirza Hayit, Kadir Egemkul and Ergesh Shermet. Kayyum Han and Baymirza Hayit were contacted, and they began working with the Americans.[21]

The Americans had decided to send a group of Turkestanis to find out about the situation in Central Asia and they asked Kayyum Han to find some candidates for them. He recommended four people, who went through intensive training. However, one of them mentioned the forthcoming operation to his girlfriend and she told her family about it. The Americans and Germans discovered this and stopped the operation.[22] Veli Kayyum Han's collaboration with the Americans was not very productive in general, and this failure brought it completely to an end.

Professor Gerhard von Mende and Sir Olaf Caroe, the British scholar of Central Asia, had meanwhile drawn the attention of the British government to the Turkestan problem. As a result, the British began giving assistance to Veli Kayyum Han, who met with Baymirza Hayit, Ergesh Shermet and other Turkestanis in the town of Minden in the province of North Rhine-Westphalia, in the British Occupation Zone.[23]

Around this time, a former legionnaire officer called Rahimi was working as a doctor in one of the camps run by the United Nations. He had been the doctor in a Turkestani unit which had been transferred during the war from the Eastern Front to France and then to the Netherlands. There it was supposed to fight against Dutch partisan groups. However, Rahimi and other soldiers in the Turkestani unit were in contact with the partisans. There were also connections between these Dutch partisans and Soviet intelligence. After the war was over, Soviet agents got in touch with Dr Rahimi and he began to work for the Soviets. Rahimi was married to a Russian woman, who was modest, sensible and beautiful.

One cold winter's day, Ruzi went to have tea with Dr Rahimi and his family. They lived in a house which a German family had given them, close to the Red Cross building in Munich. When he set out for home, while waiting for a tram near their house, Ruzi noticed that a fair-haired woman was waiting there too. But although a number of trams went past, the woman did not board any of them. After a while the woman asked Ruzi in Russian where he came from. Her accent made him think that she was probably not Russian but Serbian. Ruzi said that he was from Turkestan and asked her why she was outside on such a cold day. When she replied that she was waiting for Dr Rahimi, he asked why she didn't go to his house, which was nearby. 'His wife is at home,' she replied. Dr Rahimi's wife was extremely attractive, and this woman was not, so Ruzi thought it highly unlikely that she was his mistress.

Rahimi could easily have gone to the United States as an immigrant, but just when it had become possible for many former Turkestani legionnaires to go to Turkey, Rahimi suddenly changed his mind and decided to go there too. Ruzi began to have suspicions.[24]

There was an American officer called John Spiegler in Rosenheim who was working for the CIS. Ruzi had met him through his father-in-law and they had become friends. On returning from his visit to Dr Rahimi and his wife, Ruzi called in at Spiegler's office. Over coffee, Spiegler told him that they were on the trail of a GPU agent and showed Ruzi a photograph. Ruzi was astounded to see that the woman in the picture was the one he had met that morning near Dr Rahimi's house. He told Spiegler about their conversation. It turned out that the woman was a top-level member of the Cominform and an important NKVD-GPU agent.

The CIS immediately began watching Dr Rahimi's home. A young American lieutenant was put on duty at the house, but the weather was very cold and, when he started shivering, he took shelter in a café. Just at that moment the Russian agent arrived at Rahimi's house, and then shortly afterwards left again. The young officer had missed her, and she escaped.[25]

The Turkestani refugees hoping to be accepted into Turkey were waiting in a camp at Augsburg for the day when their journey would begin. Dr Rahimi and his wife visited them frequently. One day while they were there, Ruzi arrived at the camp in a car which had been provided for him by Spiegler, the CIS officer. He told the camp's officials that he wanted to say his farewells to his fellow countrymen, and he did so. Then he met Dr Rahimi and his wife in the camp's canteen. Ruzi told the doctor that he wanted to discuss something with him in private and they went over to a corner. Ruzi then told him that he knew about his connection with the GPU agent. Rahimi was astonished and asked how he could possibly have found out. Ruzi told him that all their activities were known to the Americans and there was no use in trying to hide them or deny them. The right thing would be to talk to the Americans and confess the full truth. If he wanted, Ruzi could arrange a meeting with them, but in the circumstances it was not possible for him to go to Turkey.[26]

Some time later, Dr Rahimi went to the CIS office in Rosenheim and explained on record, bit by bit, when he had begun to work with the

Soviets, where and how he had handed over information, through whom, and on what subjects. He and Veli Kayyum Han had frequently met. When Kayyum Han had had a bit too much to drink, he would talk about all his contacts and in particular his work with the British. Rahimi passed on this information to the Soviets, which led to the capture of hundreds of Turkestanis. He said the reason he was going to Turkey was to work there for the NKVD-GPU.[27]

This information was extremely useful to the Americans, and as a result they did not arrest Rahimi but gave him permission to go home. Their aim was to use him as bait and then deliver a heavy blow to Soviet intelligence. A little later Nureddin Namangani, an imam for the Turkestan Legion during the war, arrived in Munich and visited Dr Rahimi. He rang the doorbell but no one came. When he tried to look through the keyhole, he realised that the door was locked from the inside and went and found the landlord, who told him that Dr Rahimi and his wife had not gone out for several days. When they put a ladder up against the window and looked inside, they saw the doctor's wife lying in a pool of blood and Rahimi lifeless with a syringe in his arm.[28]

CIS officials and German police quickly arrived at the house. Dr Rahimi had left two letters. The first ran to six pages in Russian and the other was two and a half pages in Uzbek. John Spiegler asked Ruzi to translate and report on them. They contained important information about how the NKVD-GPU worked and how successful they were in recruitment, infiltration and disinformation. Though the Cold War had only recently begun, the letters described how they had been successful at covering Western Europe with a network of spies. Members of Communist parties in the Cominform were all potential GPU agents. Many Communists inside anti-Fascist resistance groups which had struggled against the Nazis, receiving American, British and Soviet support, had begun to work for the NKVD-GPU in their countries after the war, just as Dr Rahimi had been put in contact with the Soviets by Communists inside the Dutch resistance. The letters went on to describe how Rahimi had informed GPU agents where hundreds of his countrymen lived and thus sent them to their deaths. He declared that his wife had no connection at all with these actions and that he had done everything on his own.[29]

In the letter written in Russian, Rahimi explained that after being unmasked as an agent, he had thought long and hard, but there was no aspect of his treachery and the murders he had committed which could be forgiven either by people or by God. He had informed on those who had clasped him to their bosoms, fed him and trusted him, and he had not even hesitated when he revealed the places where they were hiding and so got them murdered. He wrote that although he looked like a human being, he was in fact a bloody devil, and to stop that devil committing more murders it was necessary to slay him. He would commit one last murder by killing his wife without causing her pain, and then he would put a stop to his own life. He had in fact killed his wife with an axe-blow to her head and ended his own life with an injection of poison.[30]

Opposing the Soviet Union

Those countries which wished to take advantage of the $13.7 billion aid allocated in the Marshall Plan were obliged to reserve the equivalent amount in their own country's currency. Officials of the Marshall Plan diverted 5 per cent of these funds to the CIA to carry out anti-Soviet operations in every corner of the world. Thus, at the very outset of the Cold War, $685 million had been placed at the disposal of the CIA.[31]

In every corner of Europe, Communist-aligned associations, publications, student organisations, political parties and trade unions, all directed from Moscow, had long since gone into action. They were the USSR's Trojan horses. The Americans felt obliged to set up similar channels to use against the Soviets. In a secret decision dated 18 June 1948, numbered NSC 10/2, the US National Security Council gave instructions that covert operations should be organised against the Soviets in virtually every corner of the globe. It was decided that a clandestine unit should be set up within the structure of the CIA to direct this undercover war. The unit was given a commonplace name in order to conceal its activities: the Office of Policy Coordination (OPC). Though it was part of the CIA's structure, it would report only to the secretary of defense and the secretary of state.[32]

Two organisations were established in the context of these developments with the support of the US government: the Free Europe

Committee and the American Committee for Liberation from Bolshevism, created on the initiative of the CIA chief, Allen Dulles, and the US diplomat George Kennan, exponent of the policy of Soviet containment. The members of these bodies were American writers, journalists and thinkers, and others from the worlds of arts and politics who enjoyed high reputations. In 1948 Frank Wisner was made head of the American Committee for Liberation from Bolshevism. Wisner had previously been head of the State Department's Office for Occupied Territories. Along with other prominent personalities, the members of the new committee's board included General Eisenhower, Henry Luce Booth, chairman of the boards of *Time*, *Life* and *Fortune* magazines, and the Hollywood director Cecil B. DeMille. In late 1948 and early 1949, plans were made to establish Radio Liberty and Radio Free Europe, but the stations only started to broadcast after two years of preparation.[33]

Until the Bolsheviks took power in Russia in October 1917, the country had been ruled from February to October that year by Alexander Kerensky. He had then fled the country and in the 1950s was then living in the US. His first task had been to bring together all the anti-Communist Russian organisations in Europe under the Committee for the Liberation of the Russian Peoples. At its first meeting, organised by Russian émigré groups in Stuttgart, the Liberation Committee took various decisions about the principles of the struggle it would wage.[34] The committee emphasised that nationalities should determine their own destinies, but that the break-up of Russia would not serve their interests and that, after the end of Communism, a new Russia would have to be established on the basis of federation and national cultural rights, with the unity of the nationalities of Russia preserved. A Liberation Council of the Russian Peoples would be set up with sixty members, of whom twenty would be Russians, twenty from the non-Russian nationalities, and the remainder chosen from important people without regard to nationality. Thus Kerensky's Liberation Committee declared itself against the withdrawal of post-Bolshevik Russia from the non-Russian republics and against the establishment of an independent Azerbaijan, Georgia, Ukraine or Turkestan. The implication of this was continuing Russian occupation and colonial rule for the non-Russian peoples then living in the Soviet Union.

It was impossible for representatives of the non-Russian nationalists struggling for the independence of their own peoples to accept these decisions. The NTUC published a statement in which it rejected cooperation with the Liberation Committee of the Russian Peoples: 'There is no connection between the Liberation Council of the Russian Peoples and the National Unity Committee of Turkestan. The NTUC does not recognise this body. It is a body for Russians only and has no right to speak for the people of Turkestan. The people of Turkestan are not Russians. Kerensky desires the continuation of Russian imperialism. Our aim is to establish a national independent state of Turkestan.'[35]

The Anti-Bolshevik Bloc of Nations (ABN), which was established in 1946 under US protection and was led by the Ukrainian Yaroslav Stetsko, announced that it would refuse to work with Russian émigré organisations opposed to the independence of the non-Russian nationalities.[36] The groups representing the other nationalities published similar declarations. Both the Free Europe Committee and the American Committee for Liberation from Bolshevism declared that the decisions made by the Russian organisations at the Stuttgart meeting would be accepted in full and that the nationalities problem was not one for the present but for the future. It would be taken up only when Communism had collapsed.

Stalin was extremely sensitive about the nationalities question. During the Cold War, the Soviet secret service was firmly opposed to the activities of the non-Russian nationalities and did not hesitate to commit large numbers of brutal murders when it felt these were necessary. Ruzi's friends Abdurrahman Fethalibeyli Dudenginski, chairman of the Azerbaijani National Committee, and Stepan Bandera, the Ukrainian patriot, were among the leaders whom the GPU felt most concerned about.

Ukraine had become a Soviet republic in 1922. Its struggle for independence had been continued by the Organisation of Ukrainian Nationalists (OUN) and the Ukrainian Revolutionary Army (URA), which possessed an underground organisation extending to every part of the country. When the Nazis invaded in 1941, the Ukrainians initially greeted them joyfully: Ukrainian women even had flowers in their hands. They supposed that the German armies had arrived to liberate them and that they would be able to establish an independent state. Instead, the Nazis brought cruelty and bloodshed.

The OUN, led by Yaroslav Stetsko and Stepan Bandera, established a new independent Ukrainian government in Lemberg (Lviv) on 30 June 1941. Shortly afterwards, however, the Germans dissolved the government and sent its ministers to concentration camps. In September 1944 Bandera was released and he lived secretly in Germany until the end of the war. After the war he joined the ABN together with his friends.

During the era of the Cold War, Bandera's anti-Soviet activities greatly disturbed Moscow, and he was tried in absentia and sentenced to death. In October KGB agents found out where he lived in Munich and murdered him with a poisoned bullet shot from a weapon resembling an umbrella. The murderer, a secret agent, was later caught and sentenced to eight years' hard labour. Thus Ruzi lost a friend of whom he was very fond and for whom he felt great respect.[37] Other Ukrainian nationalists, including Symon Petlyura and Jehen Knowaleg, were also murdered by Soviet agents around this time.[38]

The Killing of Fethalibeyli

Major Fethalibeyli Dudenginski, the chairman of the Azerbaijani National Committee, had left Germany after the war and lived in Egypt. He was aware that the GPU attached special importance to capturing him. After the situation in Germany had begun to return to normal and Washington had made clear its new strategy of combating Stalin, Fethalibeyli came back to Germany to renew his work against the Soviets, along with some former legionnaires. Fethalibeyli began publishing a magazine called *Azerbaijan* with financial support from the American Committee for Liberation from Bolshevism.[39] He received letters of praise and encouragement from former legionnaires.

Around this time it was decided that Radio Liberty, which the Americans had set up in Munich, should make broadcasts in the languages of the peoples of the Soviet Union, including Azerbaijani Turkish. Fethalibeyli was made head of the Azerbaijani section. The day it began broadcasting was like a festival for Fethalibeyli. In his first transmission, he addressed the people of Azerbaijan: 'Listen to this, listen to this. Today Radio Liberty is beginning its first broadcast. Even if the terror of Stalin's police succeeds in making us silent in our own home, we are able to speak freely outside our homeland. Our thirst for freedom increases every day. Our first duty is the call to freedom. Despite every kind of oppression, our people continue to resist the Communist regime. We Azerbaijanis and the other peoples of the Soviet Union are determined to destroy Communism and take back the rights that have been violently seized from us. Wherever we may be, whether in the Soviet Union or outside it, we have only a single wish. It is for the destruction of Kremlin rule. We here, with our young people and our old ones, are together with you who are enduring pain under the oppression of Stalin.'[40]

The chief editor of the Azerbaijan section listened to Fethalibeyli's radio talks in Azerbaijan and thought they were very effective. Moscow wanted to use every means that it possessed to silence this courageous voice. The outcome was that a death sentence for Fethalibeyli was signed at GPU headquarters. The task of assassinating him was given to Georgi Vladimirovic, a GPU officer codenamed Muller. Vladimirovic thought that it would be more fitting for Fethalibeyli to be killed by an Azerbaijani, and so he delegated the job to one of his staff, Mikhail Ismailov, making him various promises.

The GPU knew that Fethalibeyli was soft-hearted and well-intentioned. Ismailov was instructed to win his confidence and become his friend. At his first meeting with Fethalibeyli, Ismailov told him that he was a GPU agent and that until then he had served the Russians but now he felt pangs of conscience and wanted to work for the independence of Azerbaijan. He also explained to Fethalibeyli that the last duty he had been given by the GPU was to kill him. Fethalibeyli thought it was quite impossible that a son of Azerbaijan could be a traitor. He began meeting Mikhail Ismailov frequently and gave him help.

On 21 November 1954 Fethalibeyli and Ismailov had dinner together. After the meal they went to Fethalibeyli's home at 6 Alpenplatz in Munich. While Fethalibeyli was in his sitting room, preparing the radio talk he was going to deliver the following day, Ismailov crept up behind him with a hammer which he had previously hidden in the kitchen and struck him violently on the head. The blow made Fethalibeyli lose consciousness and roll onto the floor, but he was still alive, and Ismailov killed him by strangling him. Next, Ismailov went to Frau Boehm, Fethalibeyli's landlady, and said that Fethalibeyli had gone to the radio studio to prepare the talk he was to give the next day. He asked for a bottle of liquor and said he would drink it in the kitchen and probably sleep there overnight. Ismailov sipped his drink with one hand while with the other he dragged Fethalibeyli's lifeless body into the kitchen. He took his identity papers and replaced them with his own, then silently left the house.

The next morning, the eighty-year-old Frau Boehm entered the kitchen to do the cleaning and thought that the body lying face down on the floor with blood oozing from its head was that of Ismailov. The police who came to the house found Ismailov's identity papers on the corpse. People who picked up the next day's *Abendzeitung* were met with the following two-line news item: 'The body has been found at No. 6 Alpenplatz of an Azerbaijani called Mikhail who was murdered by a person or persons unknown.'

Fethalibeyli's friends were struck by the fact that he did not come to work during the two days after the killing and that no news of him could be obtained. So, on the day of the funeral of the supposed Mikhail Ismailov, they asked to see the body. When they examined it, they saw it was that of their friend and leader.[41] The German newspapers gave extensive coverage to the murder. Long reports were published in *Quick* and *Der Stern* magazine.[42]

Moscow had struck a heavy blow to the Azerbaijani independence movement by eliminating one of its most important leaders. On 5 December 1954, Fethalibeyli was laid to rest beside his brother Seyfullabey, who had lost his life in a car accident in 1951, thousands of kilometres away from his homeland. The funeral ceremony was crowded. His comrades in arms in Germany did not abandon him. With Fethalibeyli's murder, Ruzi had lost yet another friend.

Philby and the Beginning of the Spies'War

During the early years of the Cold War, the Soviet side was much more successful than the West when it came to intelligence, subversive activities based on conspiracies, underground organisations, secret operations and assassinations. The Americans had no alternative but to work with Soviet émigrés in Western European countries, people who possessed a stock of knowledge about the USSR and who had previously participated in anti-Soviet intelligence activities. At the start of 1949, they were so desperate that they would have cooperated with the devil against Stalin.

The US intelligence services began working with General Reinhard Gehlen, who had directed anti-Soviet espionage during the war in Foreign Armies East. Gehlen told them that he possessed a sound intelligence network inside the Soviet Union and in Eastern European counties. He believed that the conflict between East and West would inevitably end with the destruction of one side, and that the foremost duty of every German citizen was to ally with the Americans in the war against Communism in order to defend the Christian values of the West. He told the Americans that they needed agents who were not only well trained and experienced but who also believed in democracy.

Known as the Gehlen Organisation, his intelligence network carried on for some time without the Americans interfering in its internal affairs. But in July 1949, under pressure from the Pentagon, the Americans took over control of the organisation and renamed it the Federal Intelligence Service (BND). It would eventually emerge that Russian agents had managed to infiltrate its most important departments and that the BND had been largely taken over by the GPU. The general who was head of its counter-intelligence department would be arrested and charged with being an agent of the GPU and would confess his guilt.[43]

In 1949 the CIA office in Munich began preparing to infiltrate a group of Ukrainians behind the Iron Curtain. Shortly before this, a group of Hungarians opposed to the Soviets had hijacked a passenger plane and forced it to land in Munich; the same group would be the crew of the aeroplane on this mission. Steve Tanner, an agent in the CIA's Munich office, was assigned to handle the operation. A sizeable group of trained Ukrainians would be dropped into the country by parachute at night and would make contact with anti-Bolshevik groups there. The CIA knew that the group being dropped in the forests of Ukraine would not be able to gather information about Soviet weaponry or strategy, but it would have a great psychological effect on Stalin to discover that the Americans could carry out an operation behind the Iron Curtain.[44]

On the night of 5 September 1949, the Ukrainians whom Tanner had trained were dropped by a C-47 transport plane in the Carpathian Mountains, singing military marches and Ukrainian folksongs. Shortly afterwards they were all captured by the NKVD-GPU and either executed or given life sentences. This event demonstrated once again the strength of Soviet counter-intelligence.[45]

In October 1949 the CIA landed nine Albanian agents, trained in Malta, on the coast of Albania. Three of them were killed the moment they set foot on land. The remaining six were caught shortly afterwards and executed. Later, a larger group of Albanians were trained in Munich and then sent to Athens, before being taken to Albania in a CIA plane and dropped by parachute. Shortly afterwards, almost all of them fell into the hands of the Albanian police and were executed.[46]

At this period, James J. Angleton was the man in charge of secret operations at the CIA headquarters, whose job it was to protect the organisation from infiltration and double agents. He shared all the information about these operations with Kim Philby, the head of the counter-espionage division in the British intelligence service MI6. When the CIA was being established, MI6 headquarters had sent Philby to Washington to help in setting it up. From then on, Philby had handled relations between the two organisations. Philby shared an office with Angleton in Washington. In the evenings, the two friends, with glasses of gin or whisky in their hands, would chat together for hours about the agents who were going to be sent behind the Iron Curtain and the secret operations in progress in this area.[47] Angleton thus kept Philby informed, and Philby then passed all this information on to the Soviets.[48] When Philby escaped to Moscow in 1963,[49] the reason for the failure of all the CIA operations became clear. Angleton, who had nourished Philby with priceless information, was later promoted and made head of the CIA's counter-espionage office.[50]

While Soviet intelligence was carrying out successful operations in every part of the globe, the Americans were suffering defeat after defeat. Hundreds of CIA agents were sent to their deaths in the Soviet Union, Poland, Romania, Ukraine and the Baltic countries. Even today the fates of some remain uncertain.

In 1949, a CIA plane flying over Alaska detected traces of radioactive contamination in the atmosphere. The CIA investigated and reported to President Truman that it would be impossible for the Soviet Union to manufacture an atomic bomb within the next four years. Just three days later, the president had to announce to the world that Stalin now possessed an atomic bomb.[51]

As the USSR drew all the countries of Eastern Europe into its sphere of influence, Moscow became a serious threat to the security of Western Europe, and the prospect of the Cold War turning into a hot war increased. The view in the West was that Germany needed to be rearmed, but in a way that would not threaten her neighbours, and that European security would need to be permanently supported by the United States. These factors culminated in the birth of the North Atlantic Treaty Organisation (NATO), set up by the Treaty of Washington on 4 April 1949. In the event of an attack on any NATO member country, all the countries of NATO would act together against the aggressor. In 1952 Turkey and Greece were accepted as members of NATO.[52]

Don Lewin and Karis Kanatbay

While Ruzi was selling herbal teas and trying to carry on with his life as a small businessman, he also continued to work as the NTUC's representative to the Anti-Bolshevik Bloc of Nations (ABN) in Munich and to the other anti-Soviet organisations there.[53]

The North Caucasian Abdurrahman Avtarhanov remarked to Ruzi one day that the ethnic and geographical structure of Northern Caucasia was quite different from Turkestan. Many different peoples lived in the Northern Caucasus and because of this it would be very difficult for the territory to become independent. Only by cooperating with the Russians could they gain political and cultural autonomy. He hoped to reassure Ruzi about the fact that he worked with anti-Soviet Russians, unlike the other North Caucasian leaders, Alihan Kantemir and Ahmet Nabi Magoma, who kept their distance. Avtarhanov wanted to work solely for his country.[54] He was the publisher of a magazine called *Independent Caucasia* (*Svaboni Kavkaz*), set up by a North Caucasian committee working with Kerensky's umbrella group for Russian émigrés, the Committee for the Liberation of the Russian Peoples. Kantemir and Magoma were publishing a magazine called

United Caucasia (*Obyedinyeniye Kavkaz*) which the North Caucasian National Committee had set up with financial help from the Americans. It appeared in Russian, English and Turkish.

At this time, the NTUC was trying to stay afloat at Minden in the British zone. British financial assistance enabled the committee to resume publication of its journal, *National Turkestan*. The Ukrainian ABN, meanwhile, had allowed many groups that did not want to work with the Russian émigré organisations to join forces with them. There was fierce rivalry. These sentences in an ABN statement attracted attention: 'Through news that is not true and by falsifying history, Russian émigré organisations are trying to make people in the West believe that the non-Russian people living in the Soviet Union were opposed only to Bolshevism and that their sole desire was for it to be brought down and that they wanted to continue to live within the borders of Russia together with the Russians. This is nothing other than a denial of the truth.'[55]

Around that time Don Lewin, the president of the American Committee for Liberation from Bolshevism, arrived in Munich from the US and was interviewing members of the various émigré organisations there. Lewin was the child of a family which had migrated to the US from Russia in 1906. He was now a well-known writer and journalist. He and Ruzi met in a café near Munich's railway station. At this time Ruzi was in a rather difficult economic situation. He had no steady job and was still living in the home of his father-in-law in Rosenheim.

Lewin suggested that Ruzi work with the Americans and that they would be stronger together. The struggle against the Soviets could not be done on an empty stomach—if he would join them, he would be much more comfortably off. Ruzi rejected Lewin's proposal. In tactful language he explained why he could not work with Kerensky's Committee for the Liberation of the Russian Peoples. He said that his struggle was not simply against Bolshevism; it was also against Russian colonialism. There was no difference between the situation of his country in the Tsarist and Soviet periods. In the words of Akmal Ikram, first secretary of the Uzbekistan Communist Party whom Stalin had murdered in 1938, only the name plate on the door had changed. Ruzi would feel able to work with anti-Bolshevist organisations only if they agreed to Turkestan becoming an independent state. On that note they parted.[56]

Ruzi felt emotional and tears came to his eyes. He had no money, and Lewin had tried to buy him. One day it occurred to him to try to embarrass Lewin in public. Shortly afterwards, Lewin arranged a meeting with representatives of organisations that had refused to work with the Committee for the Liberation of the Russian Peoples in a bar in Munich. Leaders of Ukrainian, Azerbaijani, Belorussian and other non-Russian groups were there. Since Veli Kayyum Han and other leading members of the NTUC were in Minden, only Ruzi was able to attend the meeting on their behalf. Don Lewin again spoke of the usefulness of working together, trying to convince his audience that by cooperating they would be able to overthrow Bolshevism. At the end, he asked if they had any questions. Ruzi put up his hand and asked Lewin in Russian who he was, what nationality he belonged to, and whether he was an American citizen. 'Ruzi, you know perfectly well who I am,' replied Lewin. Ruzi said, 'If you are an American, then you should concern yourself with the problems of America. Stop bothering about the people being oppressed by Russian colonialism and about Russia.' Thereupon everyone attending the meeting, led by the Ukrainian representative, applauded.[57]

Ruzi remained in contact with his friends in Minden, but he now decided to continue on his way alone. On 17 September 1947, his daughter, Sylvia (in Turkish, Zulfiye), was born, the delight of the entire household in Rosenheim. Linda was now the mistress of her own kitchen in their wing of the country house. She too was happy.

Around the same time, the Bavarian government set up an aid organisation for Soviet émigrés on the initiative of Theodor Oberländer. During the war, Oberländer had served as an officer in the North Caucasian Legion. Between 1953 and 1960 he would be the Federal German minister for displaced persons, refugees and victims of war in the Adenauer cabinet and a member of the Bundestag. Ruzi had known Oberländer during the war, and now his assistance enabled him to become relatively comfortable in financial terms.[58]

American insistence that the émigré organisations should work together with Kerensky's Liberation Committee began to cause schisms. Don Lewis was trying to persuade them to work together and had also started making contact with opposition forces within the various organisations who were prepared to cooperate with the US.

The group headed by Karis Kanatbay within the NTUC had been opposed to Veli Kayyum Han since the war years, when they had supported Vlasov. Recently they had gone to Turkey. Kanatbay and his colleagues, Aman Berdimurat, Taci Murat and Veli Zunnun, made contact with Don Lewin and set up a new body called the Turkeli Committee (i.e. the Committee from Turkish lands). Zeki Velidi Togan took part in the establishment of the Turkeli Committee, whose preparatory meeting was held in 18 September 1950. The Turkeli Committee got financial aid from the Americans and its moral support from Zeki Velidi Togan. At the meeting in September 1950, it changed its name to the Turkestan Independence Committee and began publishing a magazine called *Turkeli* in Russian and Turkish.

To undermine Kayyum Han, Kanatbay began spreading rumours that he had killed Mustafa Shokay in 1941 by poisoning him. Ruzi knew that these claims were slanderous and one day he asked one of Kanatbay's close friends why he was trying to spread lies of this sort, since information about the death of Shokay was freely available. The friend said that he had personally asked Kanatbay the same question and had received this answer: 'Before the October Revolution, when Lenin was publishing the newspaper *Iskra* [*Spark*] in Zurich, one of the Menshevik writers fiercely criticised the theses that Lenin was putting forward about the nationalities question and the articles that he had written. Lenin went to the *Iskra* offices and told the editor, "Give an answer to this man, but don't give it more than one or two sentences. Just write that this man is a bourgeois agent and an enemy of the proletariat, that's enough." The editor replied, "But this man isn't an enemy of the proletariat or a bourgeois agent!" Lenin answered, "If you write it once, they won't believe it; if you write it twice, they won't believe it. But if you write three or four times that he is an agent and an enemy of the proletariat, then they will believe it." And if we repeat often enough that Kayyum murdered Shokay, they will certainly believe it.'[59]

Kanatbay defended himself in an article in *Turkeli* magazine: 'Drawing the democratic forces that exist today among the refugees into a single centre against Bolshevism is one of the most important duties for refugees. The Turkeli Committee has been established to found a national independence government in Turkestan without Bolshevism. It will support the efforts of Don Lewin, president of the American Committee, to bring together all the democratic forces among the émigrés. Even though the Turkeli Committee may not have accepted the resolutions of the five Russian organisations on the nation-alities question completely, it will support them because they are a force against Bolshevism.'[60]

Kerensky's Liberation Committee for the Russian Peoples held its first meeting between 3 and 7 November 1951, with eleven émigré groups taking part, five Russian and six non-Russian. During the meet-ing the Russian groups struggled to get the others to accept their views and arguments broke out. Even Karis Kanatbay and Devlet Tagiberdi, who were determined to cooperate with Kerensky, felt obliged to make the following statement: 'The Turkeli Committee would never wish to be just an appendage of one person or one organisation … although we support the idea of forming a united front against Bolshevism, we can never accept a Russian imperialism which seeks to impose the Russian name on us … Turkestan has never been a part of Russia and never will be … Our committee is ready to play a part in any cooperation centre that may be established. But we do not want the Russians to interfere in our affairs.'[61]

Just as the US was unsuccessful in covert operations in the early stages of the Cold War, they were also unsuccessful in controlling the émigré organisations against the Soviets. For a start, the US administra-tion was influenced by the strong Russian lobby in America. After the Revolution, hundreds of thousands of Russian refugees had gone to the US, many of whom dreamed of a restored Russian empire. In their view, the Crimea, Tataristan, Bashkurt, Azerbaijan, North Caucasia, Georgia, Armenia and Turkestan were all parts of Greater Russia.

In 1953 the US government officially accepted its failure in this respect and announced that it would withdraw its financial support for projects of this kind. When their funds were cut, organisations like the Turkeli Committee, which had been set up with American finance and had no serious base among the people of their own country, were obliged to close down their activities.[62]

10

RUZI GOES TO AMERICA

Archibald Roosevelt Asks to Meet Ruzi

One day in 1951 Ruzi received a letter from the US consulate in Munich. The letter said that an important person had arrived from Washington and wanted to meet him. It gave a telephone number. Astonished, Ruzi phoned the number and was given an appointment for the following day. At the agreed hour, Ruzi arrived at the consulate and, as soon as he gave his name, he was ushered into a sitting room full of classical American furniture. There he was greeted by a middle-aged gentleman, tall, fair-haired and extremely smartly dressed.

'Welcome,' he said, showing him to a seat. A translator asked him if he would like to have the conversation translated into German or Russian. The American then introduced himself as Archibald Roosevelt.

Archibald Roosevelt was the son of the former US president Theodore Roosevelt. He explained that he had heard very favourable things about Ruzi—that he was extremely moral, clever, cultured and brave—and was an admirer of the civilisation and culture of Turkestan. The ensuing conversation lasted several hours. Ruzi and Roosevelt discovered that they had many points in common, that both of them knew the history of Russia and Turkestan well and that they both loathed Bolshevism. Roosevelt explained that he had been appointed deputy chief of mission to the American embassy in Turkey and that he was stopping off in Munich on his way to Ankara in order to see Ruzi and various other people.[1] During the war, Roosevelt had served as American military attaché in Iraq. He spoke a little Arabic, and was keen to learn Turkish before taking up his post in Turkey.

The Munich *Abendzeitung* ran a front-page story about Roosevelt's arrival in the city. Though he had told Ruzi that he was going to Ankara as deputy chief of mission, Ruzi had already learnt from his American friends that his real post was as CIA station chief. After the war, Roosevelt worked in the Office of Strategic Services and, when the CIA was set up, he had joined it.[2]

During their meeting at the consulate, Roosevelt said to Ruzi that he would be staying a few days in Munich and would like to see him again. And, indeed, a day later they met for a second time. Roosevelt told Ruzi that he had been very impressed with his views on Central Asia, the Soviet Union and the nationalities problem. The US government did not have enough specialists who knew about the Soviet Union and its problems. He said, 'Mr Ruzi, the USA needs you. We want you to come to America—that is, of course, if you wish to do so.'

Ruzi was pleased at the interest being shown in him but was astonished by this invitation, which he had never expected. 'Why not? But I don't think it is technically possible,' he replied, mentioning an immigration law of 1905 which debarred him. Roosevelt smiled and replied, 'Leave that to us. The Pentagon, the State Department and the CIA all have their own immigration contingencies. If we need a specialist, we'll find a way to get him to the USA.' He added that if Ruzi did not want to live permanently in America, he could come just for a few years.

Ruzi asked what he would live on while he was there. Roosevelt replied, 'How much do you live on here?' Ruzi's mind did not really stretch to money matters. At that time, a family in Germany could get by on 400 or 500 German marks a month. One dollar at this time was the equivalent of 4.25 marks, so he thought that $300 or $400 a month would be enough and said so. Roosevelt replied that he could guarantee Ruzi at least $500 a month.[3]

Ruzi enquired of his American guest whether he wanted to meet the president of the National Turkestan Unity Committee, Veli Kayyum Han. When the answer was in the affirmative, he informed Kayyum Han of his discussion with Roosevelt and told him that the latter would see him if he came to Munich. Kayyum Han did so and met Roosevelt in a café. Roosevelt did not speak German, and Veli Kayyum did not speak English. Luckily, Fuat Emirjan, an Azerbaijani friend of Ruzi's from the war years who spoke good French, happened to be in Munich, and Ruzi asked him to act as interpreter. During the meeting, Ruzi was once more able to confirm that Roosevelt followed the Turkestan question closely and possessed extensive knowledge of the current situation in the Central Asian republics.[4]

After the war, Roosevelt had asked, through the US embassy in Moscow, to be allowed to visit the Central Asian republics and Uzbekistan, but the Soviets had turned the request down. Roosevelt had therefore gone to China, identifying himself as an American diplomat, and then crossed into East Turkestan and gone through a Soviet–Chinese border post into Uzbekistan. After visiting the places that he wanted to see, he returned by train from Tashkent to Moscow. Roosevelt was a risk-taker and he loved adventure. A truly courageous personality was required to engage in such a journey during the Cold War years.

Roosevelt had been able to observe the latest situation in Central Asia personally. He asked Kayyum Han a lot of questions and was not impressed by his exaggerated replies, in particular his claim that he had three or four thousand men with war experience following him in Turkestan and that through them he could start an armed rebellion there at any time. During the previous few years, the US secret services had attempted operations of this kind in Ukraine, Albania and other countries of Eastern Europe, and they had all failed, at the cost of hundreds of lives. Once they realised the strength and abilities of the Soviet secret service, they had halted operations of this kind.[5] After that interview no further meeting ever took place between Kayyum Han and the Americans.[6]

Ruzi in America

Ruzi had spent the first twenty-five years of his life in a country where there was a Communist government and then the next ten years in Germany. Of those, four had been lived under the Nazi regime, and six under the Allied Occupation and the newly founded Federal Republic. Now a new period was opening in his life.

His youth under the Communist regime had been full of bitter, bloody and tragic events. Ruzi had seen first his brother, then those he loved, then the most valued intellectuals of his country, its men of religion and its most talented politicians and statesmen accused of being enemies of the regime, sent to concentration camps and murdered.[7] Millions had died of hunger during the years of collectivisation. Ruzi had been unable to understand how people could become so brutal. Amid all those sufferings, the spirit of his family home, full of love and confidence, had given him comfort. Even in the years when there had been such great suffering in Uzbekistan and he had felt the chilly breath of fear and danger at every moment, his father's house had been the only refuge where he felt safe. Frequently the only thing that he longed for was that ambience of love, peace and safety. He missed his mother very much. She had raised him, together with his grandmothers, and the day he had gone off to join the army, she had said to him, 'Now go, my son. I know you. Wherever you happen to be, you will listen to the voice of your conscience. Whatever you believe to be the right path is the one you will follow. My wish for you is that you will always remain like this. You will often come to crossroads in your life. If on one side of you there is the right path, albeit one whose outcome is uncertain and full of dangers, and on your other a path crooked and wrong but full of material riches, choose the right path, even if it is full of dangers. Look away from the crooked path, even if there are limitless treasures there.' Now once again he was at a parting of the ways.[8]

Ruzi talked to his wife, Linda, and his father-in-law, whom he loved and respected and whose knowledge and experience he admired. His father-in-law told him that because the Germans would not easily accept foreigners, no matter how talented they were, he had no future in Germany. He said that there were two countries to which Ruzi could go. One was Turkey and the other was America, and he had to make a choice. 'If you go to Turkey, I have no doubt that you will quickly find your way there. In the US you may have a lot of difficulties at the beginning, but you will suffer no hardship there. No one will tell you that you are a foreigner. If you choose the US, when conditions are ripe and the opportunity arises, you can always go on to Turkey and try to do something there. But if you go to Turkey, it will be difficult afterwards to go to the US.' Ruzi reflected that if he went to the US, he would be able to help his own country more and that this choice would be more appropriate for his family too. He decided that was where he would go.[9]

He made his preparations. He was to go by boat from Bremerhaven on 1 November 1951. Professor Gerhard von Mende and Veli Kayyum Han came to see him off. Ruzi had known the professor since the war and felt great respect for him. His efforts had saved hundreds of thousands of Turkestanis, Azerbaijanis, Tatars, North Caucasians and others who would not otherwise have survived. It was also thanks to Mende's efforts that the NTUC had been able to operate freely.[10] So Ruzi was especially delighted that he had come to see him off. He told his friends that the services that the professor had done for Turkestan were of immeasurable value and that one day a statue of him should be erected in Tashkent. He spoke to Mende and Kayyum Han about colleagues in the NTUC. On the professor's recommendation, Sir Olaf Caroe had secured scholarships for some of them. Baymirza Hayit and Mümincan Teşebay were working on doctorates at Munich University. Veli Kayyum Han told him that Mümincan was not very well. Indeed, soon after Ruzi left Germany, Mümincan died.

Ruzi bade farewell to his relatives and friends, and boarded the ship which would take him to New York.[11] During the three weeks of the journey, he took stock of the past. He had never had such a long holiday before. The cool, clean winds of the Atlantic clarified his mind. He thought over his past life in the minutest detail and he examined his conscience about his decision to go to the US.

He remembered what his father had said to him two days before he died: 'Bury me according to the rules of the religion in which I believe.' He had carried out his father's will. Because of it he had almost been arrested as an enemy of the regime. God had protected him. He remembered how the president of Uzbekistan, Feyzullah Hojayev, had been denounced because he buried his elder brother according to Islamic rites. What sort of system was it in which, because of a few funeral prayers, people could be arrested, exiled, sent to concentration camps, left to rot in jail or executed? Once more Ruzi remembered his mother's words, the day he had gone off to the army. 'Go then, my son, and may you have an open path and good fortune. I will always pray to

God to protect you. Unless He wills it, even a leaf cannot stir. God accepts the prayers that mothers and fathers offer for their children. He will always protect you. No one will ever be able to do you any harm. Never forget your country and your people. Do not be cruel to others. Wherever you happen to be, if you find anyone in need of help, do not hesitate to give them it. Take care not to stray from the way you know to be the true one. Always choose what is right, not what happens to suit your interests. Choose not what is easiest, but what is right and beautiful, even if it is difficult.'[12]

After every great war the world is formed anew. If the new order is full of wrongs and injustices, then it carries within it the seeds of great wars in the future. Had not a Cold War begun immediately the Second World War was over? And when this war ended, the world would be reordered again.

Ruzi believed that for his country to be liberated and for his people to have an independent state which respected their human rights and freedoms, the Soviet Union would have to lose the war. Nazi Germany was the second totalitarian regime which Ruzi had been obliged to live under. The Nazi ideology was an enemy of humanity, incomprehensible and cruel. He had cooperated with the German army only in order to help bring down the Soviet system. When he asked himself which totalitarian regime was worse, he was unable to make a choice. Both were evil, brutal and merciless. Neither had the least respect for human honour and dignity or human life. It was impossible for Ruzi to withdraw into a corner and wait for the end of the Cold War without becoming involved in either side.

During the voyage he ran through all these things in his mind, point by point. He would follow his mother's advice to stick to the right path. In this new war, he had decided to go to a country which he did not know and whose language he did not even speak, in order to make his own contribution.

Manhattan

On a cold winter's day in December 1951 the ship carrying Ruzi approached New York harbour and the skyscrapers of Manhattan appeared on the skyline. After Margilan with its green trees, old build-

162

ings and mosques decorated with exquisite examples of Islamic calligraphy, and then the historic cities of old Europe, New York seemed like a city from a fairytale or out of science fiction.[13]

Ruzi realised that he had stepped into a completely different world. The first emotion which gripped him, in this foreign country where he knew nobody, was a sense of loneliness and sorrow. If only he had been together with his wife and daughter, at the side of his mother, and in his fatherland. If only he had been able to make an Uzbek pilaf in an Uzbek teahouse with his friends. Then Ruzi told himself, 'Stop this sentimentality and grief! The most dangerous thing in life is when someone feels sorry for himself or herself. Pull yourself together, hold your head high and carry on along your way.' He had to get to know his surroundings and learn the language of the country straight away.

Ruzi had thought that he would get along easily with the $500 he was to receive from Columbia University each month. They had rented an apartment for him in Forest Hills, a pleasant district, in a beautifully appointed building with a large garden and a staffed gate. He would pay $180 a month in rent. That left $320 for himself and his family. He soon found that this did not amount to much, so while working at the university and studying English he also looked for a second job.[14]

About that time, the *Voice of America* radio station had started transmissions in Uzbek. The Uzbek section was headed by a former legionnaire from Kokand called Maksut Bey. Maksut had got his job on the station through the assistance of Archibald Roosevelt. He had been able to come to the US because he was married to a Russian woman. *Voice of America* was having difficulties preparing broadcasts in Uzbek and finding staff who could write articles and present programmes. Maksut proposed that Ruzi work for them as a freelance journalist and presenter. He would be paid $50 for each article he wrote and $15 for each one that he read out. This would add up to about $500 a month in additional income, making him very comfortable.[15] At that time Ruzi's English was still poor, and so in order to follow events in the world and the US he subscribed to two newspapers, one German-language and the other Russian. The Russian paper was *Novoye Russkoye Slovo* (*Word of the New Russia*) and from it he gained news of what Russian émigré organisations were doing.

Ruzi's first few months in the United States were difficult. While he was in Germany, certain Russian émigrés had been unhappy that he was going to the United States: they were people who still lived mentally amid dreams of Tsarist Russia and wanted Turkestan to remain a Russian colony for ever. These people now began a campaign against Ruzi. It is possible that Soviet agents played a part in it. Articles were published in the *New York Times* alleging that he was a bourgeois nationalist who supported Hitler and was a former SS officer. Archibald Roosevelt's friends contacted Ruzi and told him that they knew the claims were untrue and that he should not be uneasy or upset by them. Despite that, Ruzi felt upset at not being able to do anything to stop the rumours.

In 1954 a Middle East Institute was set up at Columbia University, including departments on Turkey and Turkestan. Roosevelt introduced Ruzi to some of the institute's academics, and they proposed to him that he join the Turkestan department, which was headed by a Hungarian professor. Ruzi began working there as a specialist on Central Asian and Turkestani affairs. His analyses and articles evoked a considerable response both inside and outside the US. In a short space of time, he made good progress with his English and found that he had begun to adjust to American life.[16]

Argus

As an adversary of the Soviet Union, Ruzi was a talented, serious, determined, well-educated and experienced opponent. During his work for US intelligence, his independent and objective attitude was widely appreciated. US officers found themselves dealing with someone who did not give in on substantive issues, even in the difficult conditions of those days; someone who would not be an ordinary agent or run-of-the-mill civil servant; someone who could not be bought. Even as a member of the CIA, Ruzi succeeded in maintaining his independent position until he retired. He never worked with the American Committee for Liberation from Bolshevism, as a matter of principle. The Russian émigré bodies active in the committee had decided that questions of nationality would only be discussed once Communism had been destroyed. Ruzi believed that the non-Russian nationalities had been deceived by Lenin and his companions, and they did not want to be deceived again. If the Russian émigré groups would accept the right of the non-Russian peoples to establish independent states and determine their own destinies, only then he would be prepared to work together with them. He met the chairman of the committee and its State Department representatives and cooperated with them on some issues, but he never acted jointly with them.[17]

During his time working in Turkey, he would tell CIA headquarters that the Turks regarded him as one of themselves, that they did not conceal even their most important state secrets from him, and that he had no right to exploit their sympathy for him. He would therefore not be involved in intelligence-gathering operations directed against Turkey. This was a moral issue for him. He would only work in support of the underground activities of the Soviets against that country and try to organise counter-measures.[18]

One day Ruzi read in the New York-based Russian newspaper, *Novoye Russkoye Slovo*, an article entitled 'Gossip and Facts' by a writer who used the pseudonym of 'Argus'. Argus produced satirical articles five days a week. In that day's piece Argus compared the Prophet Muhammad to Stalin and made fun of both Stalin and the dictators. Ruzi was disturbed by the attempt to equate the Prophet of Islam with one of the blood-thirstiest tyrants in history. As a Muslim who was respectful towards all religions and opposed to fanaticism, he felt deeply wounded.

That night, after his wife and daughter had gone to sleep, Ruzi filled his vodka glass and wrote a long letter to Argus. In it, he made clear that as long as people lacked respect for other faiths and regarded those with different beliefs as enemies and murderers, enmity and onflict in the world would never cease. In his article, Argus had insulted and wounded millions of Muslims who had faith in the person of the Prophet Muhammad.

When he got hold of the following day's *Novoye Russkoye Slovo*, he saw that Argus had written an article directly addressed to him. It began, 'I have learnt many things today from a Turkestani friend of mine called Ruzi. He has helped educate me, even at this age.' Argus went on to apologise to Ruzi and to all Muslims. In his letter to Argus, Ruzi had frequently used harsh expressions. Indeed, at several points he had insulted him. Now, as he read Argus's response, he thought to himself, 'If I had written more gently, it would definitely have been better.'[19]

One day he had just finished teaching his class at Columbia University when one of the staff told him that someone called Argus was there to see him. Ruzi found himself looking at a short person of around sixty years old, with a long nose and a sympathetic face which made him want to smile back—he had great difficulty in keeping himself from doing so. Argus told Ruzi that he had been much moved by his letter and wanted to apologise in person. He invited Ruzi to dinner at the Russian Tea House on 48th Street in Manhattan, a favourite haunt of well-known writers, artists and politicians. This was the first step in a long friendship.

Argus, whose real name was Mikhail Eisenstadt-Jeleznov, was a Jew who had been born in Russia. He had been educated in a Russian high school in Riga before the October Revolution. When the Bolsheviks seized power, he had come to the US as an immigrant. He worked for a Lithuanian relative who had a furniture shop in New York and in his later years had begun to write his newspaper column. He had written several satirical books, including the bestselling *Moscow on the Hudson* and *A Rogue with Ease*. *Moscow on the Hudson* lampooned Russian immigrants to the US.[20] Argus was clever, cultivated and widely experienced, and Ruzi learnt a great deal from him. Through Argus he was to meet many new friends, including Ukrainians, and was able to raise their awareness of Soviet colonialism.[21]

11

FIRST VISITS TO THE MIDDLE EAST

Hamid Rashid and the Hajj

One day Ruzi was waiting for a bus at a metro station in Manhattan. A tall, fair-haired Germanic-looking person greeted him with a nod, but Ruzi didn't recognise him and went on reading his newspaper once they both boarded the bus. When they reached the stop near his home and he got off, the man got off too. Smiling, he came up to him and said, 'My goodness, Ruzi. I have been staring at you for half an hour thinking you would recognise me, but you still haven't managed to do so.' It was only then that Ruzi realised he was looking at an old friend. 'Oh Hamid, my brother,' he cried. 'Where have you sprung from? Out of the earth or down from the sky?' And they embraced each other.[1]

Hamid Rashid Islamkulof came from a Tatar family. In Tsarist times, his father had been educated in Islamic sciences in Bukhara and for many years had been an imam in Orenburg, a city in the far south-east of Russia, close to the border with Turkestan. But after encountering major problems with Russian officialdom, he and his family had left Orenburg and settled in Margilan. Ruzi's father had helped the family, finding a house for them and work for the father in one of the mosques. Hamid Rashid was born there in 1910.[2]

Hamid Rashid's father and Ruzi's became close friends. Jamshid felt great respect and affection for this enlightened clergyman who had sound national feelings and was open to modernisation and innovation. Hamid Rashid was seven years Ruzi's senior. They had last met in Margilan in 1941 when Ruzi was about to go into the army and Hamid Rashid, who was then a geography teacher at the high school, had called to wish him good luck. Hamid Rashid was called up in his turn and sent to the Eastern Front. There he had examined his conscience and decided that it would be wrong to fight for the Bolsheviks. He went over to the Germans, endured his share of hardships in a prisoner-of-war camp and then served in the Tatar Legion. For some time after the war, he had lived in a camp in Poland and there he registered himself as a Finnish Tatar. Large numbers of Kazan Tatars had gone to Finland since Tsarist times; there are about a thousand Tatar families in Finland today. The Helsinki Muslim community was well organised, with many successful business enterprises, and Hamid Rashid was able to get help from some of these people. Although he had married in Margilan and had two children, when he understood that he no longer had any chance of returning home, he had married the pretty daughter of a Belorussian family. At the first opportunity, they had gone to the US. Ruzi was delighted to run into him in New York. He introduced him to his wife, Linda, and the two families began to meet frequently. [3]

One day when they were chatting at home, Hamid Rashid said, 'Ruzi, my friend, we have come through blood and fire. Thanks to God, both of us narrowly escaped death many times. The Angel of Death took the lives of hundreds of people just beside us, but never rang on our doorbells. I believe that God will preserve us from countless dangers from now on too. I have a proposal to make to you. Let's go together on a pilgrimage to Mecca; let's visit the Kaaba and the lands where our prophet was born and where his tomb is.'

Without even thinking, Ruzi immediately accepted. 'Fine, Hamid my brother, let's get ready and go on the hajj,' he replied. Ruzi had some money saved up and he depended on nobody.

In those days, air travel meant going by old-fashioned propeller planes. Someone who bought a ticket between Saudi Arabia and New York would travel by whatever route he wished, staying in whichever cities along the way he chose. [4] Today's John F. Kennedy Airport was then only a tiny terminal called New York Airport, smaller than that of Rome. Ruzi and Hamid Rashid flew from New York to Rome and stayed there three days. They saw the Colosseum, the Pantheon, the Vatican City, everything that they could in the time available, and they talked at great length.[5]

Ruzi had not received much of a religious education, but Hamid Rashid had learnt many things from his father, the imam. He explained the religious and moral aspects of the hajj to Ruzi, along with its economic and social side. After worshipping at their local mosque, people would talk about the news of their neighbourhood and discuss how to help those in need. After Friday prayers in the big mosques, they would talk about not just the affairs of their own neighbourhood, but wider issues. Public worship in the mosques was thus also like a meeting of a people's assembly. In the same way, the hajj resembled a worldwide meeting of Muslims, where people would make commercial connections and exchange news about the important issues in their countries.

While Hamid Rashid was explaining all this, a thought struck Ruzi. 'In that case, I know what we are going to do in Mecca and Medina,' he said. 'Since there are will be people there from all over the Muslim world, and these people will be talking to each other about their troubles, difficulties and joys and the state of their countries, we should tell people on the pilgrimage about the situation of the Muslims of Turkestan. We can write out a statement to the Muslims of the world and have it printed there. Then we distribute it to people as they come.' Ruzi also said that they should try to meet statesmen and other important people to brief them about the Turkestan problem.

They put their heads together and wrote a few pages that described the suffering of the Muslims in the Soviet Union, the cruelties of the Communists there, and the situation in Turkestan. When they read through what they had written, they felt that their message was short but clear.[6]

Egypt

From Rome, Ruzi and Hamid Rashid flew to Cairo. The Egyptian king Farouk had been overthrown by a military coup a year previously, in July 1952.[7] In his place General Neguib was appointed head of state, with Colonel Gamal Abdel Nasser as the general's deputy.[8]

Ruzi suggested to Hamid Rashid that they should go to the presidential palace and visit General Neguib, whom he had met in Germany.

'Are you out of your mind?' Hamid Rashid replied. 'Are two foreigners travelling on the hajj just going to go to the palace and ask to meet the president? And do you think that General Neguib, the Egyptian head of state, would accept them?'

'Let's go and have a try,' said Ruzi. 'If he doesn't see us, at least we will have been there and had a look at the presidential palace from the outside, so what do we have to lose?' They got into a taxi and arrived at the palace. Ruzi told the guards at the gate that he knew General Neguib from Germany and that they had come on a visit to congratulate him on his appointment as head of state. The official vanished for some time, and then returned, telling them that General Neguib was awaiting them.

General Neguib was an honest, well-intentioned and modest man. On seeing Ruzi, he exclaimed, 'My brother from Turkestan!' and embraced him. Ruzi explained that they had called in at Cairo on their way to Mecca and that they intended to tell Muslims from all parts of the world about the Turkestan problem, about the oppression that Muslims were suffering, and about the hostility of the Communists to religion.

'What an excellent idea,' replied the general.[9] He was well aware that Central Asia was a colony of Russia, and regarded the country with affection and sympathy. His cook was a former legionnaire, an Uzbek from Kokand, and they often spoke about Turkestan.

The general gave his visitors tea and asked them if they needed anything. Ruzi told him that they would like to visit Colonel Nasser. President Neguib said that he had left Cairo to go on the hajj a few days earlier. 'But you can see him there,' he added. He took out a card with his name and the Egyptian government crest on it and wrote down a few sentences in Arabic.

'Gamal is staying in the State Guest House in Mecca. If you show this card to the men at the door, they will immediately take you in to see him.' And he held out the card to Ruzi.

General Neguib would occupy the presidency of Egypt for less than two years. In 1954, after a republic had been declared in Egypt and a treaty signed which provided for British withdrawal from the Suez Canal, he was removed from office and put under house arrest, leaving Nasser free to emerge from behind the scenes and become the undisputed ruler of Egypt.

Ruzi and Hamid Rashid put the final touches to the statement which they had drafted in Rome. They now had to get it translated into Arabic. But who could carry out the task?[10] The two friends decided to try and find an acquaintance of Ruzi's called Alimjan Idris, who had settled in Cairo after the war.[11] Educated in the madrasas of Bukhara, he had gone to Germany during the First World War and been an adviser on Muslim prisoners of war. During the Second World War he had advised the German Foreign Ministry and the Ministry of Propaganda. He had a good command of Russian, German, Turkish, Arabic and all the Turkic Tatar dialects. At one point he had lectured in a school for Muslim clergy set up in Dresden to meet the spiritual needs of the legionnaires. After the war he had been one of the three administrators of the German Muslim Council, along with Abdurrahman Avtarhanov.[12] Alimjan Idris developed close contacts with government circles and the leaders of the Arab League and made them aware of the pitiful situation of the Muslim legionnaires after the war. He collected and distributed food parcels which helped many Turkestanis at that time, including Ruzi.[13]

Alimjan Idris greeted Ruzi and his friend cheerfully and entertained them royally. He said that he could translate their statement into Arabic but that it would take him two days. Ruzi and Hamid Rashid would have to leave Cairo just one day later. Alimjan Idris told them not to worry: he knew an Eastern Turkestani who had worked with him at Al-Azhar University in Cairo and who was going on the hajj three days later. He would finish the translation and hand it over to them in Mecca.

Ruzi and his friend spent their final day in Cairo visiting the pyramids and going around the city's historic buildings, looking at magnificent houses from the time of the Mamluk dynasty and the Ottomans.[14] They then set off by plane from Cairo's tiny airport to Jeddah.

Arabia

In the two holy cities of Islam, Mecca and Medina, there was a substantial community of Turkestanis, who were known there as Bukharans. For centuries they had come to Mecca and Medina for the hajj and for commerce and had settled there so that they could end their days in the lands sacred to Muslims. Turkestanis had made important contributions to the history of Islamic civilisation. After the Koran, the most important sources of their faith for Muslims are the books of Hadith and Sunnah,[15] collections of the sayings and doings of the Prophet Muhammad. Many of these were put together by Turkestani scholars called Muhaddis.[16] Academics from Central Asia wrote highly regarded works on law, Koranic interpretation and other Islamic studies. Indeed, the first grammar of the Arabic language was written down by Turkestani linguists.

At the time of Ruzi's visit the famous Islamic scholar Altunhan Töre, who had taught younger members of the Saudi royal family, was among the Turkestani clergy living in the country. He was a writer and poet as well as a theologian and had produced an annotated translation of the Koran into Uzbek.[17] Ruzi and Hamid went to visit him. He embraced these fellow countrymen with great affection and gave them an invitation to his tent during the hajj.[18]

Three days after Ruzi and his friend had reached Jeddah, Alimjan Idris's friend brought them the finished translation of their statement. There were now two important issues for them to solve: how to get it printed and how to distribute it. Ruzi and Hamid Rashid held a meeting with the leading Bukharans. They read out the statement and asked for their help. The Bukharans enthusiastically approved of the statement and quickly arranged to have 250,000 copies printed. It would be distributed to the hajj pilgrims by youngsters from Turkestan.[19]

In those days the hajj was a gruelling experience. There were virtually no facilities for drinking water and ablutions. The size of the crowds of pilgrims led to large-scale accidents and crushes. When Ruzi performed the hajj in 1953, there was a panic during the ceremony of the stoning of the devil at Mount Arafat and hundreds of people lost their lives, among them large numbers of pilgrims from Turkestan and Turkey. Ruzi and Hamid Rashid were rescued from the melee only with difficulty. In later years, King Faisal would construct vast infrastructure, solve the problems over water, toilets and accommodation, and turn Mecca into a city in which millions of people could perform the hajj comfortably.[20]

Ruzi's attention was caught by the careless and overexcited behaviour of young Bukharans—Central Asians—in Mecca and Medina. Saudi Arabia was a country ruled by an absolute monarchy. Cinemas were forbidden, as was listening to records or selling them. People who were not native Saudis were followed closely by the security services. Saudi Arabian citizens did not even have the slightest right to form an organisation, and the government did not look kindly on gatherings of foreigners.

At this time the Saudi Arabian army contained many officers who were Turkestani Uzbeks, the children of families who had settled there either in the years when the armies of Tsarist Russia had occupied their country or after the Bolshevik revolution. The government of Saudi Arabia had admitted all the Turkestani officers in its army as citizens, whereas it refused to open its armed forces to Palestinians, among whom there were strong leftist movements. The Palestinians objected to this situation and put pressure on the Saudi government. Thereupon the Saudi administration announced that Bukharans who were not Saudi citizens would also be prevented from joining the army.

Various young Bukharans had made contact with the NTUC in Germany and began forming their own groups in Mecca and Medina. On 9 April 1952 the NTUC had held a meeting in Germany and emphasised the need for Turkestani émigrés to unite. Baymirza Hayit was given the task of setting up Turkestani organisations in Turkey and the Arab countries.[21] When meeting young people involved in these groups, Ruzi tried to explain the need for care and discretion, but his warnings had little effect. In 1956 Veli Kayyum Han visited the country.[22] He met several of the Saudi royal family, but the Saudi government was displeased that the flag of the Turkestan legionnaires flew on the tent in which he stayed and that the young Turkestanis made more noise than was necessary. Ten of them were arrested. Ruzi, who was by this time working in Washington, heard about it from Joseph Danachau, a friend of his who was cultural attaché at the US embassy in Jeddah. Danachau enjoyed hunting in the desert. His guide was an Uzbek from Margilan, and he was one of those detained after Kayyum Han's visit. Danachau took Ruzi to see Crown Prince Faisal, and Ruzi briefed the prince on the situation in Central Asia, the hardships that Muslims were suffering, and the oppression of the clergy. He said that the young people who had been arrested had no evil intentions towards Saudi Arabia and had not engaged in any seditious activities, but were simply inexperienced and overexcited. He requested that they be set free. As a result of Ruzi's representations and a second, secret visit by Kayyum Han, the arrested men were released. The youngsters never found out that Ruzi had been involved in freeing them. Had not Ruzi's mother always said, 'A good action has as much value with God as the degree to which it is kept secret'?[23]

On his first visit to Saudi Arabia, during the hajj, Ruzi was able to hold long conversations with Altunhan Töre in his tent. Töre approved the work that was being done outside the Soviet Union and gave it his support. In his opinion the real struggle was inside the country: the Soviet Union would be brought down not by attacks from outside but by being undermined from within. This was because atheistic, cruel and unjust regimes were sick at root. Because of this fatal illness, the Soviet system would rot from within and one day the republics of Central Asia would become independent.

In his youth Ruzi had heard his father praying that one day God would grant him the chance to go on pilgrimage. 'How good it would have been if my mother and father had been able to go on the hajj,' he said to Altunhan. The old man replied that even if they had passed away, a hajj could be performed in their names. And indeed, years later, Ruzi would go a second time to Mecca and Medina and make the hajj on behalf of his mother and father.[24]

The 250,000 statements which Ruzi and Hamid Rashid had prepared were handed out to pilgrims from the four corners of the world. News items about it appeared in the Saudi papers, and on his journey back to the US, Ruzi learnt that the German press had reported on it too.

A Meeting with Gamal Abdel Nasser

The hajj was just about to draw to a close. Animal sacrifices were being offered and people were congratulating each other. During the days of the pilgrimage Ruzi had got to know a young Uzbek lieutenant from Kokand. The young officer never left his side and helped Ruzi with everything. Ruzi told the young man that he had met General Neguib in Egypt and that he wanted to meet Nasser while in Saudi Arabia. He knew where Nasser was staying, and the young man could go with him and act as interpreter if he wanted.[25]

There was a guesthouse in Jeddah built by the Saudi government for foreign statesmen. Here Nasser and some other foreign dignitaries were staying during the hajj. It was a two-storey building with no architectural pretensions—ordinary, ill-shaped and modern.

Ruzi gave the lieutenant the card which General Neguib had written for him. The lieutenant spoke in Arabic to the sentries and they took them immediately into the waiting room. When a delegation that had gone in before them came out of Nasser's room, the officials took Ruzi, Hamid Rashid and the lieutenant from Kokand to meet him.[26]

Gamal Abdel Nasser greeted them with a smile. The visitors introduced themselves and sat down cross-legged on the carpet. Nasser took Ruzi by the hand and sat him on his right. He was tall, impressive and handsome, with slightly curling black hair, a pleasant face and a broad forehead. There was no arrogance or pride in his expression; he looked kindly and modest. Ruzi was sitting beside one of the most interesting statesmen in the world, one who would play a key role in the political life of Egypt and the Arab world for nearly twenty years.[27]

Nasser was a revolutionary Arab nationalist and he had come to power promising to make improvements in a country which was riddled with corruption. In Egypt he was pursuing pan-Arab, anti-imperialist and anti-colonial policies. Ruzi spoke about the Soviet Union, the nationality problems there, and the oppression of Islam and the Islamic clergy. Nasser told his visitors that the age of imperialism was over and that colonised countries would one by one achieve their independence. He was sure that the colonies of Russia would one day attain freedom. Egypt had not yet been completely liberated from British colonialism, but they would go soon. In his opinion, countries liberated from colonialism had to cooperate and help others to achieve independence. The meeting lasted nearly an hour and as it was ending, Nasser said, 'Let's pray for the independence of Turkestan. Prayers said here in these sacred lands for the oppressed are accepted by God.' They all held up their hands and prayed that the Soviet republics of Turkestan might one day achieve independence.

The Uzbek lieutenant from Kokand discharged his duties as an interpreter very well, but Nasser spoke English and frequently addressed Ruzi and Hamid Rashid in that language. At one point he turned to Ruzi, saying, 'I hope we will meet again. When you come to Cairo, don't forget to call me.' They made their farewells and parted.[28]

After Ruzi had offered his sacrifice at Mecca and completed the hajj, he went on to Medina. There too he held meetings with his fellow countrymen. He felt it necessary to give them a few warnings. He visited the grave of the Prophet Muhammad at the Al-Masjid al-Nabawi mosque and prayed for his mother, his father, those who were close to him, and his people.[29]

During the hajj Ruzi had felt the serenity and happiness that came from being on sacred ground. He had succeeded too in doing something for his people and his country, which increased his happiness further. But physically he was very exhausted. The rituals of the hajj, his intense activity and the heat had all caused him to lose weight.

The two friends decided to fly from Jeddah to Beirut. When you arrived at a Saudi Arabian airport at this time, only God would know when your plane would actually take off. An influential person from the Saudi royal family might arrive at the airport and commandeer the plane that you were about to board, and you would be left waiting. The situation only changed after Faisal came to the throne.[30] After waiting a few days in Jeddah airport, they finally arrived in the Lebanese capital, Beirut.

Until the First World War Lebanon had been part of the Ottoman empire, ruled by the Turks for 400 years. It had been occupied by the French during the First World War and only became independent in 1943. At this date more than half the population was Christian and the remainder was Muslim. Beirut, a beautiful city between sea and mountains, was a centre of rest and recreation for rich Arabs. Ruzi and Hamid Rashid set out to relax and enjoy the rich Lebanese cuisine. Ruzi regained some of the kilograms he had lost in Saudi Arabia.[31]

A First Visit to Turkey

From Beirut, they flew to Ankara. Ruzi felt excited as he set foot in Turkey for the first time. It was the first visit there for both him and Hamid Rashid, and Ruzi had no idea that he would later spend more than ten years in the city. Though it was Turkey's capital, Ankara at this date was still only the size of a small town. Mustafa Kemal Atatürk and his companions had directed the Turkish War of Independence from there and afterwards made it Turkey's new capital. Only twenty-nine years had passed since the proclamation of the Turkish Republic. Immediately after the First World War, the Turks had gone through the most difficult and critical period in their history. The Ottoman empire had collapsed, and

Britain, France and Italy had occupied Turkish territory. Backed by the British, the Greek army had invaded Turkey's western territories, dreaming of creating a Greater Greece. The victory won by Atatürk and his companions was a victory over imperialist colonisation. [32]

Turkey and Turkestan resembled each other in language, religion and culture. Turkey's indigenous people were the descendants of clans which had migrated there from Central Asia from the tenth century onwards. The Central Asians accepted Turkey as part of their fatherland and the Turks of Turkey as their brothers and close relatives. During Turkey's national struggle, the people of Turkestan had given whole-hearted support to those fighting for independence. The People's Republic of Bukhara had sent its entire treasury, accumulated by its khans over centuries. [33] Ruzi had first learnt about Turkey from Nogay Hoja, who had told his pupils about Mustafa Kemal and the fight he was putting up against the occupiers of his country. [34]

During the Second World War, the rulers of Turkey had succeeded in remaining neutral and thus saved the country from a massive disaster. [35] During those years, there had been a question in the minds of Ruzi and his friends as they fought in the Turkestan Legion: what would they do if Nazi Germany were to attack Turkey? [36] They decided that in that case they would go over to the Turkish side at the first opportunity. The issue was discussed in the NTUC, and the German High Command was informed that under no circumstances whatsoever could the legionnaires fight against Turkey. [37] The NTUC's chairman visited Turkey in 1942 and, during his talks with officials, he declared, 'If the Germans open a new front against Turkey, Turkestani soldiers will never take Germany's side.' [38] Thankfully, the situation had never arisen.

Amid a changing postwar world, Turkey was now trying to develop its relations with the West. [39] Turkey applied to become a member of NATO, the North Atlantic Treaty Organisation, in order to guarantee its security against the Soviet Union, but in 1950 its application was rejected. Seeking allies against the Soviet Union and eager to join NATO, Turkey then sent a Turkish brigade to the aid of the US-backed Republic of South Korea, which was under attack from the Soviet-backed North Korea. At a subsequent meeting of the NATO Council it was resolved that Turkey should be invited to join, and on 18 February 1952 Turkey became part of NATO. [40] This reduced fears of a Soviet assault on Turkey, since the

NATO treaty specified that an attack on one country would be regarded as an attack on all the others and they would come to its assistance. Ruzi was among many who felt reassured.

On this visit to Ankara, Ruzi was entertained by Professor Ibrahim Yarkın and Professor Sayit Ali Ankara. Ibrahim Yarkın had been born in 1902 in Tashkent. In 1922 he had been sent to Berlin to study, and from 1929 he had been active in the Turkestan nationalist movement. The following year he arrived in Turkey and became a professorial assistant in the animal technology section of Ankara University. In 1951 he became head of this department.[41] Ruzi, Hamid Rashid and the two academics swapped views about the activities of the NTUC and the work that needed to be done outside Turkestan.

Ruzi particularly wanted to visit the sociologist Professor Tahir Şakir Çağatay, to whom Ergesh Shermet and Baymirza Hayit had written after the war, unsuccessfully proposing that he take over the leadership of the Turkestan liberation movement. Çağatay was another of the students sent to study in Germany in the early 1920s and had worked on *Young Turkestan* magazine. In 1931 he married Saadet İshaki, the daughter of Ayaz İshaki, one of the leaders of the Idel-Ural Movement,[42] and in 1939 they arrived in Turkey. After working for a while as an adviser in the Turkish Ministry of Agriculture, he joined the Faculty of Languages, History, and Geography in Ankara University in 1948.[43] Ruzi was unable to meet him, however, as he was not in Ankara just then.

Ruzi's final destination was Istanbul. There he visited Abdulvahap Oktay and his wife, Saide, who was also Turkestani. They had moved to Turkey in 1939. Until then, Abdulvahap had edited the magazine *Young Turkestan* for a decade in Germany.

Ruzi and Hamid Rashid also visited the Uzbek Sufi *tekke*[44] in the Üsküdar district and met Necmettin Efendi, its joking and witty sheikh. The *tekke* had an important place in relations between Turkey and Central Asia. It had been founded in 1752 by Yesevi and Naqshbandi dervishes from Bukhara. Under the Ottoman empire pilgrims on the hajj from Central Asia would stop at Istanbul before going on to Mecca and Medina. They were given hospitality at the *tekke* before being taken into the presence of the Ottoman sultan by its sheikh. During the Turkish War of Independence the *tekke* had been one of the most important headquarters of the secret Karakol Society, which organised the smuggling of weapons and men from Istanbul to Anatolia. Many famous Turkish wartime figures had visited there, among them İsmet İnönü, Adnan Adıvar and his wife, Halide Edip Adıvar, Mehmet Akif and Yunus Nadi.[45]

Sheikh Necmettin fastened his eyes on Ruzi with a piercing gaze that seemed to go straight through him, and told him that he had a long life ahead of him and that in the years to come he would return to Turkey and remain there for a long time. He also told him that his mother in Margilan was still alive and healthy and that she prayed every day for her son. Ruzi had heard of people who had the ability to perceive things which others could not see, a power which the Buddhists call the third eye and which Sufis call 'the eye of the heart'. He asked Sheikh Necmettin if he would see his homeland and his mother again one day.

'Ruzican, sometimes we can talk through our hats,' the sheikh replied. 'Sometimes we get it right and sometimes we don't. So let's have a go at answering your question and see if we get it right. New things await you in Washington. You must be ready for them. Years later a day will come when you will return to your homeland. You will be greeted there by crowds. I cannot tell whether you will see your mother, Tajinissa Hanim, but you will meet your sister, Shemsihan, again."

Ruzi had not told Sheikh Necmettin the name of his mother or his sister. They had never met before, and he had arrived unannounced at the *tekke*. So how did the sheikh know their names?

As Altunhan Töre had prophesied during their pilgrimage to Mecca, Sheikh Necmettin said he believed that the Soviet Union would collapse one day, not because of a war or an external attack, but brought down from within. Years would have to pass before this happened. But he agreed with Töre: 'Don't you stop. Do whatever you can to undermine the Soviets, for that system is a cruel one and your duty is to work to destroy it.'

Everything Sheikh Necmettin said that day to Ruzi was later fulfilled to the letter. So why had he said, 'Sometimes we get it right and sometimes we don't'? Ruzi later learnt the reason for this. Muslim holy men regard it as undesirable to show that they may have the ability to foretell things. Sheikh Necmettin had said 'Sometimes we talk though our hats' to hide the fact that he was making a prophecy.

Ruzi and Hamid Rashid stayed in Istanbul for nearly a week. In those days Istanbul was not yet an ugly forest of apartment blocks. It had a population of little more than half a million, divided between the old city within the walls, Kadıköy and Üsküdar on the Anatolian side, and Eyüp on the European side. They visited the Topkapı Palace, where the Ottoman sultans had lived for hundreds of years, Ayasofya Museum and other mosques and monuments. Then they flew to Munich in another propeller-driven aeroplane.[46]

A re-encounter with Veli Kayyum Han

In Munich, Ruzi saw old friends, his parents-in-law and some of his wife's other relatives, and various people who had helped him after the war. They recalled past times together. He had arranged to meet up with Hamid Rashid afterwards in Hamburg, where he was visiting relatives of his Belorussian wife.

Friends in the NTUC invited Ruzi to visit them in Minden, where they were based in a building that had belonged to senior Nazis but been taken over by the British army. The NTUC had been publishing its magazine *National Turkestan* from Minden, in Turkish, Arabic and English, but had had to stop producing the Arabic and English-language versions because of financial difficulties. Ruzi was met by Hussan Ikram and Ergesh Shermet at what was then Düsseldorf's tiny airport. For the first day he stayed in the NTUC office. With Ergesh he reminisced about the war years and with Hussan about the time the two of them had spent in Rosenheim after the war.[47]

The following day Veli Kayyum Han invited Ruzi to dinner in his home in Düsseldorf. When Ruzi arrived at the house, he saw that Professor Ibrahim Yarkın was there too, whom he had met in Ankara. Professor Yarkın was in Germany as the guest of a university there and wanted to take the opportunity to visit Kayyum Han. They were friends, but there were serious differences of opinion between Kayyum Han and the professor and his colleagues.

Professor Yarkın would later say about these disagreements: 'When Veli Kayyum came to Turkey after the war, he met us and asked us to join the national movement. But we—and first and foremost Tahir Çağatay—as members of the Turkestan National Union, did not find Germany's policies towards the Turkic lands that were prisoners of the USSR acceptable. Germany had conquered the Crimea but it had not given it independence. It had conquered Ukraine and the Baltic countries and turned them into colonies. When Tahir said this, Kayyum Han replied that the Germans had promised him that they would grant Turkestan independence. Indeed, he had possession of a document that showed that the Germans had recognised Turkestan as an independent country, signed by various people. But I did not know who the signatories were. We were not persuaded. So we did not accept Kayyum Han's request.'[48]

In the course of the evening, they discussed the people Ruzi had met on his journey. Veli Kayyum Han said, 'Ruzi, you talked at length with our youngsters in Saudi Arabia and you told them, "Stay clear of the NTUC and don't get involved with the work of the committees." How could you do that? I would never have expected it of you.'

Ruzi was extremely upset. He said that Kayyum Han had been misinformed and that he had not said anything of the sort. 'I did not meet them just once but lots of times,' Ruzi said. 'We printed 250,000 leaflets and handed them out to the pilgrims. But I tried to explain to the youngsters that the Saudi state is an absolute monarchy and that even Saudi citizens are absolutely forbidden to establish organisations, and so they should act extremely carefully to make sure that their work is carried on without interruption.'

Thereupon Kayyum Han showed him a letter he had been sent from Saudi Arabia. The youth who wrote it had given a truly nonsensical account of the matter. Ruzi said that Kayyum Han had known him for years and he should not pay any attention to such lies.[49]

Kayyum Han said that he had established perfect relations with the leaders of the Saudi state and that nothing bad was going to happen to the young activists. But Ruzi was proved right not long afterwards, when the young people working for the NTUC in Saudi Arabia were arrested by the security forces. The activities of the NTUC in the country thus came to an end. This heated exchange in Veli Kayyum Han's house in Düsseldorf was to be Ruzi's last meeting with him.[50]

12

THE BANDUNG CONFERENCE

Ruzi Goes to the Bandung Conference

Ruzi read in the newspapers that a conference of non-aligned nations was to meet in the city of Bandung in Indonesia in April 1955.[1] India, Pakistan, Indonesia, Ceylon, Burma and Egypt had recently shaken off colonialism, and a group of leaders from these countries— Jawaharlal Nehru of India, President Sukarno of Indonesia and Gamal Abdel Nasser of Egypt—argued the need to create a bloc of countries that were not aligned with either the Eastern or Western protagonists in the Cold War.[2] The newspaper reports said that Tunisia, Algeria and Morocco, then still French colonies, would attend as observers at Bandung.

Ruzi thought that as his country was a colony of Russia, he should find a way to attend the Bandung Conference as an observer and representative. A friend suggested he might be able to go as a newspaper correspondent. Ruzi had met some Indonesian diplomats in the mosque in the Islamic Centre in Washington. He paid them a visit and collected information about Indonesia's history and its political, economic and social situation. He prepared an analysis for the CIA explaining the importance of the Bandung Conference in the era of the Cold War. The conference was expected to adopt resolutions condemning colonialism, and efforts had to be made to include the colonialist Soviet

Union in this condemnation. The report had the desired effect and the CIA decided to back Ruzi's Bandung adventure financially.[3]

Having solved his financial problem, Ruzi next began to rack his brains about how he could get an invitation to Bandung. He had got the information he needed about Indonesia from his contacts in the Indonesian embassy. Prime Minister Sastroamidjojo was a friend of the Soviet Union and the People's Republic of China, and President Sukarno was under his influence. However, a former Indonesian prime minister, Mohammad Natsir, took a critical view of the USSR and China. Natsir was now chairman of the Masyumi Party, a moderate Islamic party which was the largest political force in Indonesia. The smaller Social Democrat Party was also opposed to the Soviets and China. Ruzi thought that once he was in Indonesia he could make contact with them and take part in the conference as an observer with their support.[4]

About two weeks before the conference began, Ruzi flew from New York to San Francisco and from there to Hawaii. During this long journey he got talking to the passenger in the seat beside him. This young American was an idealist doing aid work for underdeveloped countries struggling with famine and infectious diseases. Ruzi explained to his companion why he was going to Indonesia. The young man said he was a friend of the former US Senator Homer Ferguson, whom President Eisenhower had appointed ambassador to the Philippines and who was on holiday with his wife in Hawaii. If Ruzi wanted, he could arrange a meeting. Ferguson was an influential person in US politics and so Ruzi accepted the suggestion.

In Hawaii Ruzi briefed Ferguson on the Soviet Union and explained his reasons for wanting to attend the Bandung Conference. He said that the Soviet Union and the Chinese would try to exploit the conference for their own political ends and that the US's European allies still had colonies in Asia and Africa. The situation in those countries would be discussed at the conference and they would be denounced. He went on, 'The most merciless colonising country today is Russia. The five Central Asian republics, the Baltic countries, the southern and northern Caucasus and Ukraine—an area of approximately eight million square kilometres—are all colonised by Russia. The fact that the Soviets and the Chinese People's Republic are colonialist countries needs to be on the agenda of the conference and they ought to be condemned. That is what I am going to work for at Bandung.'[5]

The ambassador listened with interest and gave his word that he would draw Washington's attention to the issue.[6] His secretary made meticulous notes. From Hawaii, Ruzi was due to fly to Manila, the Philippine capital, and then on to Jakarta, the Indonesian capital. The ambassador said that he too would be flying to Manila in two days' time with his wife and that if Ruzi wished, he could accompany them. Ruzi accepted with pleasure and said he would be honoured. The ambassador had Ruzi's economy-class ticket converted into a first-class one. Ruzi thanked him and they said goodbye until they met again in the aeroplane.[7] Thanks to this, Ruzi was able to stay a further two days in Hawaii, then a heaven upon earth that had not yet been spoilt by ugly buildings. He travelled around the island and enjoyed himself, while at the same time preparing for Bandung.

A large propeller-driven plane took them to Manila. There were places for a maximum of six people in first class. By day the first-class passengers could have a good time in an exquisitely furnished room where they were served fine food and drinks. At night there were beds where they could sleep. As he boarded the plane, Ruzi observed that among the other first-class passengers was Elizabeth Taylor. The actress was then only twenty-three and already a renowned beauty. She had divorced Conrad Hilton Jr, her first husband, and married her second, the actor Michael Wilding. On board the plane, Ruzi attracted her interest. They chatted and drank champagne together. That night, when the air hostesses were preparing the passengers' beds, Ruzi told them in a loud voice, 'Make the beds up so at least my feet and Elizabeth's can touch each other.' The other passengers responded with roars of laughter.

When they landed, the ambassador proposed to Ruzi that he stay in Manila for a few days. But at that time there was only one plane from Manila to Jakarta a week. The opening date of the conference was fast approaching. Ruzi thanked the ambassador and said that he had to travel immediately.[8]

When Ruzi got onto the plane from Manila to Jakarta, he ran into someone he knew, an Indonesian diplomat whom he had met in the mosque of the Washington Islamic Centre. The young Indonesian was the son of one of his country's richest families. He had resigned his diplomatic position in order to run the trading firms owned by his family. He had gone to Japan to visit the company's Tokyo office and establish new business ties there and was now returning. Ruzi explained to his fellow traveller what he wanted to do in Jakarta. But, he said, he had still not been officially invited to the conference. Ruzi's companion gave him the telephone number of the chairman of the Masyumi Party and former prime minister of Indonesia, Mohammad Natsir.[9] When Ruzi arrived in Jakarta, he made contact with Natsir and arranged a meeting.

Mohammad Natsir was a very cultivated man, a Muslim who was strongly opposed to every form of extremist thinking and colonialism, while respectful towards all religions. When Sukarno, the leader who had led Indonesia to independence and to whom the Indonesians had given the name of 'father of the nation', began to fall under the spell of Ali Sastroamidjojo, who sympathised with Russia and China, Natsir had gone into opposition against him.[10]

Mohammad Natsir knew very well that an Islamic renaissance had been achieved in the Middle Ages by scholars from the Transoxiana region of Central Asia. 'You are the child of lands which have produced great Sufis, lawyers, religious scholars, philosophers, mathematicians and astronomers. I know that your country is a colony of Moscow. I am going to use all the influence I have here to try and help you,' he said. His words gave Ruzi hope and courage. He added that he knew President Sukarno well but that there were serious disagreements between them. He would not ask for help from Sukarno for Ruzi, but rather from the vice-president, Professor Mohammad Hata.[11] Natsir said that he would talk that night with his friend Professor Hata and would ring the organisers of the conference himself the following morning. Early the next day Ruzi received a call from the conference's press office, asking him to call and collect his invitation as an observer delegate for Turkestan. Ruzi learnt that a place had been reserved for him as a guest at the hotel in Bandung where the conference would take place. Mohammad Natsir called the chairman of the Bandung branch of the Masyumi Party and told him to look after Ruzi during the conference and give him any help he needed.[12]

The Bandung Conference

The conference was attended by twenty-nine independent countries from Asia and Africa. Those present as observers did not have the right to address it or to vote, but they could engage in whatever activities they chose outside the sessions. Ruzi began by meeting the observers from Tunisia, Algeria and Morocco. He told them that his country too was a colony and asked for their help in having the Soviets and China officially condemned by the conference. He would assist them in having the same resolution passed against France.[13]

The chairman of the Masyumi Party in Bandung stayed in touch with Ruzi all the time. He spoke on behalf of his party to the other delegates from Muslim countries and kept Ruzi constantly informed. Ruzi learnt from him which delegations were pro-Soviet and pro-Chinese and which opposed them. He met the head of the Iraqi delegation, the chairman of the Foreign Affairs Committee of the Iraqi parliament, Muhammad Fadhel al-Jamali, and the country's education minister. Both men were uncomfortable about the activities of the Soviet Union in the Middle East. Ruzi had polished up the statement which he and Hamid Rashid had prepared on the hajj. He gave a copy of the text to the Iraqis. 'It would be a very good thing if the Turkestan problem could be discussed during the conference,' he told al-Jamali. Al-Jamali said nothing but shook his head with a smile. Ruzi later saw that he was one of those who spoke up most strongly about the Turkestan problem during the conference.[14]

The most popular person at the conference was Jawaharlal Nehru, who headed the Indian delegation. The head of the Egyptian delegation was Colonel Nasser, now the new ruler of the country, its president and chairman of the Revolutionary Council. Another member of the Egyptian delegation was Anwar Sadat, who would eventually succeed Nasser as head of state. At the head of the Philippine delegation was the country's foreign minister, General Rómulo. Pakistan brought a large delegation, led by its prime minister, Muhammad Ali Bogra. Ruzi met him and got a promise of support and an invitation to visit Pakistan. Ruzi also made friends with the Thai foreign minister.[15] Fatin Rüştü Zorlu, Turkey's foreign minister, headed the Turkish delegation.[16]

The plane bringing the delegation from the People's Republic of China crashed, with the loss of all passengers. A day before the confer-

187

ence started, a second Chinese delegation arrived in Bandung, headed by their prime minister, Chou En-lai. Ali Sastroamidjojo welcomed Chou at the door of his plane. The Indonesian government had allocated one of the most beautiful villas in Bandung for them, and though the other members of the Chinese delegation stayed there, Chou did not. Indonesia's richest industrialist and businessman was Chinese and he hosted Chou in his own villa.

On the second day of the conference, Chou asked for the floor and made a speech. The head of the most populous country in the world was dressed extremely modestly, in a collarless shirt, a simple military jacket with no markings and plain trousers. He spoke very slowly. Beside him there was a Chinese-American interpreter, who translated Chou's speech into English word by word. In the speech, the words 'Soviet Union' did not come from Chou's mouth even once. He said that China would always stand beside countries which had been liberated from colonialism and achieved independence, and he strongly criticised those countries which still had colonies in Asia and Africa. He said that there were minorities within the borders of the Chinese People's Republic. Of these the Tibetans and Uyghurs possessed every right in their countries within the frontiers of China and lived in peace. They administered their own affairs and their national languages were official languages alongside Chinese. They had schools which provided education in their national languages. They had decided of their own free will to live together with the Chinese within the frontiers of the Chinese People's Republic.[17]

In fact, of course, the blood spilt by the Chinese armies when occupying Tibet in the early 1950s had not yet dried. Eastern Turkestan had been occupied by Mao's forces in October 1949 and the Uyghurs' struggle to live freely and under humane conditions in their own country had been bloodily put down by the Chinese army. Tens of thousands had been murdered and thousands more arrested. The whole world knew that Tibet and Eastern Turkestan were colonies. Chou was telling a lie to the faces of the delegates.[18]

Ruzi felt that something had to be done to counter Chou's lies. He did not have the right to speak at the conference, but he was able to organise a press conference for the journalists who had come from the four corners of the world to cover the event, including around thirty from the USSR. Ruzi told the press office of his plans, and they informed journalists and delegates of the press conference to be given by Ruzi Nazar, observer delegate from Turkestan and a former officer in the Turkestan Legion. Meanwhile, the chairman of the Bandung branch of the Masyumi Party told Ruzi just half an hour before the press conference was due to begin that a North Caucasian guest called Seyit Shamil had arrived from Turkey. He had been unable to take part in the conference, as he had not been invited.[19]

Ruzi told the chairman that he should bring this guest straight in and seat him beside himself at the press conference. Seyit Shamil was the grandson of Sheikh Shamil, the national hero of the North Caucasus, who had fought for its independence against the armies of the tsars. Seyit Shamil had wanted to come to Bandung along with the Uyghur leader Isa Yusuf Alptekin, the former prime minister of the Republic of East Turkestan, which had been broken up by Chinese armies in 1949. But Shamil was the only one to obtain a visa, as the Chinese government had put pressure on the Indonesian government to stop Alptekin being given one. They had gone together from Istanbul to Karachi, where Alptekin had again applied for a visa and been turned down. The Uyghur leader decided to wait in Pakistan for Shamil to return.[20]

Ruzi placed Seyit Shamil on his right and began to speak, welcoming his audience. 'I don't speak Chinese,' he said, 'but the word "Lai" in Mr Chou En-lai's name is "lie" in English. I say this because the honourable prime minister began his speech with a lie and ended it with a lie. Haven't the armies of the People's Republic of China bloodily occupied Tibet and brought its independence to an end? Has China not made Tibet into a Chinese colony? Hasn't the United Nations condemned this occupation? Weren't the territories of East Turkestan occupied by the armies of the Chinese People's Republic just six years ago and its government disbanded? Hasn't this conference been convened to reject colonialism and to condemn the colonialist countries? I strongly condemn France for still occupying Tunisia, Algeria and Morocco, and the other Western countries which have colonies. But at the same time I also condemn the Soviet Union and China, which are the greatest colonialists. I am astonished that a prime minister can tell a lie in front of the whole world while looking delegates from twenty-nine countries in the eye and I condemn him utterly.'[21]

When Ruzi finished this speech, he said, 'My friend here is now going to give you more information about Soviet colonialism,' and gave the stand to Seyit Shamil. Seyit made his speech in Turkish and a translator who had come with him from Turkey translated his words into English.[22]

News about Ruzi's press conference appeared in newspapers world-wide the following day. Before the conference was even over, Ruzi had achieved his aim, at least in part. His argument that the Soviet Union and the People's Republic of China were colonialist countries had been widely quoted in the world's press.

At one point Ruzi met the head of the Turkish delegation, Fatin Rüştü Zorlu. During the conference, Zorlu argued that neutrality and non-alignment were a mistake during the Cold War while the Soviet Union and China maintained their aggressive attitude. He had established a bloc together with Iraq, Pakistan and Ceylon. Against it was ranged a group consisting of India, the People's Republic of China, Indonesia, Egypt and Burma. Zorlu explained that Turkish security had faced a serious threat from the Soviet Union after the Second World War and that as a result Turkey had been obliged to enter NATO. He declared that if non-aligned countries set up a separate bloc, this would simply serve the expansionary policies of the Soviet Union.[23] Zorlu told Ruzi that what he had done at the conference had been excellent and asked him to carry on in the same vein. He explained that Turkey was unable to support him openly, otherwise the Soviets would accuse Turkey of engaging in pan-Turkism. Ruzi was delighted that the foreign minister of Turkey had spoken so openly with him and showed him such affection and concern.[24]

The conference witnessed fierce arguments between the group headed by Turkey and the states siding with India, but ten points which had been agreed were announced in a statement. Thanks to the efforts of Ruzi and his friends, all colonialist and imperialist countries were condemned, including the Soviet Union and the People's Republic of China. The statement declared that many former colonies were now independent and that the imperialist countries had lost their monopoly of power there, that colonialism and racism had been rejected, that economic and cultural relations should be fostered between societies, and that Palestine should be supported against Israel.[25]

Ruzi had not only succeeded in getting Soviet colonialism con-demned. He had also managed to get Turkestan, which included five

Soviet republics, represented for the first time at an international conference, albeit only as an observer. The Turkestan question had come onto the international agenda. Ruzi had met nearly all the delegates at close quarters and briefed them on Soviet and Chinese colonialism, the nationalities problem in the Soviet Union and violations of human rights in the Soviet and Chinese colonies.[26]

Before leaving Jakarta, Ruzi once again visited Mohammad Natsir. Natsir asked his young visitor about Turkestan. He told him that he admired the Sufis of Central Asia and that he wanted to visit Samarkand and Bukhara one day, as they were among the most important centres of Islamic culture. He asked Ruzi for more information about Turkestan and the Turkestani problem. As soon as Ruzi returned to Washington, one of the first things he did was to send Natsir scores of books and documents about Turkestan and the Soviet Union.[27]

While the Bandung Conference was taking place, the Soviet Union held its own hastily arranged conference at New Delhi in India. Well-known writers from the five Central Asian republics and many other Asian countries were invited. The meeting was aimed at uniting the countries of the Third World in an Asia Solidarity Organisation linked to Moscow. Zülfiye, Uzbekistan's most famous woman poet and writer, was invited, as well as the writer Mirzo Tursunzade from Tajikistan, along with Kazakh, Kirghiz and Turkmen writers. At a second conference two years later in Cairo, attended by 500 delegates from the countries of Africa and Asia, the name was changed to the Afro-Asian People's Solidarity Organisation. Anwar Sadat, the future president of Egypt, was appointed its secretary-general.[28]

After Bandung

After the conference, the foreign minister of Thailand flew Ruzi in his own plane to visit his country. Ruzi stayed for a week in Thailand. The king and queen of Thailand were at that date much loved by the ordinary people. In Bangkok Ruzi gave talks to a group of Thai diplomats about the Soviet Union.[29]

Ruzi had promised the prime minister of Pakistan that he would go on there after his visit to Thailand. Seyit Shamil and Isa Yusuf Alptekin were waiting for him in Karachi. Alptekin told Ruzi about Communist

Chinese oppression in Turkestan and how the Uyghurs, who had inhabited their lands for several thousand years and in the past had established mighty civilisations, were being destroyed. The Uyghur Autonomous Region of Xinjiang, as it was known, extended over an area of 1.6 million square kilometres and was rich in uranium, gas and petroleum reserves. The Beijing government was systematically settling Han Chinese there and the Uyghurs were becoming a minority of second-class citizens.

Ruzi told Alptekin that it would be impossible to succeed against China through armed force. The only way to get any results would be to keep world opinion informed and so create international pressure on the Chinese. He told him that to this end they had to cooperate with the Tibetan independence movement.[30]

During this visit Ruzi also met the prime minister of Pakistan, Muhammad Ali Bogra. From Karachi Ruzi went on to Ankara, where he revisited his old friends Professor Yarkın and Professor Tahir Çağatay and explained what he had been doing in Bandung. The two academics had been following developments at the Bandung Conference in the press. They embraced him, offered their congratulations and expressed the wish that his good work would continue. Ruzi had, they said, achieved a great success.[31]

After a short trip to Istanbul, where he met Turkestanis who had read about his work at the Bandung Conference in the Turkish press, Ruzi went on to Munich. There he saw his colleagues who were working for Radio Liberty at the Soviet Union Research Institute. Both the radio station and the institute were controlled and financed as part of Washington's new strategy adopted after the US government realised that it was not going to get results from working with the American Committee for Liberation from Bolshevism. More than fifty specialists worked at the Soviet Union Research Institute, the vast majority of them refugees from the USSR. In 1955 the institute began to publish a quarterly magazine in Turkish and monthly bulletins in English and German. The magazine's editor was Edige Mustafa Kirimal, while Nikolai Golay was in charge of the bulletin. The institute published books and arranged conferences. From 1958 onwards it produced an English-language magazine, the *East Turkic Review*, dealing with the regions where Turkic peoples lived. Temirbek Devletshah was its editor. Ruzi offered congratulations to Edige Kirimal on the success of his magazine, and to Mirza Bala, an Azerbaijani academic friend of his, on the excellent research being published.

While he had been in Bandung, the president of the American Committee for Liberation from Bolshevism and the assistant secretary of state called Ruzi and asked for a meeting when he was back in Washington. On his return, the president of the committee told him that he had scored a great professional success, but asked why he was still not working with the committee. Ruzi replied that he had talked repeatedly about this topic with the people concerned and that the reason was very clear. If the Russian émigré organisations within the committee's structure would agree that once the Soviet Union had broken up the non-Russian republics could immediately become independent, then the obstacle would disappear. Otherwise it would be impossible for him to work with them.[32]

The foreign affairs representative on the committee was Erik Kunihal, a Finnish-American diplomat. Kunihal had graduated from West Point Military Academy, after which the US government gave him and four other young officers special training which prepared him to become an expert on the Soviet Union. Kunihal then served as US consul in Riga, the capital of Latvia, one of the Baltic republics. He knew a great deal about the nationalities question and felt an affinity for the republics of Central Asia. Ruzi met Kunihal frequently, and cooperated with him on some projects and became a friend of his family.[33]

During the Bandung Conference Muhammad Fadhel al-Jamali, the head of the Iraqi delegation, had invited Ruzi to Iraq and asked him to give a series of lectures at Baghdad University about the nationalities issue in the Soviet Union. So towards the end of 1955, Ruzi flew to the Iraqi capital and met al-Jamali, who told a young member of the Iraqi parliament to take care of Ruzi and help him with whatever he needed. Ruzi stayed for a week in Baghdad, holding discussions with students and tutors in the university and giving lectures about the Soviet Union.[34]

One afternoon, the parliamentarian invited Ruzi to go with him to a house in Baghdad on the right bank of the Tigris. They caught carp from the river. A fire was lit and the fish was served smoked. Apart from Ruzi, there were twenty-five guests from various Arab countries. They spoke among themselves in Arabic and the Iraqi parliamentarian translated into English for Ruzi. These people mentioned Nasser with admiration and believed that he was going to achieve great things for the Arab world. Ruzi understood from their conversation how popular Nasser was in their countries. [35]

Ruzi bade farewell to al-Jamali, expressing the hope that they would meet again, and then returned to Washington. Two years later he was to travel to Baghdad again.

In 1958, the pro-Soviet General Abd al-Karim Qassem led a bloody coup and overthrew the government. Members of the royal family were savagely murdered. The prime minister, Nuri al-Said, was tied to the tail of a horse and torn to pieces. [36] Following this bloody coup, Ruzi wondered what had become of his friend al-Jamali. Finally he learnt that al-Jamali, who was popular with ordinary Iraqi people, had gone into hiding and eventually found a way to get out of the country. He settled in Tunis. Ruzi was able to correspond with him, but the two men never met again. [37]

13

UNDERCOVER WORK IN
INTERNATIONAL CONFERENCES

On 26 December 1957, a conference of the Afro-Asian People's Solidarity Organisation convened in Cairo, in the wake of the Suez Crisis. Representatives of states, leftwing parties and national independence movements that supported the fight against Western colonialism were invited. Colonel Nasser wanted to demonstrate to Britain and France, which had invaded Egypt at the time of Suez, that his country could not be isolated. His military advisers suggested to him that the conference should take a decision to set up a permanent secretariat-general in Cairo, run by Egyptian officers. Egypt would thus be able to steer the national independence movements and would gain a major advantage over the Western colonialists.

More than 500 delegates from forty-six countries in Asia and Africa took part. Iran, Saudi Arabia, Pakistan, the Philippines and Turkey did not participate. The head of the Soviet delegation was Sharof Rashidov, president of the Praesidium of the Soviet Republic of Uzbekistan, one of the most important of the fifteen Soviet republics. Safronov, the editor of *Ogoniok*, one of the most important Soviet magazines, was there as his deputy. To emphasise that Central Asia was not a colony, Moscow took care to include a large number of Central Asians and Azerbaijanis in the delegation, as well as many Muslims. The first secretary of the Uzbekistan Komsomol, Murtazayev, was present, as were leading writers and poets from those regions, including Zülfiye and Tursunzade.

The conference was a continuation of Bandung, and Ruzi wanted to attend it too, representing his country. He was invited as an observer by the president of Al-Azhar University and the president of religious affairs in Egypt. He stayed in the same hotel as the Soviet delegation.[1] Ruzi had prepared a statement that described Soviet colonialism in his country and had it translated into Arabic and English and distributed to delegates at the conference. Most of the Central Asians in the Soviet delegation were afraid to meet him, but some of them were brave enough to have a conversation. Six Turkestanis who lived in Saudi Arabia learnt that Ruzi was an observer at the conference and came to visit him in Cairo. One morning when they were sitting in the hotel lobby, Rashidov, the head of the Soviet delegation, came in. Ruzi told his guests who he was, and they said in Uzbek to Rashidov as he went past, 'My brother, please, let's drink a glass of tea together. We are Uzbeks living in Saudi Arabia.' Rashidov politely declined, saying that he was waiting for someone, and indeed not long afterwards Safronov appeared and they left the lobby together. Ruzi understood that Rashidov had been embarrassed by his presence and that he had not wanted Safronov to see him meeting the Turkestanis from Saudi Arabia.[2]

Ruzi did have the opportunity to meet Murtazayev, the chairman of the Uzbekistan Komsomol, several times. Murtazayev was an easy-going man. He went to the hotel's sauna, he would joke and chat with the other delegates and in the evenings he would sip beer in the hotel bar. Murtazayev told Ruzi that they were aware of the problems of the Soviet Union and Central Asia and that they knew all about the liquidations in the Stalinist period, but he felt they could achieve something for their country by staying within the system and gaining influence. Murtazayev did indeed continue to rise within the Party. In 1959 he became vice-president of the Komsomol organisation for the entire Soviet Union. But in later years he dropped from sight. He was appointed party chairman of an unimportant town in Uzbekistan, where he fell ill and died at an early age. The Soviet system found it difficult to digest Central Asian intellectuals like Murtazayev who felt qualms about their nationality.[3]

Zülfiye was one of the few people at the conference who had no hesitation about meeting Ruzi. She was one of the best known and most popular poets not just in Central Asia but in the entire Soviet Union. Her poems had been translated into many languages. Zülfiye had been born in 1915 and had married a man named Hamid Alimjan. He had died in a tram accident in Tashkent in 1944. It was rumoured that because he was an opponent of the regime, he had been pushed under the tram by GPU agents. Another rumour was that he had committed suicide because he was unhappy. While in conversation with Zülfiye, who was a classical Central Asian beauty, Ruzi brought up the subject of Hamid Alimjan. Her eyes filled with tears. 'We were so happy—why would my husband commit suicide?' she asked. Ruzi sympathetically changed the subject. But he understood Zülfiye had hinted that her husband had been murdered. For years afterwards, whenever Ruzi remembered this meeting, he would grow sad.[4] On another occasion he said to her that he hoped their own fatherland would one day gain its independence. Zülfiye looked around nervously and said, 'I wonder whether we will see those days or not,' and then quickly left. Ruzi thought that he had upset her unnecessarily. The death of her husband had deeply affected Zülfiye. The bitterness of loss and her grief could be clearly felt in her poems. However, she did live to see her country become independent before her death in 1995.[5]

Another person who was happy to meet Ruzi frequently in Cairo was the head of a Kazakh *kolkhoz*. He was a tall, fatherly, cheerful man who had achieved great success at the collective farm and had been proclaimed a Hero of Socialist Labour. One day when Ruzi asked if he was not afraid to be seen with him so often, he replied smilingly, 'I have found a brother here whom the winds of change have blown so far from the fatherland and I am helping ease his homesickness. Didn't you know the Kazakhs are completely fearless?'[6]

One of the most interesting personalities in the Soviet delegation was Ziyaeddin Babakhanov, head of the religious organisation for Muslims in Central Asia and Kazakhstan. He was a Muslim clergyman who, like his father, Eshan Babakhan Abdulmejidhanoglu, had collaborated with the Communist Party in the Soviet period and interpreted Islam in terms of the instructions of the Party. Babakhanov had been born in 1908 and had studied Islamic theology and Arab language and literature in Communist-controlled Uzbekistan. He had been sent by the Party in the 1940s to study in Egypt at Al-Azhar University, graduating in 1947. Between 1941 and 1943 he was secretary of the religious administration in Uzbekistan and from 1943 to 1957 he was its deputy head and a member of the executive committee of the USSR's World Peace Committee. Under the guise of a man of religion, he was in fact an important Soviet functionary inciting hostility towards religion on behalf of the Communist Party, one of the most important agents of the GPU and later the KGB.[7]

At the Cairo conference, Babakhanov was elected a member of the executive committee. When Ruzi met him, Babakhanov told him that religious freedom of every kind existed in the Soviet Union and that it was a great sin to accuse the Communists of being enemies of religion. It was Lenin who had given Soviet Muslims their freedom. He explained that the Western imperialists wanted to make Central Asia and Kazakhstan into their colonies and were conducting a campaign of lies and slander against the Soviets. Ruzi told Babakhanov that because he was senior in age and had a very important position he felt obliged to be respectful to him, but that he himself knew of the oppression being carried out against Islam and its clergy.[8] To this Babakhanov replied that the Communist Party protected real Muslim clergymen but took measures against reactionary Islamic clergy who deceived the people and exploited them. When Ruzi said that during the Soviet period the Communist Party had closed down more than 30,000 places of worship, Babakhanov replied that these mosques had been shut because they were centres of exploitation and sedition and that by taking this step the Communist Party had prevented people from being deceived by clergymen who exploited Islam.

Getting up, Babakhanov said that the time for the *yatsı namaz*, the Muslim night prayers, had arrived. He said he would pray for Ruzi and ask Allah to show him the right way. Ruzi called out to him, 'Please pray to Allah like this: Whoever is on a crooked path, let God show him the true way.'[9]

Mahmut Aykarli and Mubashirhan Terazi

During the conference, Ruzi happened by chance to witness a significant meeting, which enabled him to establish that one of the leading figures of the Turkestani independence movement in Afghanistan and the Arab countries was a KGB agent. Mahmut Aykarli was an important Soviet intelligence operative outside the USSR. He had come to Iran from the Soviet Union in 1931 and won the trust of Mufti Sadreddin Han,[10] a leading figure in the Turkestan independence movement. He then worked for twenty-four years for Soviet espionage in Afghanistan, Iran and Pakistan. During the Second World War he had gained the trust of the German embassy in Afghanistan. He supplied them with some bits of information known to Soviet intelligence and then passed back information to Moscow about German anti-Soviet activities in the area. He also succeeded in becoming the representative of the NTUC in what became Pakistan, and kept the KGB informed about its activities there. In 1955 he set out from Pakistan, intending to go first to Turkey and then on to Germany, but changed his mind and went from Iran to the Soviet Union with the assistance of the Soviet embassy in Tehran.

With the help of Soviet agents inside the Afghan government, Aykarli had ensured that Sadreddin Han was compelled to reside in the city of Herat in 1944 and was thus prevented from working actively. A letter written by Sadreddin Han to Mustafa Shokay reveals that Aykarli was made the leader of the Turkestan National Independence Movement in Afghanistan on the endorsement and advice of the mufti. As someone well acquainted with the mufti's dealings, he established contact with the embassies of Germany, Japan, Turkey and Britain, passing on to them information of which KGB-GPU headquarters was aware and getting valuable information back from them in exchange, which he relayed to the Soviets. During the years of his activities Aykarli caused the deaths of large numbers of people in the Soviet republics of Central Asia who were in touch with the liberation movements outside the country. After returning to the Soviet Union, he was given an important post in the KGB and received the Lenin Service Medal. In fact, he had been withdrawn because of the defection to the West of a senior KGB-GPU official who knew that he was a Soviet agent.[11]

In Afghanistan Aykarli had been in contact with a member of the Turkestan independence movement called Mubashirhan Terazi. Terazi was an important cleric and he enjoyed influence within the Afghan royal family because he gave lessons in Arabic and Farsi language and literature to its younger members. During the Second World War he had been appointed to lead the armed anti-Soviet resistance which the Germans were trying to start in Turkestan with men of the former Bukhara khanate, which had resisted Soviet rule until the 1920s, former Basmati[12] leaders and soldiers from the Turkestani legions. The operation was given the code name 'Hansa'. The minister in the German embassy in Kabul, Hans Pilger, was in communication with Terazi.

Terazi was extremely conservative in religious terms. He used to describe *Young Turkestan* as 'that prayerless magazine' and found it too liberal. In later life Terazi migrated to Cairo, settling there.

Late one night during the Cairo conference of 1957, Ruzi was returning to his room from the hotel bar and happened to see Mufti Ziyaeddin Babakhanov and, behind him, the youngest son of Mubashirhan Terazi struggling to carry two large suitcases. Babakhanov and the young man looked around to make sure that no one was in the lobby and then went outside. Ruzi was behind a pillar and they did not notice him. Where could the mufti of the vast lands of Central Asia and Kazakhstan be going with the young man at this hour of the night? Ruzi went out of the hotel in time to see the two get into a taxi. He jumped into another taxi and told the driver, who spoke English, that the old man was ill and could not be left on his own, so they had to follow his taxi. They went a long way through the deserted Cairo streets. Then the taxi they were following stopped in front of a building. The mufti and the young man got out of it and went into the house. Ruzi paid the taxi which had brought him there and then positioned himself in a place where he could easily watch what was going on inside the house.[13]

Mubashirhan Terazi greeted the arrivals, embracing the mufti as cordially as if he was his oldest friend, and they began a long discussion. Ruzi could not hear what they were saying but he could see that Terazi was talking and the mufti was continually making notes. At one point the mufti opened the suitcases and presented what seemed like precious gifts to Terazi. Before they left, Terazi gave the mufti a roll of paper. Ruzi could not see what was written on it but it was not difficult for him to guess that it was information and reports prepared for the KGB. The most important activity of Soviet intelligence was infiltration. The KGB-GPU's experience and knowledge in this area was unmatched by any other intelligence organisation in the world. The Mahmut Aykarli operation was as important as the Kim Philby operation. Mubashirhan Terazi's activities as a Soviet agent were no less important than Philby's.

After returning to the United States, Ruzi arranged for the matter of Mubashirhan Terazi to be given close scrutiny, and unfortunately his suspicions proved to be correct. Terazi, one of the most important people in the Turkestan independence movement, the friend of Mahmut Aykarli, the close favourite of the Afghan royal family, the instructor of the king's sons and the professor at Al-Azhar University, turned out to be a Soviet agent.[14]

TheWorldYouth and Student Festival

The World Federation of Democratic Youth was set up in 1945 in London under the control of the KGB and GPU, and in the circumstances prevailing after the Second World War it expanded rapidly. But as the Cold War began, a significant number of its Western members withdrew.

The most important activity organised by the federation was the World Youth and Student Festival, which was first held in Prague in 1947, attended by 17,000 delegates from seventy-one countries. These festivals, held every two years, were an extremely important propaganda tool of the Soviet Union and up to 1957 were held successively in the Eastern bloc cities of Budapest, East Berlin, Bucharest, Warsaw and Moscow. Through the festival the Soviet bloc demonstrated to the world the importance it attached to youth and art. By projecting propaganda about the Soviet system to tens of thousands of young people from various countries, it attempted to win over Asian and African youngsters, possible future rulers of their countries, to Communism. The Soviet delegation to the festival was selected from the young people who had been the most successful in the Komsomol and the most loyal to the Communist ideology. They were also used for intelligence work.[15]

In 1959 the seventh World Youth and Student Festival was held for the first time in a city in the Western bloc, in Vienna, and this was of great importance to both sides. The Soviet Union spent $56 million on the project, a very large amount in those days. Invitations were issued to nearly 20,000 young people belonging to socialist youth and student bodies in 112 countries. The Soviet Union was the largest participant with a delegation of 360. The CIA took a close interest in the event, as did the Austrian intelligence services. Thanks to his colleagues in Austrian intelligence, Ruzi was invited to the festival as an observer. In addition, he had placed his own contacts in the American delegation, which consisted mainly of sportspeople and artists. The chairman of the Soviet delegation was Murtazayev, the Uzbek who had previously been first secretary of the Uzbekistan Komsomol and was now the second secretary of the Soviet Komsomol.[16] The Soviet delegation also included the first secretary of the Tashkent Komsomol, Obeidullah Abdurazakov, and the chairman of the Namangan Komsomol. Abdurazakov was the kettle-drum player of the delegation, while the Namangan chairman was there as a bodyguard of the Uzbek Spring Band. Years later, when Uzbekistan gained independence, Ruzi and Abdurazakov would become close friends. But in 1959, although both their hearts nurtured the dream of independence for their country, they were in different camps. During the festival, Abdurazakov met two Uzbeks whom Ruzi had planted in the American delegation. In a veiled way he hinted to them that the desire for independence was still alive in the country and that resistance against Bolshevism continued. When Uzbekistan did become independent, Abdurazakov would be his country's first foreign minister and later its ambassador in Turkey.[17]

Ruzi's contacts in the American delegation were two ethnic Uzbeks, Isakcan Narzikul, who was a worker in a machine factory in Philadelphia, and Ali Jan, who had been born in India, grown up in Turkey and then studied engineering in Germany. Later he had gone to America and got a job in the Uzbek section of *Voice of America*. He had not seen his mother since he went to the USA and had asked that a Jeddah–Washington air ticket be bought for him. Ruzi put the two men through a short training period and told them to be careful.

Narzikul and Ali Jan arrived in Vienna separately from Ruzi. They made contact with the Uzbeks in the Soviet delegation, ate with them and drank vodka together, and then passed on what they learnt to Ruzi. Ali Jan possessed remarkable talents. He had mastered all the Western dance forms superbly and had even made use of this skill in the night-clubs of Germany. Women would come to the clubs to dance with him and the club owners would pay him for it. In Vienna Ali Jan succeeded in extracting much information from the beautiful girls in the Soviet delegation who admired him for his fine dancing. Meanwhile, Ruzi had met a beautiful woman in the East German delegation who was working with the KGB staff within the festival administration and persuaded her to pass on information to him too. At the same time KGB officers in the Soviet delegation were trying to recruit young people from the delegations of other countries whom they could use as intelligence operatives after they returned home.[18]

Through the help of his Austrian intelligence colleagues, Ruzi managed to enter the camp where the Uzbekistan Spring Band was staying. He introduced himself as the son of Uzbek parents who had settled in Vienna in the Tsarist period. One evening Murtazayev, the head of the Soviet delegation, had dinner with the delegation's other members, including Obeidullah Abdurazakov, and Isakcan Narzikul and Ali Jan. He told these two that he had heard Ruzi was in Vienna and that he would like to meet him, but they replied that they didn't know him. This was because he had warned them to be careful. When he met Ruzi again years later, Abdurazakov would tell him that Murtazayev had known that Ruzi was in Vienna and that Isakjan and Ali were working for him. He had been informed of this by the KGB in Moscow.[19]

There were also members of the Turkish Communist Party (TKP) at the Festival. During the Cold War the TKP was considered to be the fifth column of Moscow and was not allowed to operate in Turkey. Its general secretaries lived in Russia or East Germany and worked from East Berlin. Its members were tracked by the security forces and arrested at every opportunity. The most wide-ranging arrests took place in 1951 and 1956. When the TKP's general secretary, Dr Şefik Hüsnü Değmer, died in prison at Manisa in 1958, he was succeeded in the post by Yakup Demir (an alias used by another veteran Turkish Communist, Zeki Baştımar). In 1960 Demir fled Turkey and subsequently carried on his work in Moscow and East Berlin.[20] Radio stations controlled by the KGB transmitted to Western countries in the same way that Radio Liberty and Radio Free Europe operated under CIA control. The most important of the stations broadcasting towards Turkey were the *Voice of the TKP* and *Bizim Radio* (Our Radio). Moscow Radio also had its own Turkish transmissions.

During the festival Ruzi concentrated on the activities of TKP members. A large number of young people had come from Turkey,[21] as well as young Kurdish people from Turkey, Iran, Iraq and Syria. The TKP had selected the membership of the Turkish delegation. During the conference, the TKP arranged for a secret meeting to be held in Vienna at which Kurdish delegates from Turkey, Iraq, Iran and Syria took part. At this meeting a debate was held about whether an armed Kurdish movement in Turkey would have any chance of success in the short and medium term. The general opinion was that it would not. As a result, it was decided to concentrate on work in Iraq.[22]

When the Soviet-backed Mahabad Kurdish Republic was set up in December 1946, Molla Mustafa Barzani was its commander-in-chief with the rank of major-general. President Truman put pressure on Moscow, as a result of which the Mahabad Republic was wound up in 1947. Barzani together with 500 armed men had then gone to the Soviet Union through Iran and Turkey. When General Qassem seized power in Iraq and the royal family and cabinet members had been executed, Barzani reached an agreement with him and returned once more to Iraq. There he set up the Peshmerga forces. His younger son, Masud, was jointly responsible with him for military affairs. In the final years of a life of continual struggle, Barzani would see the Kurds of northern Iraq enjoying certain rights within an autonomous region.[23] In this way the results of the decisions taken at the Vienna meeting began to emerge over time. Even in those years before he went to Turkey, Ruzi grasped that one day the Kurdish problem would give Turkey serious headaches.

A Meeting with Nâzım Hikmet

In Vienna, Ruzi was astonished to find that the Turkish poet Nâzım Hikmet had come to the city to take part in the World Youth and Student Festival. Ruzi had known Nâzım's name from his youth. His poems had been published in Soviet literary journals in the 1930s. Ruzi liked him as a poet and man of art but did not agree with his political preferences. In particular he strongly disliked the politically motivated poems Nâzım had written praising collectivisation and lauding to the skies the Communist Party of the Soviet Union and the Russian proletariat. In Ruzi's view, they might be well written but their content was perverse.[24]

Nâzım had first gone to Moscow with high ideals in 1921, when intellectuals were still intoxicated by the October Revolution and flags of revolt had been raised across the world against colonialism and exploitation. Before the Revolution, Lenin had described Tsarist Russia as the world's largest prison. The oppression of Central Asia by Tsarist Russia was worse than anything the colonists of Europe had done in Asia and Africa. The people of Central Asia were slaves deprived of every basic human right and liberty. Lenin and his colleagues had given their support to the Turkish War of Liberation, and the intellectuals of Azerbaijan, Turkestan and Bashkurdistan supported the Bolsheviks during the first years of the Russian Revolution. Sultang Galiyev in Kazan, Zeki Velidi Togan in Bashkurdistan, Neriman Nerimanov in Azerbaijan, and Turar Ryskulov, Feyzullah Hojayev and Akmal Ikram in Turkestan— and hundreds of others—listened to Lenin's appeals and took up posts in his party.

Nâzım had studied economic and political science at the Sun Yat-sen Communist University of the Toilers of the East, which had been established in Moscow in 1921. This university was the most important of the four universities operating under the auspices of the Communist International. Years later it was given the name of Patrice Lumumba, the Congolese leader who struggled against Belgian imperialism and achieved independence for his country. Many future leaders from Africa and Asia completed their studies at the University of the Toilers of the East. They included Liu Shaoqi, who followed Moscow's line when the Sino-Soviet split emerged, proclaimed his opposition to Mao and was killed, as well as the Indian Communist Manabendra Nath Roy, and Şevket Süreyya Aydemir, Vâlâ Nurettin and the Communist Party leader İsmail Bilen in Turkey.[25]

Until Nâzım escaped from Turkey to the Soviet Union in 1951, he spent much of his life in prison. In the harsh conditions of prison it was certainly not easy for him to follow developments in the Soviet Union or find out that the CPSU was no longer Lenin's party. For him the Soviet Union was still the homeland of the peoples of all the colonies in the world.

Ruzi understood all this and felt respect and admiration for the great poet. In Ruzi's view, the revolt against injustice should be respected. He himself had worked with the Nazis at one time in order to struggle against injustice, and was he not now cooperating with the Americans? Years previously he had read Nâzım's *Epic of the War of Independence* and had told himself that it was something which could only have been written by a very great poet. Nâzım had begun writing this poem in 1939 and, after working on it in three different prisons, had finished it in 1941. It had a great impact on Ruzi.

Ruzi felt both proud and moved by the fact that *The Epic of the War of Independence* told the story of a Turkestani popular hero:

With pinched eyes,
Sparse beard
And light machine gun,
Turkestani Haji Ahmet
Wandered to the mountain top,
In the morning, in the midday heat, and early evening and the moonlight
    and the starry night.
Whenever things were tough for our fellows
He would suddenly appear, as if he sprang from the ground,
And fired and scattered the enemy
And then disappeared again in the mountains.

Ruzi loved the lines which told how the people living in Turkey had come to Anatolia from his own country.

Galloping from distant Asia,
Thrusting into the Mediterranean like a mare's head,
This land is ours.
With bloody ankles, clamped teeth, and bare feet,
And land like a silk carpet,
This heaven, this hell is ours.
Close the doors of the country, never to open again,
Destroy the slavery of one human to another.
This is our invitation—
To live alone and free like a tree
And also in brotherliness like a forest.
This is our longing.

Ruzi thought that after Nikita Khrushchev's revelations about Stalin to the 20th Congress of the Soviet Communist Party in 1956, Nâzım must have grasped the reality of the Soviet Union in the Stalinist period. He had to find a way to talk to the poet while he was in Vienna. When they encountered each other at the festival, Ruzi said that he would like to meet him and Nâzım agreed.

Ruzi went to Nâzım's hotel as they had arranged. Nâzım greeted the young Turkestani with warm smiles. Ruzi told his life story to the poet.

He explained that he now lived in the US and that in his struggle for his country's independence, he was working with the Americans.[26] It was impossible for Nâzım not to guess which organisation Ruzi was cooperating with.

Nâzım was now fifty-eight years old. He was handsome and had an ability to make people relax and feel confident in his presence. He replied that he had often gone to Ruzi's Central Asian homeland and had many friends in Uzbekistan who were poets and writers. He mentioned the Azerbaijani poet Samet Vurgun, who was one of the greatest poets of the Turkish world in the twentieth century.[27]

Ruzi could see that Nâzım was tired and that his years in Turkish jails had done him severe damage. He said nothing about whether he was happy with his life in the Soviet Union. He simply remarked to Ruzi, who had lived far away from his own country and his dear ones for many years, 'I know very well what it means to long for one's homeland.' Nâzım told him to take advantage of the opportunities offered in the US, particularly in education. When they said goodbye, he looked at Ruzi with his sea-blue eyes and said in a sad voice, 'Take care not to get involved in politics. One shouldn't get mixed up in politics and eat shit.' Nâzım added a few more words implying that one should avoid becoming a plaything of the great powers and being used by them. In the circumstances there was nothing he could have said which would have been more explicit.[28]

Ruzi understood from Nâzım Hikmet's words and expressions that he was unhappy in the Soviet Union. Documents emerged after the break-up of the Soviet Union in the 1990s which showed that Ruzi had been right. Indeed, some of the poet's Azerbaijani friends said that he had been trying to find a way to return to Turkey.[29]

Isakcan Narzikul and Ali Jan

Isakcan Narzikul and Ali Jan, whom Ruzi had planted in the American delegation for the World Youth and Student Festival in Vienna, had interesting life stories.

Isakcan Narzikul came from the province of Jizzakh in Uzbekistan. In the 1930s his geography teacher at high school had been Sharof Rashidov, who went on to be first secretary of the Uzbekistan

Communist Party and an alternate member of the Politburo of the Soviet Communist Party. With Rashidov's help he joined the Tashkent military academy.[30] While he was still a student, the Second World War began. Training was speeded up. Narzikul became a captain in the Red Army and was sent to the Eastern Front, opposite the German units in the Baltic.

Like the great majority of young Turkestanis, Narzikul was an opponent of Russia and in favour of independence for his country. One day he shot himself in the leg with his revolver and allowed himself to be taken prisoner by the Germans. Because of his attitude, he did not endure much hardship in the prison camp before he joined the Turkestan Legion. He was sent on a training course in the school in Alsace-Lorraine where Ruzi was an instructor, but he could not take the exams and was forced to leave and become a civilian.[31]

This was the time when there was serious rivalry between Himmler's SS and the German High Command. The SS did not have sufficient knowledge of some military matters and so it opened its doors to former soldiers from the legions. Narzikul joined the SS as a lieutenant.[32] The Turkestan Regiment had become an SS unit as the result of pressure from Himmler on the NTUC.[33] Under the command of Gulam Alim this brigade did sterling service on the Eastern Front.[34] Indeed, on one occasion it was the only unit which was able to break through an enemy encirclement and save other units from certain annihilation. Alim and his officers were awarded medals and prizes. Alim was a tough soldier. When an Uzbek youth assaulted a German girl in a village close to where he was dug in, Alim killed him on the spot.

SS Major-General Gottlob Berger gave the Turkestan Regiment a mission in Poland. While carrying it out, Gulam Alim and the officers under his command robbed a Polish bank and returned to their quarters in Czechoslovakia with a sizeable amount of gold. They took the view that what they had done was not theft but war booty.[35] The legionnaires were fighting and trying to enjoy life at the same time.

When the Vlasov dispute erupted, Gulam Alim defied orders from General Berger and refused to join Vlasov. On Christmas night his unit—including Isakcan Narzikul—killed their German SS officers and became partisans.

Officials of the NTUC found Narzikul's SS greatcoat in their headquarters. It was full of bullet holes. His fellow countryman Jizzakli

Chorabay, who worked in the propaganda radio station in Berlin with Ergesh Shermet, personally saw the holes in the coat. Everyone assumed that Narzikul had died, and a funeral service for him took place in Berlin.

In the closing days of the war, Narzikul was captured by Red Army soldiers but managed to escape. Because he had become a partisan he could not cross over to the German side, and because he had fought for years against the Red Army he could not return to the Russian side. So finally he took refuge in a Catholic church. The priest liked him and helped him. Isakcan spoke both Russian and German very well and was good at languages, and so he learnt Slovak, telling the priest that he wanted to become a Catholic, although no one later on was sure if this was from conviction or expediency. He was baptised and changed his name to Ilya Narzikov.[36]

After the war, he settled in a Slovak camp belonging to the UN on the banks of Lake Tegernsee near Munich. Nureddin Namangani, one of the imams of the Turkestan Legion, told Ruzi and his friends that Narzikul was alive. Baymirza Hayit and Ergesh Shermet went to the camp and questioned him intensively, suspecting him of being a Soviet agent. Ruzi told them to leave him alone and think about what they themselves had experienced while living under wartime conditions.[37]

Narzikul, alias Narzikov, then migrated to the US as part of a Slovak immigrant contingent. He got a job as a worker in a machine factory near Philadelphia. After his trip to Vienna with Ruzi he returned to his factory job. The factory owner was buying new machinery to replace his old equipment. Narzikul and a Hungarian friend put up $700 each and bought one of the old machines. The two friends stored it in the garage of the house they were living in and, after their work hours in the factory were over, they continued manufacturing its products at home, selling the pieces they produced to the owner. After a few months the Hungarian got back his $700 and took his share of the profits and left the partnership. Narzikul bought a second and then a third old machine. Later he set up his first factory, then a second one, and then a third. He joined the ranks of American multimillionaires. He gave financial assistance to old friends from the legion and to the leadership of the NTUC. When the Turkestan Society bought a building in New Jersey, he gave the society practical assistance.[38]

At that time, Narzikul's biggest concern was to make a good marriage with a woman from Turkestan. But the women suspected that he might genuinely be a Catholic and would not go near him. At the US airbase at Incirlik in Turkey, there had been a talented and beautiful girl from Turkestan working as a secretary. She won the hearts of the American women there and they collected enough money to send her to study in the US. Narzikul met her and proposed marriage, but she, like the others, refused. All his wealth did nothing to solve his problem. In the end he married a German girl whom he had got to know in the factory in which he was first employed. He died of cancer in 1993.[39]

When he died, a Catholic ceremony was held for Ilya Narzikov in the local Catholic church. Later on, his old friends gathered in his house and held an Islamic ceremony for him. One of the guests pointed out that no funeral *namaz* prayer had been performed for Isakcan Narzikul. One of the others answered, 'We performed a funeral *namaz* for him in his absence in Berlin in 1945.' Those who heard had some difficulty in preventing themselves from bursting into laughter.

Was Isakcan Narzikul or Ilya Narzikov a Catholic or a Muslim? Catholics accepted him as Catholic and Muslims as a Muslim. But he believed in the unity of God, and that Jesus and Muhammad were prophets.[40]

Ali Jan's family had left Turkistan in the 1920s and settled in India, where he had been born. Ruzi met him in Germany, and he later came to Washington with Hussan Ikram to work for the *Voice of America*, staying initially with Ergesh Shermet. Ali Jan was fun-loving and witty, but he had one personal failing. He loved boasting. When the Soviet Union broke up and Uzbekistan achieved independence, he began travelling regularly to Tashkent where he had various small trading ventures. One day as he was going through customs at Tashkent airport, the officers asked him if he had anything to declare. He said in a loud voice, 'I have very little money on me—not more than 25,000 dollars.' Some people heard this and followed him back to the house where he was staying. They broke into the house, knifed him and took his money. Thus Ali Jan, who loved boasting, paid for his error.

14

RUZI IN TURKEY

SOLDIERS, PLOTS AND POLITICS

Altemur Kılıç

In 1956 Ruzi and his family moved to a rented apartment in Arlington on the bank of the Potomac River. It was at this time that he got to know Altemur Kılıç, who was then the press attaché in the Turkish embassy in Washington.

Altemur Kılıç was the son of Kılıç Ali, a hero of the Turkish War of Independence whose real name had been Emanullahzade Asaf Bey. His father had been the chief aide-de-camp to Nuri Pasha,[1] commander-in-chief of the Caucasian Islamic Army, which had liberated Azerbaijan from Armenian occupation. In 1919, while Kılıç Ali was getting ready to take part in the struggle for independence which Enver Pasha had started in Central Asia, he met Mustafa Kemal Pasha, the future Atatürk, at Amasya on the recommendation of Mahmut Celâl Bey.[2] He joined the national liberation movement which Mustafa Kemal had begun and organised the national independence forces against the French in the provinces of Antep and Marash.[3] After the War of Independence, Kılıç Ali became president of the courts known as the Independence Tribunals. Altemur Kılıç was a Bukharan Uzbek on his mother's side, and the son of a father who felt great love for Turkestan.

Selim Selçuk, a leader of the Azerbaijani Turks in Washington, was a close friend of Ruzi and Altemur Kılıç. He worked at the National Science Foundation in Washington, a body which translates scientific works published in various countries of the world into English. The friends would get together regularly and discuss the problems of the Turkish world.[4]

Altemur Kılıç introduced Ruzi to a young officer called Agasi Şen, who was an assistant attaché in the Turkish embassy. Agasi Şen in turn told Ruzi about Alparslan Türkeş, a staff colonel who had been posted to the Pentagon as the NATO representative of the Turkish General Staff. Ruzi knew his name from newspaper reports but had not met him.

Towards the end of 1944, when it had become obvious that Nazi Germany was going to lose the war, the president of Turkey, İsmet İnönü, ordered the arrest of thirty Turkish intellectuals who wanted independence for Azerbaijan, Turkestan, Caucasia and the lands of Idel-Ural and who felt sympathy for the Turkish peoples of Russia. His aim was to show Stalin that Turkey was not interested in the Turkish communities living within the borders of the Soviet Union. Among those who faced a martial-law tribunal in Istanbul was Lieutenant Alparslan Türkeş.[5] The trial ended with his acquittal and Türkeş returned to the army.

Ruzi was familiar with the activities of the Soviets in Turkey and other countries, and so could see how the Soviet fifth column in Turkey must have exerted itself to get Türkeş and the others arrested. Years later Türkeş would speak about it as follows: 'The people making the accusations were Marxists and Communists controlled by the Soviets. At these dates the great majority of the Turkish peoples were prisoners of the Soviets and of Communism. The Communists in Turkey were utterly blind supporters of friendship with Russia and consequently tried to scare people with our ideas. Local Marxists under the influence of Soviet propaganda did whatever was necessary to discredit us. In fact we did not approve of Hitler's movement and thought it was harmful. During the Second World War we were always anxious about Soviet expansionism. We took the view that if a Communist government were formed in Turkey, the new regime would surrender Turkey to the Russians. For we had witnessed many examples of this. We had seen how Czechoslovakia and Poland had passed into the hands of the Soviets and the way in which Romania and Hungary had succumbed to the embrace of the Soviets. The Soviets were demanding territory from us in Turkey at that date. That was why we opposed the activities of the Communists. Criticisms began that our attitude was unfair. Turanism[6] was alleged to be fascism. But after the passage of fifty years, the correctness of our views emerged.'[7]

Ruzi was pleased when Alparslan Türkeş was posted to Washington. Towards the end of 1955, he called his friend Altemur Kılıç and invited him and Türkeş to dinner at his home in Arlington, along with Selim Selçuk and Agasi Şen. Linda and their daughter, Sylvia, had gone to visit her family in Germany for the Christmas holiday. Ruzi prepared fine *meze* and cooked a good Uzbek pilaf.[8]

Ruzi's friendship with Altemur Kılıç continues to this day. Kılıç later went on to hold senior posts such as press attaché in Bonn, director-general of press and information, and minister in the Turkish delegation to the United Nations. Ruzi would visit Kılıç in 2008 in the beautiful Mediterranean city of Alanya.[9]

When the military seized power in Turkey on 27 May 1960, Agasi Şen was offered a place in the National Unity Committee but refused it, saying, 'We did not make the revolution in order to govern the country but to put a stop to a quarrel between brothers. We promised the people that after the intervention, we would return to the barracks.' The chairman of the National Unity Committee and acting head of state made him his chief aide-de-camp. After leaving the army, Agasi Şen became general manager of Turkish Airlines. Ruzi stayed in contact with him for the rest of his life, until his death early in the 1990s.

After the 1960 take-over of the government, Selim Selçuk was made press attaché in Washington by Alparslan Türkeş, who held the post of undersecretary of the prime minister's office though in reality he exercised the powers of a prime minister. However, on 13 November 1960 Türkeş was abruptly sent into exile in India and Selçuk was removed from his post by the other members of the committee in a purge of Türkeş's friends.

Türkeş was a key figure among the officers who led the 1960 military coup. He was dubbed 'the Powerful Colonel of the Revolution'. One of the most interesting figures in Turkish political life over the last half–century, he left a deep mark on his country's recent history. Ruzi's friendship with him continued right up until Türkeş's death.[10]

A DARK PATH TO FREEDOM

The 27 May 1960 Military Coup in Turkey

Ruzi spent 1959 in Washington, giving lectures on the Soviet Union to officers from NATO member states. He travelled frequently to Germany and held meetings with *Radio Liberty* and the Soviet Union Research Institute in Munich.[11]

In the Middle East at that time, the Soviet Union was trying to expand its influence in the Arab countries. Moscow had set up military bases in Egypt, Syria and Iraq, thereby placing Turkey under siege from the south. In Iraq General Qassem seized power in a bloody coup in 1959 and then signed a defence and cooperation agreement with the Soviet Union. In 1952 Turkey had been admitted as a NATO member and thus managed to obtain a guarantee for its security vis-à-vis the Soviet Union. It was in this context that Ruzi was sent to Turkey in December 1959. He worked as an intelligence officer in the US embassy in Ankara over eleven years, living through the coup of 27 May 1960, Talât Aydemir's attempted coups of 22 February 1962 and 21 May 1963, and the coup of 12 March 1971. In the course of eleven years he would strike up friendships with large numbers of Turkish statesmen, politicians, business people, artists, bureaucrats and soldiers. In Ankara Ruzi experienced events as a government official of the United States, one of the world's two great empires, and passed his own judgement upon them.[12]

Two years had passed since the Democrat Party won the general election of 1957, its third victory since the introduction of free elections in Turkey in 1950. The Democrat Party (DP) received 48 per cent of the vote and won 424 seats in the Grand National Assembly, while the opposition Republican People's Party (RPP) won 42 per cent and 178 seats. The total number of votes cast for all the opposition parties had been larger than those for the Democrat Party, but the electoral system gave the DP far more seats in the house. Violent rivalry between the DP and the RPP had begun during the election campaign and was exacerbated by these results. Most of the conservative popular masses supported the DP, but the military and civilian bureaucracies and the vast majority of educated people supported the RPP.

As time passed, the government's attitude grew steadily harsher. Demonstrations supported by the RPP and university professors spread to every part of the country. The RPP leader İsmet İnönü's tours of the provinces of Uşak, Kayseri and Istanbul were wrecked by popular protests incited by the government. The Turkish people seemed to be divided into two hostile camps. Censorship of the press increased and many journalists were arrested. The DP tried to dampen down the opposition by all possible means. İnönü invited the country's armed forces to act, and the professors of the Law Faculty in Istanbul issued a *fatwa* for military intervention. Just before it took place, İnönü made the following call from the podium of the Grand National Assembly. 'We said there should be a democratic regime and it was established. It is something very dangerous to divert this democratic regime from its course and turn it into a system of oppression. If you continue to go down this road, even I will not be able to save you. When conditions are ripe, revolution is a legitimate right for nations.'[13]

As the demonstrations increased and the atmosphere grew tense, Fletcher Warren, the US ambassador, addressed his staff in the embassy garden. Warren told them that Turkey's domestic politics were going through a very stressful time and that the country's stability was extremely important for the US. He expressed the wish that they should not meet their Turkish friends for a while in order not to expose themselves to mistaken interpretations, other than when necessary in the course of their work as embassy officials.[14]

Ruzi had left Linda, their daughter Sylvia and their son Erkin in Rosenheim with Linda's father until the house they were due to occupy in Ankara was ready. He had rented a house with a garden belonging to a former chief of the armed forces General Staff in Third Avenue in Ankara's Bahçelievler district. For now he was living in a small apartment next door to the Ministry of Agriculture. Because of the ambassador's warning, he did not inform any of his old friends of his arrival in Turkey.

According to Ruzi's account of the events of that time, the claim that the 1960 coup was engineered by the United States is utterly mistaken. Warm relations existed between the US administration and Turkey, and the DP government and the administration viewed the Turkish prime minister Adnan Menderes and his colleagues sympathetically. The US was uneasy about leftist groups inside the RPP rather than the DP. It is true that in 1959 the Soviet ambassador had invited the Turkish foreign minister, Fatin Rüştü Zorlu, to lunch and initiated a positive dialogue.

In statements which Zorlu later made about this invitation, he said that the DP government had tried to make relations with the Soviet Union more flexible but had acted with great caution. Plans for a visit by Menderes to the Soviet Union were being considered, as well as for cooperation in various investments in heavy industry, but all these moves were undertaken in tandem with negotiations with the US.[15]

A dispatch written by Ambassador Warren in 1960 about a meeting he held with Menderes states that the prime minister did not make any difficulties over the affair of the U2 spy plane which took off from the Incirlik Air Base and was obliged to make a forced landing in the Soviet Union. Warren said that there could be no better ally than Menderes. A message the ambassador sent to Washington on the morning of 27 May 1960, the day of the coup, ran as follows: 'The Turkish Armed Forces seized power at 4.00 a.m. this morning in an extremely well organised coup. The Embassy is of the view that the uprising stems entirely from domestic political concerns.' In a later message the ambassador reported that he had been visited by officers belonging to the National Unity Committee and that they had told him that the coup was directed against the Democrat Party, not against the US.[16]

At that time there was no reason which might have made it necessary for the US to instigate a coup in Turkey. Among the officers who carried out the coup were people who wanted to bring the RPP to power. The US government's view of the RPP, on the other hand, was less positive.[17] Ruzi is certain that the leaders of the 27 May 1960 coup carried it out on their own initiative and were not in contact with any foreign power.

Less than six months after the revolution, the fourteen officers on the National Unity Committee who were allegedly pro-American were arrested by its other members and sent into exile, under the guise of appointments as 'government advisers' to Turkish diplomatic missions abroad.[18] The fourteen men were purged by General Cemal Madanoğlu, who had excellent relations with the RPP and who was even implicated in later years in a pro-Soviet attempted coup. This would surely have been blocked by the Americans if the US had had a role in the coup.

Shortly before the 27 May coup, nine officers of the Turkish armed forces had formed a conspiracy aimed at overthrowing the government. Their leader was Staff Lieutenant Colonel Samet Kuşçu. He began to suspect that his fellow conspirators were hatching a plot against him and so informed the Menderes government. Kuşçu himself was arrested and received a jail sentence of two years. The other eight officers were acquitted. This was just one of the conspiracies which had been cropping up inside the Turkish army since the mid-1950s. US intelligence certainly knew about these activities, but they were not involved.[19] American interests required a stable Turkey. In order to avoid giving the impression that the US might be connected with these coups and coup leaders, the US ambassador had warned embassy personnel, CIA operatives included, that they were not to talk to Turkish citizens except in case of necessity.[20]

This was a time of coups across the countries of the Middle East. Nasser and his colleagues had come to power through a coup in Egypt and so had Qassem in Iraq. In the wake of the coups, Iraq had left the Baghdad Pact and drawn closer to the Soviets, while Egypt had established very good relations with Moscow. It was inevitable that young officers in Turkey would be affected by the coups happening in neighbouring countries. According to Ruzi, the conspiracies being formed inside the Turkish armed forces were a result of the initiatives of younger officers. The endless mistakes of the DP and the fact that İsmet İnönü had been sympathetic to the idea of a revolution prepared the way for the 27 May 1960 coup.[21]

One of the most serious failings among certain Turkish intellectuals was that they always tried to explain events in terms of a single cause. In their view, the CIA or the KGB or some other murky power always lay behind any event. They were unwilling to understand that highly complex factors led to social and political events. If Turkish politicians had shown more common sense prior to May 1960 and succeeded in cooling down the high political temperatures in the country, if the riots against İsmet İnönü in Kayseri, Manisa and Istanbul had not happened, if the RPP had not spread around the lie that hundreds of young people had been ground to pieces in mincemeat machines, if university professors had not issued appeals to revolution and so exacerbated tension, then the period of coups would not have begun in Turkey.

On the night of the coup, President Celâl Bayar and Prime Minister Adnan Menderes, as well as DP parliamentarians and generals who supported the government, were arrested and taken to the military academy. Alparslan Türkeş and his friends supported the idea of sending Bayar and Menderes and fifty other leading DP members to Switzerland at the expense of the state and setting the DP parliamentarians free. Türkeş raised the idea with General Cemal Gürsel, chairman of the National Unity Committee, who responded favourably to it.[22]

On the morning of 27 May, various academics from Istanbul University's Faculty of Law were brought by air from Istanbul to Ankara. They included many leading Turkish law professors. In accordance with a decision of the National Unity Committee, they formed a commission entrusted with drafting a new constitution. The members of the commission said that if the DP members were released, the coup would lose its legitimacy and therefore they would have to be placed on trial.[23]

Inside the National Unity Committee, the gap in outlook between those of its members who were in touch with the RPP, such as Sami Küçük and Cemal Madanoğlu, and the group headed by Türkeş and Orhan Kabibay was growing daily. Türkeş and his friends were against placing the former DP leaders on trial. Ekrem Acuner, who represented the RPP wing of the committee, and others all said that 'beef steaks and revolutions could not be bloodless', and that the DP leaders had to be called to account. They were trying, with General Madanoğlu, to have the government handed over to the RPP.[24]

When the conspirators made preparations for the 27 May 1960 coup, they needed a five-star general to be their leader. General Cemal Gürsel had settled in Izmir and was no longer involved. The deputy chief of General Staff, Cevdet Sunay, had rejected their proposal. Then one day Orhan Kabibay said to Türkeş, 'I know Major-General Cemal Madanoğlu, head of land forces logistics, from Korea. Let me go and talk to him. What can we do? If not a full general, then it will have to be a major-general.'

They went together to Madanoğlu's office. Türkeş waited in the room of his adjutant while Kabibay went in to see Madanoğlu and spoke with him. He said, 'Pasha, I have come here to talk about something extremely important with you. If you agree, just reply in a couple of words. If you don't, then say no. But what I am going to say is highly secret and whether or not you agree, you must keep it secret. Countermeasures are in place if you reveal it.'

Upon this Madanoğlu leapt from his seat, crying out, 'Good heavens, man, what are you going to say?'

Kabibay replied, 'Pasha, we are going to overthrow this government: we have a secret organisation. We want you to join us. Say yes if you agree, and no if you don't.'

Madanoğlu replied, 'You wretched donkey, you know that I have balls but no brains.'

Kabibay replied, 'Well, we have both.'[25]

Kabibay gave Madanoğlu twenty-four hours to think things over. When he returned, Madanoğlu said, 'Is manhood dead then, man? Count me in.' After 27 May, however, Madanoğlu and his group, being RPP supporters, were at odds with Türkeş.[26]

After the coup Namık Gedik, who had been minister of the interior in the Democrat Party government, was kept prisoner at the military academy. It was alleged that he had committed suicide by throwing himself out of the window. The Gedik family never believed this. Though more than fifty years have passed, the veil of secrecy shrouding this event has never been lifted. Ruzi is of the opinion that it was murder.

Claims were frequently made later, especially among the Turkish left, that Türkeş worked for US intelligence. Türkeş did in fact believe that Turkey's interests made it necessary to cooperate with the United States. He was very familiar with Soviet imperialism. But he never pursued a policy of submission to the US.[27] During the period when the DP was in power, close cooperation had existed between Turkish security bodies and US intelligence. The Americans had opened an office in the Turkish Ministry of the Interior known as the Joint Working Office against Subversive Activities. After a while this office had in effect taken control of the entire correspondence of the ministry. Immediately after the coup, Türkeş discovered the existence of this office and gave an order for it to be closed immediately. Thereupon William H. Doyle, first secretary at the US embassy, visited Türkeş and asked him to reopen it. Türkeş, learning that Doyle was the CIA's station chief in Ankara, gave him this message: 'Yes as regards working together against Communism. No to a CIA office in the Ministry of the Interior.'[28]

All these facts make it possible to conclusively dismiss the suggestions that the 27 May 1960 coup was instigated by the CIA and that Türkeş was the puppet of the Americans.

Alparslan Türkeş

One day after the coup, an American woman invited Ruzi to her home for dinner. She had settled in Ankara many years before and spoke very good Turkish. She admired Turkish culture and the Turks, and it might be said that she herself had become Turkish to some extent. Also present at the dinner were some officers who had recently left the army. One of these said that the officer who had announced the coup on the radio on the morning of 27 May 1960 was Alparslan Türkeş. That was when Ruzi learnt that Türkeş was one of the most important members of the National Unity Committee and had even been the leader of the coup. He wished the crisis in Turkey could have been overcome without military intervention. But he thought to himself, 'It's lucky for the country that Türkeş is involved in this business.'[29]

About ten days after this dinner, Ruzi was walking back to his flat from Ankara's famous Kerpiç restaurant. Three of Türkeş's daughters were walking in the opposite direction and, when they saw Ruzi, they recognised him from the time in the mid-1950s when their father had been Turkey's NATO representative in the Pentagon. 'Uncle Ruzi,' they said, 'what a nice coincidence. Have you seen our father?'

Ruzi told the girls that as he had just come to Turkey, he hadn't called him yet but would do so soon.

'Well, we are not going to let you go now,' said the girls. 'If our father hears that we have seen you and not taken you to him, he will be upset. So come on, let's go and see him now.' Ruzi accepted and they went together to the prime minister's office.[30]

At that time, Türkeş was officially the undersecretary in the office but he was in reality acting as prime minister, deputising for Cemal Gürsel. The girls went in through the large waiting crowd and shortly afterwards Türkeş emerged from his room with his arms outstretched, crying, 'Welcome.' He embraced Ruzi and asked when he had arrived in Turkey. Ruzi told him that he had done so six months earlier but that he had not called him in order to prevent gossip about US activities. 'I told the girls that I only arrived three days ago, so please don't tell them when I really came and show me up as a liar,' he said.

Türkeş asked Ruzi whether he had settled in yet and found a house to live in with his family. He offered him any assistance he needed. Ruzi could see that large numbers of people were waiting outside to speak to Türkeş and so he said he had to leave. But Türkeş would not let him go and they chatted for a while. Then they said goodbye, promising to meet again as soon as possible.[31]

Linda and the children arrived from Germany a few days later. The Türkeş family called at Ruzi's house to welcome her. When Türkeş's arduous day's work was over, he would often call on Ruzi and have a drink and they would chat. But Türkeş was fairly abstemious where alcohol was concerned. Their dealings continued like that until 13 November.

Ruzi's daughter, Sylvia, was a good friend of Türkeş's daughter Çağrı. Some nights Çağrı would stay at the Nazar home and some nights Sylvia would stay with the Türkeş family. On the night of 13 November, when Alparslan Türkeş and his colleagues were arrested by the Madanoğlu faction, Çağrı was staying over with Sylvia. That night Türkeş was taken to the Mürted military air base outside Ankara. Ruzi then acted on his own initiative and got the American authorities to urge President Cemal Gürsel to ensure that the fourteen arrested officers were not put to death. Madanoğlu and his colleagues had been determined to have the detainees killed.

On 19 November 1960, Turkeş was brought to Esenboğa airport outside Ankara and put on a plane to India, to be sent into exile as a 'government adviser'. The morning after he was arrested, his family was informed that his much-loved horse, which had been stabled with a military unit, could no longer be kept there. Ruzi took over responsibility for the horse and had it stabled in the Ankara Equestrian Sports Club. When Türkeş eventually came back to Turkey in 1963, he returned the horse to him.[32]

Turkish Intelligence

Contacts between the CIA and Turkey's intelligence organisation had begun in the early 1950s. Turkey's intelligence service was then known as MAH (Milli Amal Hizmetleri, or National Security Services) or the Turkish National Security Organisation. It had a past stretching back centuries. In the Seljuk period, on the advice of the Grand Vizier Nizamülmülk to Sultan Alparslan, intelligence had become a regular state institution. The Ottomans throughout their history had given

221

particular importance to intelligence services. In the final phase of the empire's history, an intelligence organisation in the modern sense, the Teşkilat-ı Mahsusa (The Special Organisation) was founded. The tradition was continued by the Karakol Society during the Turkish War of Independence and later by the MAH.[33]

The MAH was a de facto organisation which worked directly under the prime minister but had not been established by law. At the outset of the 1950s, the CIA began cooperating with it. During the same years, Staff Captain Fuat Doğu of the General Staff Intelligence Presidency visited Washington accompanied by four colleagues and received intelligence training there. Through Türkeş, Ruzi met Fuat Doğu during the time he spent in Washington. Ruzi regularly acted as an instructor on the Soviet Union and the nationalities question for officers from NATO member states being trained in Washington. Türkeş had recognised Fuat Doğu during a lesson he gave in the Pentagon. Both men were in favour of Turkey being part of the Western alliance and of cooperation between the US and Turkey, but the essential thing for both of them was that neither side should intervene in the internal affairs of the other. It was Türkeş who had shut down the CIA office inside the Turkish Ministry of the Interior.

Until MİT (Milli İstihbarat Teşkilatı) was created by a special law in 1965, the intelligence service continued to work as MAH, with its main building in the Maltepe district of Ankara. At the time when Fuat Doğu became head of MAH on 27 August 1962, with the rank of staff colonel, a floor of the Maltepe building was used by CIA officials in Ankara. Fuat Doğu managed to get the CIA to leave the building and so regained the independence of the Turkish intelligence organisation.[34]

During the years that the DP was in power, rivalry between the United States and the Soviet Union carried on relentlessly. Turkey's security was under serious threat from Moscow. The DP government did not have sufficient experience to conduct foreign relations in such circumstances and, although its intentions were good, it followed a policy of submission in its relations to the US. A letter written by the CIA station chief in Turkey, William H. Doyle, on 12 July 1960, during the period when Türkeş was undersecretary in the prime minister's office, set out the extent to which Turkey's intelligence organisation had come under the control of the CIA and how dependent it was on the CIA financially.[35] During the trials of the former DP leaders,[36] the subject was brought up by Salih Korur, who had been undersecretary in the prime minister's office during the Menderes government. Heads of MAH gave evidence at the trials.[37]

Ruzi would remind his Turkish friends that cooperation against a common enemy was essential for the intelligence organisations of different countries, but that every country had to protect the independence of its own intelligence service. Chief among the intelligence officers in Turkey for whom Ruzi felt admiration during his time was Ziya Selışık, who was twice head of MAH, between 1960 and 1961 and again in 1964–5. Selışık had worked in the Karakol Society during the Turkish War of Independence, smuggling weapons to nationalist forces in Anatolia. Selışık explained to Ruzi that major reforms were required in the Turkish intelligence service and availed himself of Ruzi's knowledge and experience. When the new MİT law was being prepared, Ruzi undertook a study for Selışık of laws and regulations on the subject in other countries. According to Ruzi, Selışık was a born intelligence officer. He possessed a mass of information and experience acquired during the War of Independence and the Second World War. He was cultured and wise, a good conversationalist, fatherly and with a sweet temper. Ruzi would always remember him as a good intelligence officer, a patriot, a good friend and a great man.

On 13 July 1965 Selışık retired. The new MİT law came into effect on the 22nd of the same month. The Turkish intelligence service now had a legal basis. It was Selışık who had taken the first steps to make the organisation independent.[38]

In the days following the coup of 27 March 1960, the Soviet Union made a proposal to Turkey which Alparslan Türkeş afterwards explained as follows: 'During the early days of the revolution, the Soviet ambassador to Ankara was Nikita Rijov. Rijov was someone who was extremely active and appeared friendly. He showed greatly friendliness and sympathy towards us. He paid me compliments and invited me to functions. One such invitation arrived from Rijov which I accepted. I took Mehmet Baydur, the deputy director of the Economics Department of the Foreign Ministry, along with me and went. The Soviet Embassy was in its old building at that date. I knew Baydur from Washington. He had been the Counsellor in the Turkish Embassy in Washington when I was in America. Mr Rijov received us in the large salon on the upper floor of the embassy. He was giving a dinner in my honour. The ambassador's speech was absolutely fitting. He declared that he was transmitting greeting to me from his First Secretary, Nikita Khrushchev, in the following words. "Mr Undersecretary, First Secretary Khrushchev sends especial respects and greetings for you. He likes you and Turkey very much. He invites you to Moscow. We are going to empty an entire 250-kilometre strip from the Turkish border in the Caucasus to the shores of the Black Sea of soldiers. We are also going to give you $500 million in aid each year. And we will give Turkey regular aid in order to help develop its economy." Ambassador Rijov paused at this point, so I asked him, "Very well, Mr Ambassador, but what do you want from us?" The ambassador gave the expected answer. "Get out of NATO." My response to this request was: "We are friends of the Soviets, not their enemies. Atatürk established this friendship. The basic principle of Turkish foreign policy is 'Peace at home and peace abroad'. That means in particular living as a friend with the Soviet Union. We are your friends too. The reason why we joined NATO was the threats which Stalin had earlier been directing at us. You asked us for territory. You asked for the Straits. You wanted a Marxist government set up in Turkey."

'This dinner in the Soviet embassy had pretty much turned into a game of chess. We were using diplomatic language, measuring our words and balancing them carefully as we spoke. At one point in this explosive negotiation, Mr Rijov replied to me as follows: "Mr Undersecretary, we come to you with a new proposal in a new situation. Our leader, Mr Khrushchev, is expecting a reply from me to this latest message of his. We want to revive the friendship which existed in the time of Ataturk. Turkey and the Soviet Union will join hands."'

The ambassador invited Türkeş to go to Moscow to discuss this and similar topics. He added that they would provide military aid and the latest weaponry and so would modernise the Turkish army more fully than the Americans had done. Türkeş rejected both the ambassador's proposals and his invitation and ended the conversation with these words: 'We will never give permission for any kind of action against the Soviets on our territory but our membership of NATO will go on. We cannot break it off or leave it.'[39]

As well as conducting diplomatic offensives of this sort, the Soviet Union also operated in the Middle East through Communist parties

belonging to the Cominform. The possibility that Turkey might termi-
nate its alliance with the West and work together with the Soviet Union
was an especial nightmare for the United States in those years. Both the
US and Turkey had been made uneasy by the signing of military agreements between the Soviet Union and Syria and Iraq and the subsequent
establishment of military bases in these countries. In these years Turkey
was extremely sensitive about the activities of Communist movements
with ties to Moscow.

Mihri Belli was a powerful Communist, a man of both action and
ideas. He had formulated the National Democratic Revolution theory,
based on his experiences in the Turkish Communist Party and during
the Greek civil war. In his view, revolutions should be carried out in
two stages, as they had been in Russia. In the first stage, there would be
collaboration with socialist army officers and a democratic bourgeois
revolution would be carried out, as had happened in the February
Revolution led by Kerensky in 1917. In the second stage, the proletar-
ian revolution would take place, just like the revolution of October
1917, which had brought the Bolsheviks to power under the leadership
of Lenin.

Türkeş and his colleagues who were purged in November 1960 had
regarded the Moscow-controlled Turkish Communist Party as Russia's
fifth column in Turkey and thus a great danger for the country. A large
section of the members of the left wing of Turkey's National Unity
Committee sought to extend their political influence by getting themselves declared life senators in the new senate about to be set up by the
committee, and were also working with socialist army officers for a
leftwing coup. The theoretician of National Democratic Revolution,
Mihri Belli, was in contact with militant youth leaders favoring an
armed revolution.[40]

Fuat Doğu, who served as head of Turkey's intelligence services
from August 1962 to 1964, had a good understanding of the Soviet
system. Although the young officers and socialist intellectuals might say
that the National Democratic Revolution movement was against imperialism and capitalism, Fuat Doğu was certain that a revolution of that
kind would make Turkey into a Soviet satellite. He infiltrated his own
men into the leftist conspirators' group and got to know how the coup
leaders' activities were controlled by the Turkish Communist Party and

thus indirectly by Moscow. The leader of this left-wing junta was General Madanoğlu, head of the group which had purged Türkeş and his companions.

General Madanoğlu

The armed forces would intervene in Turkish politics again on 12 March 1971. A few months before this, the doorbell rang at Ruzi's house in Third Avenue in Bahçelievler. Ruzi opened the door and there was General Cemal Madanoğlu. Ruzi invited the retired pasha in and took him to his drawing room. His guest said that he wanted to discuss recent political events in Turkey and the future of the country. Ruzi gave him a whisky and they began chatting.[41]

A magazine called *Öncü* (*Pioneer*) was published at that time. It was financed by the Soviets and Ruzi knew that Madanoğlu had connections with it. Madanoğlu had met Agasi Şen, the aide-de-camp of Cemal Gürsel, the head of state and chairman of the National Unity Committee, and obtained information about Ruzi from him. Şen had been a friend of Ruzi since his time in Washington.

Madanoğlu told Ruzi that he and his friends were going to stage a new coup d'état, that all the preparations needed for it within the army had been completed and that they wanted to work with the Americans. He said that both countries would benefit if the two US generals working at the Joint US Military Mission, JUSMAT, would assist them.[42] Ruzi told the pasha very frankly, possibly even a little rudely, that he was unable to help on this matter: 'Pasha, you have knocked at the wrong door. The Americans will not play any role in such a coup, either directly or from the edges. As far as I know, the USA never intervenes in the internal affairs of Turkey.'

Ruzi then informed his superiors of Madanoğlu's visit and what he had said.[43] Meanwhile, Fuat Doğu, the head of Turkey's intelligence service, had discovered through his agents that a leftwing coup was planned for 9 May 1971. Doğu saw that the civilian government was unable to take any steps against the coup leaders and so he informed the president of the republic, Cevdet Sunay, and the chief of the army General Staff, Memduk Tağmaç. On 9 March the generals and officers on active service who had been identified as members of the conspiracy, chief among them Major-General Celil Gürkan, were officially retired from the armed forces and arrests began. In Istanbul, General Faik Türün, the commander of the First Army, arrested journalists and writers in contact with the conspiracy. General Faruk Gürler, the land forces commander, and General Muhsin Batur, the air force commander, had until then been supporting the conspirators. They now withdrew their support and submitted to General Tağmaç as chief of General Staff.

On 12 March 1971 the chief of staff and service commanders sent a memorandum to the government obliging it to resign. It did so, but the resolute attitude and backing of Fuat Doğu, President Sunay and the chief of staff meant that the conspiracy was put down. Madanoğlu and his fellow conspirators were arrested. In court Madanoğlu stated that Ruzi had encouraged him to carry out a coup and that he had promised every kind of assistance. This was despite the fact that Ruzi had clearly stated to Madanoğlu that the Americans could not support the coup he was planning.

Ruzi offered the following interpretation of Madanoğlu's behaviour. 'The conspirators were in contact with the Soviets. Following the instructions they received from Moscow, they persuaded Madanoğlu to make a statement like that in order to put me into a difficult situation with both the USA and Turkish officialdom.' But Ruzi had already informed both US and Turkish officials about the conversation. So Madanoğlu's claim was a clear falsehood.[44]

Fuat Doğu

During the Democrat Party era in Turkey, the Turkish intelligence service MAH in effect worked as the CIA's Turkish branch. Turkey possessed a sound intelligence network in the Caucasus, Central Asia, Afghanistan and the Arab countries. During the Second World War the Germans had established good relations with Turkish intelligence and tried to avail themselves of its resources. Similarly, during the Cold War the Americans tried to make use of Turkey's intelligence network in the region.[45]

Until Alparslan Türkeş became undersecretary in the prime minister's office after the 27 May 1960 coup and Ziya Selışık and then Fuat

Doğu took over as successive heads of MAH, Turkish intelligence had carried out virtually no independent operations aimed at the Soviets. Only after the CIA office in the Turkish Ministry of the Interior was shut down by Türkeş, and Ziya Selışık and Fuat Doğu separated the offices of the CIA and MAH in Ankara, was it possible to speak of Turkish intelligence as an independent and national body.[46] The three people who gave Turkey's intelligence services a national and independent identity—Türkeş, Selışık and Doğu—were all close friends of Ruzi Nazar.

Under Fuat Doğu there continued to be close cooperation between MİT and the CIA. This was a relationship appropriate to the intelligence organisations of two friendly and allied countries. MİT entrusted one of its high-level officials with the task of holding talks with the CIA. This official had frequent meetings with a CIA operative nominated for the task by the CIA's Ankara station chief. It was known that the CIA provided technical assistance for Turkish intelligence and gave support in training its officers. Archival documents from that period show that Ruzi made significant efforts for Turkish intelligence to gain a national identity and independence.[47]

After Fuat Doğu took over at MİT, he launched operations against the Soviet Union that were completely independent of the CIA. His first task was to turn the Office of the Head of Intelligence into a fully modern intelligence and evaluation unit. His account of this ran as follows: 'Moscow perceived Turkey as a major threat to its own security. Russia had been the great security threat for Turkey over recent centuries. During the eighteenth and nineteenth centuries the Ottoman empire shrank steadily with Russia benefiting. During two hundred years of Turkish-Russian wars Turkey lost the Balkans, Crimea, the northern and southern Caucasus, and Azerbaijan, all of them to Russia. The whole of Central Asia was occupied by the Tsars' armies. The First World War was started in order to share out the territories of the Ottoman Empire, known as the "sick man of Europe". If the February and October Revolutions had not happened and Tsarist Russia had emerged victorious from the Wars, it would have been the end of the Turkish state. Russia emerged from World War Two as victor and demanded Turkey's eastern provinces and the Straits. Moscow's aim was to destabilize Turkey, weaken the country which it considered a danger for its own security, and then eliminate it.'[48]

Russia was second only to Britain in stirring up the Kurdish question, and it made extraordinary efforts to create an ethnic problem inside Turkey. During the Cold War Turkey always remained on the defensive. It tried to take countermeasures against Soviet operations and made efforts to assist the Americans in their activities against the Soviets. In Fuat Doğu's opinion, Turkey had to boost its defensive measures and its cooperation with the United States and also launch the independent operations against the Soviets that its own interests required. The Turkish state had a valuable stock of experience acquired on the subject of subversive and conspiracy-based work inside the borders of the Soviet Union, acquired from the period of the Ottoman empire onwards. The state should make use of this and undertake independent operations aimed at destabilising the USSR and breaking it up.

Fuat Doğu knew that the Soviet Union had two weak points. One of these was the nationalities problem and the other was the economy. The US and its allies were doing all they could to exacerbate the crisis of the Soviet economy. The US was forcing the Soviets to rearm and a large portion of the Soviet state was expended on defence. What Turkey could to do was to aggravate the nationalities problem.

During his time as undersecretary Alparslan Türkeş persuaded Cemal Gürsel, the head of state and head of the National Unity Committee, to create a Turkish Culture Research Institute in Ankara and a desk in the Foreign Ministry for Turks outside Turkey and the Turkish Cypriots. The expenses of the research institute were borne by the prime minister's office. It would conduct scholarly research on Turkic people outside Turkey and particularly on the nationalities problem in the Soviet Union. But when Türkeş was purged, the other members of the committee, as well as İsmet İnönü when he became prime minister, wanted to close down both the Research Institute and the desk for Turks outside Turkey in the Foreign Ministry. The latter was indeed closed, but Gürsel intervened to stop the institute being shut down. When Fuat Doğu took over as head of MİT, it was strengthened and he ensured that it carried on its activities for many years as a research body.

Ruzi assisted Fuat Doğu with the institute and its activities. In the late 1960s, Doğu organised a secret conference in the Marmara Hotel in the Atatürk Forest Farm on the outskirts of the city. It was known as the Marmara Conference and made the Soviets uneasy. The academic work of the conference was carried out by the institute. Representatives came from almost every region of the Turkic world, both from within the Soviet Union and outside it. Its conclusions, which emerged very clearly, were that Moscow had not resolved the nationalities problem in the Soviet Union and that the non-Russian nationalities living within the boundaries of the Soviet Union continued to desire to leave it and establish independent states.

Around this time Fuat Doğu arranged for various musicians to go to the Soviet Union and give concerts in Azerbaijan and Uzbekistan, among them the singer Nesrin Sipahi. There was great interest in the singer when she arrived in Baku and Tashkent from Turkey. Doğu's team had again made the Soviets uncomfortable.[49]

Doğu believed that preparations must be made for the break-up of the Soviet Union. In his view, what made the USSR a superpower was the petroleum of Azerbaijan, the natural gas of Turkmenistan and Uzbekistan, the wheat of Kazakhstan, the cotton of the Central Asian republics, the petroleum of the Caspian, and the uranium and other mineral resources of these territories. The destruction of the Soviet Union would only be possible when these lands broke away from it, and that was what one must work for. In pursuit of this aim, he sent students to work with the world's leading specialists on the Soviet Union.[50]

When in 1971 General Doğu had the Madanoğlu group of conspirators arrested and thus forestalled the coup the Soviets were aiming for, it was the last straw. Moscow gave the signal for its offshoots within the Turkish state to have him purged. A civilian government was set up after the March 1971 memorandum, and rivalry began between Doğu and the deputy prime minister, Sadi Koçaş. Doğu had excellent relations with President Sunay and the chief of the General Staff, General Tağmaç. But the outcome was that Sadi Koçaş and his group were successful. Doğu was removed from his post and sent to Lisbon as ambassador.[51]

Doğu had also opposed making Atilla Karaosmanoğlu, who was an expert at the World Bank, deputy prime minister for economic affairs. However, the prime minister, Nihat Erim, appointed Karaosmanoğlu after receiving a favourable opinion of him from the Americans.[52]

The role that the Soviet Union played in the purging of both Türkeş and Doğu is obvious. But the US did not stand up for either of them.

Neither Doğu's successor as undersecretary of MİT, Nurettin Ersin, nor the head of the Intelligence Office, Recep Ergün, was as far-seeing as he had been. Ersin even believed that it was a waste of time for MİT to be concerned with the nationalities issue in the Soviet Union.[53] The work that had got under way was now halted. Various young members of MİT on whom the Turkish state had spent large amounts to train them as experts on the Soviet Union were now obliged to leave the organisation. When the Soviet Union broke up twenty years later and it was understood that the real reasons for this were the nationalities question and the economy, Fuat Doğu was proved right. But his successors had stopped the work he had begun, and Turkey was thus unprepared for the disintegration of the Soviet world.

An Encounter at the Opera

As we have seen, Ruzi had a great love of music, theatre and the opera and had made many friends among actors and singers. Among them was Cüneyt Gökçer, director-general of Turkish State Theatres and Operas.

Cüneyt Gökçer was not yet married to Ayten Gökçer, the famous Turkish actress with whom his name is usually connected in Turkey. She was still Ayten Kaçmaz, one of the most successful and beautiful performers of the time. Ruzi's relationship with them was that of a true friend and a lover of the arts. Because of Ruzi's position in the US embassy, there were people who frequently exploited this.

On days when important works were being performed, Cüneyt Gökçer would invite Ruzi to the opera. Another opera lover was Turkey's prime minister İsmet İnönü. One evening when Ruzi was at the opera with his daughter Sylvia, İnönü and his wife, Mevhibe, arrived. Cüneyt Gökçer arranged for them to sit beside him and after the performance he invited the İnönüs together with Ruzi and Sylvia to have tea with him. Ruzi and İnönü chatted for a while and Ruzi told him the story of his life. He spoke of his years in the Turkestan Legion and the work he had done recently. He said that one day the Soviet Union would break up and that it was necessary to be prepared for it, and that nationalist resistance was still alive in Azerbaijan and Central Asia.[54]

By way of reply İnönü told Ruzi that the Soviet Union was a great empire and that great empires did not collapse in just eight or ten years. One had to look at history and the past to see this. 'Give this business up, Ruzi,' he said. 'By the time the Soviet Union breaks up, the Azerbaijanis, Turkmens, Uzbeks, Kazakhs, Tatars and others who live there will all have become Russian.'

Hearing this from the pasha filled Ruzi with deep disappointment.[55] He now understood why the Turkish Culture Research Institute had been shut down, along with the desk for Turks outside Turkey in the Ministry of Foreign Affairs. İnönü thought that the correct course was not to get involved with the nationalities issue and so bring down the wrath of Moscow. During the early years of the Second World War İnönü had seen the Germans occupy the whole of Europe in a short period of time and almost reach Moscow, and he had made the issue of the Turkic peoples a matter of government policy. But when he realised that the Germans were going to lose the war, he abandoned this policy. Before fifty years had passed, it was not İnönü who would be proved right but Ruzi, Fuat Doğu and the others who opposed him. It would be a vindication for the people who had been arrested and tortured in the 'Trial of Racists and Turanists', among them Ruzi's close friends Alparslan Türkeş and Fethi Tevetoğlu.[56]

15

FROM TURKEY TO BONN

The Kurdish Question

Ruzi knew that before and during the First World War the British had promoted ethno-nationalist movements in order to break up the Ottoman empire. Kurds and Turks had in fact lived intermingled for centuries in this region. Different ethnic groups enjoyed cultural autonomy in the Ottoman empire and there were virtually no Kurdish rebellions. Over the centuries Kurds and Turks married brides from each other's communities and were interrelated. After the British withdrew, Russia began to concern itself with the Kurdish problem.

Ruzi went frequently to the south-eastern provinces of Turkey and made contact with intellectuals there. After the military coup of 27 May 1960, most of the large Kurdish landowners were arrested and placed in a camp near Sivas. One of them was Kinyas Kartal. They were later released, and in subsequent years Ruzi became a close friend of Kartal's.[1]

One day Ruzi mentioned to Kartal that his first name, Kinyas, was Russian and asked him how he had been given it. Kartal told Ruzi his life story. He was the son of a great Kurdish landowner who was the chieftain of the Burkhan clan, and he had been born in 1900 in Georgia. His father had given him the name of Kinyas, meaning 'prince' or 'noble'. The Burkhans lived inside the frontiers of Tsarist Russian in

Georgia and the Caucasus. They had serious problems with the Armenians in the region, who received the support of the Russian state and army to attack them, and so they decided to migrate to Turkey. One part of the clan settled in Kars and İğdir and another in Van.

Kinyas had studied at the military lycée in Tbilisi and then graduated from the Russian military academy in Baku and had served for a while as an officer in the Russian army. He was assigned a post by the Red Army when it was created by Trotsky, but he felt uncomfortable about the Armenian units in the Red Army and did not accept it.[2] Seeing that his clan had migrated, Kinyas, together with the daughter of a Russian general who was in love with him, escaped to Turkey in 1922. He settled in Van and became chieftain of the tribe. His Russian bride took the name Leyla and they had a long and happy married life. When the Law on Surnames was passed in Turkey, he took the surname Kartal. In the 1920 he was twice exiled but eventually returned to Van. Following the 1960 coup, he entered the Assembly as Justice Party deputy for Van.

As time passed, Ruzi's friendship with Kinyas Kartal deepened. The two men both spoke perfect Russian and frequently held their conversations in that language. Kartal used to tease him, saying, 'Watch out, Ruzi, don't let them arrest you as a Communist because you speak Russian. They won't pay any attention to the fact that you are an American citizen, they'll just throw you inside.' Ruzi could not but perceive the injustice being done to so many people of Kurdish background who accepted that Turkey was their homeland and that its state was their state, and who were influential and respected in their own region. These errors would damage Turkey and play into the hands of various countries wanting to inflame the problem. During Turkey's War of Independence, Haji Bedir Agha, the head of the Bedirhan clan, had rendered great services to the Turkish state. Said-i-Nursi, a religious leader from a Kurdish background, had enrolled in the nationalist forces in the Turkish War of Independence and supported Mustafa Kemal. Kinyas Kartal was firmly attached to the state and loved Turkey. 'If Turkey had not existed, the Burkhan clan would have been completely wiped out by the Armenians. So how could I betray the Turkish state to which I owe my very existence?' he would say, unburdening himself to Ruzi.

What wounded him most were the accusations made against him when he was sent with 485 other Kurds to the Kabakyazı Camp at Sivas after the 1960 coup. He remained in the camp for nine months. The food the inmates were given was not fit for humans, let alone animals. But these things were not important for Kartal. What mattered to him were the accusations made against him. The Kurdish leaders had been accused of serving foreign ideologies and states, of exploiting religion and abusing their influence, of oppressing people and making them work like slaves. Despite all that he had experienced, his faith in Turkish justice had never been shaken. 'It is possible for the Turks to make mistakes but these fine people will one day perceive their errors and know how to reverse them,' he would say. One day he told Ruzi, 'This state has made me a member of the Assembly and even president of the Assembly. One day it will definitely recognise its mistakes, but you tell the Great Powers that they shouldn't interfere in our affairs.'[3]

In the Soviet–American rivalry during the years of the Cold War, what mattered to the United States was the stability of Turkey. At that time promoting Kurdish separatism did not accord with the interests of the US. Ruzi saw, however, that if the Kurdish problem was not solved, it would cause Turkey great anguish in the years ahead. The official policy of the Turkish state was based on denying the existence of the Kurds.

Ruzi talked about the Kurdish problem with Alparslan Türkeş while he was undersecretary of the prime minister's office and again when he returned from exile. They agreed that something could not be destroyed just by denying its existence. If the Kurdish problem was not resolved, it would be exploited to Turkey's disadvantage by other countries. Ruzi did not just talk about it to Türkeş, but he also gave strong warnings to Turkish intelligence officers. But the answer he got was not encouraging. They said, 'There are no Kurds in Turkey. They are only "mountain Turks".'[4]

Years later, when the Kurdistan Workers' Party (PKK) started its operations, Ruzi observed that it was supported by Turkey's former allies and told his Turkish friends, 'If Turkey had abandoned its policy of denial then and if the rights which have recently been granted had been extended then, it would not have been possible for the PKK's activities to have taken place.'

Ruzi never forgot the words Kinyas Kartal frequently repeated: 'From the soil in which the seeds of separation are planted, resentment and hatred spring.' Kartal is no longer alive. But in Ruzi's view, even today there are many sensible intellectuals of a Kurdish background who believe as Kartal did in the brotherhood of Turks and Kurds, and who regard the Republic of Turkey as their own state and oppose terrorism. As Nâzım Hikmet had said to Ruzi in Vienna, 'One should never be the plaything of the great powers.'

Ruzi gave the following warning to both Turks and Kurds: 'Do not forget that there are states which seek to take advantage of the quarrels between Turks and Kurds. They will attempt provocations of every kind and every sort of murky trick to keep the dispute going. Be vigilant against these games and, whatever you do, find a way to live together as brothers.'[5]

Hunting Trips

Ruzi was passionate about hunting. During the years he spent in Turkey, he would take his son, Erkin, with him and they would go hunting with friends. There are three villages inhabited by Kurdish people to the west of Ankara, called Sarayköy, Büyük Hasan and Küçük Hasan. While out hunting, Ruzi and Erkin often had to spend nights in Sarayköy, where the people would offer them hospitality. Sarayköy had a primary school and the children there spoke excellent Turkish. A large picture of President Cemal Gürsel, then head of state and chairman of the Committee of National Unity, hung in the village meeting room. However, the villages of Büyük Hasan and Küçük Hasan did not have their own schools and the children there spoke Kurdish among themselves. There was no Kurdish nationalism to be found among the Kurds living in Central Anatolia. These were people who were attached to their state and respected it. What they required was education and economic progress.

The wild natural scenery of Central Anatolia possesses an exceptional beauty. At that time it had not yet been poisoned by chemical fertilisers and was one of the richest bird paradises in the world. It was as if the true owners of this wild nature were ducks and geese, partridges, pheasants, turtle doves and quail. Deer and mountain goats wandered in herds.

Hunting has its own moral rules. It was humankind's first profession. Today technology gives mankind extraordinary power. Hunted animals no longer have any chance against the hunter. Therefore today's hunter is obliged to hunt in a way which ensures that the quarry does not die out. The first rules that come to mind are the obligation to feed animals in cold winter weather and to hunt only in the permitted season to ensure that their species survive.

During the nights Ruzi spent in the villages of Central Anatolia on his hunting trips he encountered wonderful hospitality. People who had to fight against harsh natural conditions in summer and winter would lay out their cleanest beds for their visitors and offer them their finest food. As he got to know the people of Anatolia, Ruzi observed that there were strong resemblances between them and the people of his homeland in Central Asia. Anatolian people were dignified and hard-working. They made sacrifices and were extremely generous.[6]

A Turkish official, the son of a wealthy family who had studied at a university abroad, accompanied him on one hunting trip. Ruzi was made very uncomfortable by the way in which this man looked down on the villagers and declared that if they did not make progress, then neither would Turkey. When he saw the bedding that they had put out for him, he said, 'How can we sleep in a bed that stinks so much?' When he shot a pregnant deer the following morning, it was the last straw. Ruzi called the young fellow over to him, gave him a hard slap on the cheek and yelled, 'Go to hell. You can make your own way back to Ankara on foot.' Then he left him in the middle of the steppe and carried on with his other friends.[7]

Another day he went hunting with a colonel who was commanding officer at headquarters in Ankara and a lieutenant-colonel from the same post. These people were very different from the rich kid who had studied in Europe. They talked for hours with the villagers beside the stove and listened to their problems. They ate with relish the food that the village women had made for them. Ruzi observed once more that the Turkish army was Turkey's most important institution, one on which the state rested.

On their way back, the jeep carrying the two officers collided with a truck full of watermelons. The colonel died on the spot and the lieutenant-colonel was badly wounded. He stayed in hospital for several months. After this event, Prime Minister İnönü forbade army officers to go hunting.[8]

A DARK PATH TO FREEDOM

Ruzi's Mother Appeals to Him over the Radio

In the Cold War both sides mercilessly exploited anything that was sacred to the other.

One day in 1965 Veli Zünnun, head of the Uzbek section of *Radio Liberty*, rang Ruzi and told him that his mother and his sister had made broadcasts on *Tashkent Radio* addressed to Ruzi. He would send him the recordings. 'It was a magnificent speech,' said Zünnun. 'When you hear it you will understand why I say that. From now on she is not just your mother, but the mother of all of us.'[9]

When Ruzi received the recording, he was very excited. After twenty-five years he was about to hear the voices of his mother and sister again. He played the tape. First his sister, Shemsihan, spoke. It was obvious that she was reading from a text prepared by the KGB. In a shaky voice, she declared, 'We have learnt that you are alive and we are extremely happy. Things in our country have now completely changed. We live amid prosperity, in happiness, peace and tranquillity. As you know, we are a wealthy family. We have houses and extremely valuable carpets and jewels which we inherited from our father. Half of his property is yours. Come and claim them and don't leave us, particularly your aged mother, alone.

'Goodbye, my dear brother. Now my mother will speak to you,' she concluded. Ruzi wondered what his mother would say. Was she also going to say, 'You have goods and property here. We are living in peace. Come immediately!'

The old woman began by saying slowly, '*Bismillahirahmanirrahim.*'[10] It was obvious that she was not reading the text in front of her. She went on, '*Esselamu aleykum!*' and then read a short verse from the Koran. Then she said, 'My dear son, your father prayed for you. Go on living wherever it is that you live. You will be fortunate and happy. I pray for you and the friends who are with you, all the time. Be well and be safe. However it is that God has protected you until today, may he go on doing so.'

The microphone was suddenly switched off, which meant that what Tajinissa Hanim had been saying had not pleased the KGB agents.[11] She had spoken on the live broadcast as her heart told her to, and not as they had wanted. Ruzi and his friends noticed that she had not said even once, 'Come back to your homeland.' He listened to his mother's appeal with moist eyes, a sad heart, and mixed feelings.[12]

Friendships in Turkey

During Ruzi's eleven years in the US embassy in Ankara, from 1959 to 1971, he made many friends in Turkey. He was able to talk to many of the most important people in Turkey's politics, in the arts, the civil service and business circles. He was at the centre of intelligence work against the Soviet Union in cooperation with Turkish officials. His meetings with his Turkish friends during these years were entirely outside his professional activities. They were simply the friendly dealings of a Turkestani intellectual with his friends and brothers, without any hidden intentions.[13]

At the start of the 1960s, the Turkish businessman and millionaire Ayhan Şahenk was unmarried and they frequently used to go out together to düğün parties[14] to search for suitable potential brides. Şahenk would come up to Ruzi, saying, 'I have fallen in love, brother.' Even today Ruzi remembers with a smile how he would then reply, 'But that doesn't suit you.' On one occasion they went to the Istanbul Hilton Hotel for a düğün and Ayhan Şahenk pointed to the daughter of a businessman, saying, 'I am in love, brother—I am going to marry her.' After the düğün Ruzi and his family went on their annual leave to Washington. When they got back a month later and he met up with Ayhan Şahenk, the latter showed Ruzi a ring on his finger, saying that he was engaged to the girl he had met in the Hilton. And indeed they did get married.[15]

One of the journalists whom Ruzi most admired for his intelligence and commonsense was Abdi İpekçi, the editor of the liberal newspaper Milliyet. He met him many times. Nine years after Ruzi left, İpekçi was murdered. Ruzi was of the opinion that his murder was linked to the attempt on the life of Pope John Paul II. Information which emerged after the break-up of the Soviet Union showed clearly that the Russian secret service was behind the attempt on the pope's life. John Paul II had been supporting efforts in Poland to have that country secede from the Soviet bloc. If Poland had indeed left the Eastern bloc at the start of the 1980s, this would have shortened the life of the Soviet Union and the USSR might have broken up much sooner. At a time when the Soviet Union was struggling for its life, some in Moscow may have wanted to trigger a civil war in Turkey and so prolong the life of the Soviet state. Ruzi considers the killing of Abdi İpekçi to have been a very great loss for Turkey.[16]

Another of Ruzi's friends in Turkey was Dr Fethi Tevetoğlu, a politician who was elected senator for Trabzon in 1961 and again in 1966. He was a graduate of the Army Medical School and deputy president of the Senate for a while. He was a frequent guest at Ruzi's weekend gatherings, at his home in Bahçelievler, where delicious Uzbek pilafs and other Central Asian dishes would be served and guests from the worlds of art, politics and business would be entertained. Other regulars were Cüneyt Gökçer, Aclan Sayılgan, Halit Zarbun, a member of the Constitutional Court, and Ali Naili Erdem, who was then Justice Party deputy for Izmir and who served as minister of industry and then of labour. In the 1960s Ruzi established friendships with many of Turkey's leading intellectuals, making no distinction between right and left. Among these were Çetin Altan, İlhan Selçuk, Galip Erdem, Gökhan Evliyaoğlu and Professor Aydın Yalçın.[17] In Ruzi's opinion intellectuals who put themselves at the service of another country, whichever one it was, were extremely dangerous and harmful. During the eleven years he was in Turkey, Ruzi observed sorrowfully that many Turkish intellectuals had done this.

Turkey was a country at the heart of Eurasia. It served as a bridge between Europe and Asia in both the cultural and geographical senses. It had many points in common with Azerbaijan, the lands of the Caucasus, Central Asia and the Balkan nations. If Turkey took advantage of its geopolitical potential as it should do, given its centuries of experience, it could be one of the most important and strongest states in the world. But, in Ruzi's view, one of the weakest aspects of the Turkish state was that its institutions were open to infiltration by foreign countries. Ruzi was of the opinion that Turkish security organisations were not as sensitive to the danger as they ought to be.[18]

Just as there had been adherents of Britain, Russia, France and Germany in virtually every organ of the state in the final years of the Ottoman empire, the Turkish state now faced a similar problem. The only thing that had changed was that new countries had been added to the list. Consequently the Turks had to take serious and effective measures against the threat. The security organisations of the Turkish state should end their rivalry and concentrate on this problem in particular. The Turks should not forget that today's friends might be tomorrow's rivals and that this rivalry might one day turn into hostility. A country's intelligence organisation had an important place in ensuring that that its very existence and independence continued.[19]

Bonn

Ruzi had been living outside his Central Asian homeland since 1941 and Turkey for him felt virtually like a second motherland. When in 1971 he returned to Washington for the sake of his children's schooling, it felt to him like a second separation from his homeland and he became homesick once more.

The CIA did not keep Ruzi at its Virginia headquarters for more than a year. At the height of the Vietnam War there was talk of him being posted to Vietnam. Ruzi was not unenthusiastic about the idea. But Washington believed that this important figure from the Cold War would be of more use in work against the Soviets in Germany and posted him to Bonn, then capital of the German Federal Republic.[20]

Ruzi's years in Germany were occupied with routine business against the Soviet Union. The ideological and intellectual battle between the two sides in the Cold War was then continuing apace. Richard Helms, head of the CIA between 1966 and 1973, reported to President Richard Nixon that over twenty years more than $400 million had been poured into *Radio Free Europe* and *Radio Liberty* and that their radio broadcasts kept opposition forces and groups alive in countries behind the Iron Curtain. Statements against the Soviet regime by the physicist Andrei Sakharov and the novelist Alexander Solzhenitsyn had been conveyed to the peoples of the Soviet Union by means of these radio stations under CIA control. Their broadcasts reached an audience of thirty million people in Eastern Europe. Although the Soviets spent $150 million every year to jam these transmissions, the attempt was unsuccessful and citizens of the USSR tried to listen to them by every means they could.[21] Helms also declared that more than a million books and magazines had been secretly infiltrated into the Soviet Union and the countries of Eastern Europe in the two decades since the mid-1950s.

In the early 1970s a multi-volume comparative encyclopedia was produced with the intention of showing the superiority of the West. It was entitled *The Soviet System and Democratic Society* and it contrasted the concepts and institutions in terms of the Marxist-Leninist and liberal-capitalist worldviews. It was prepared by a committee headed by Professor Boris Meissner, who at one point had been an advisor to Konrad Adenauer, the founder of the German Federal Republic, and Professor Zbigniew Brzezinski, who had served as national security adviser to President Jimmy Carter. Brzezinski, who had been born in Warsaw, was one of the ablest political scientists in the US. This work made the case that the Soviet Union had lost the Cold War at the level of ideas.[22] Indeed, fifteen years after this work was published, the Soviet bloc broke up and the Soviet Union collapsed. During his years in Germany, Ruzi was involved in expediting works of this kind, and became friends with Professor Brzezinski.[23]

The Soviets reacted with hostility to the intellectual and ideological campaigns of the West. *Neues Deutschland*, the official Communist Party newspaper in East Germany, made frequent attacks on Ruzi. It claimed that he was coordinating anti-socialist forces in the countries of Eastern Europe and that he was working in Bonn to get those countries to leave the Eastern bloc.

After working for twelve years in Germany, Ruzi returned to Washington in 1983. His priority, as always, had been the nationalities problem in the Soviet Union. He wrote several analyses about it and gave classes on the topic in the CIA's training school. He made contact with officials who came from the non-Russian nationalities in Soviet diplomatic missions in Western European countries and engaged some of those to work with his own organisation. Despite attractive proposals from CIA headquarters that he continue with his post in Germany, Ruzi chose to return. He had observed that the Soviets were fighting for survival and he thought it would be more appropriate to be at headquarters in order to hasten the end of the USSR.

During his years in Germany he had been given special assignments in other countries. He had also lived through the most exciting and dangerous moments of his life in three weeks in Tehran in 1979, the year in which the staff of the American embassy in that city were taken hostage.[24]

16

UNDERCOVER IN IRAN DURING
THE HOSTAGE CRISIS

Iran

From 1953, when the Iranian prime minister, Mohammed Mossadegh was ousted in a coup with CIA backing, the Shah of Persia, Reza Pahlavi, was one of the most important allies of the US in the Middle East. On 31 December 1977, President Jimmy Carter gave a resplendent official dinner in the White House in honour of the Shah, at which he compared the monarchy of Iran to an island of peace and stability in a sea agitated by fierce waves. This was nothing more than a restatement of views which CIA agents had stressed insistently in their reports and analyses of Iran since 1953.[1] A few weeks after the speech by President Carter, a CIA officer by the name of Howard Hart arrived in Tehran as the new station chief. He would be in the post before the Khomeini Revolution, during it and after it. Hart was a brave and experienced secret agent. At the time when demonstrations against the Shah were growing, he thrust aside a report from the headquarters of SAVAK,[2] the Iranian intelligence service, and went into the streets to find out what was really going on. He began to grasp the facts. The reality was very different from what had been presented in the reports and analyses which CIA agents in Tehran sent back to headquarters. In none of these was there any suggestion that the Shah could face problems.[3]

In August 1978 the CIA sent a report to the White House which stressed that revolution in Iran was still very remote. A few weeks after it was dispatched, supporters of the exiled religious leader Ayatollah Khomeini began large demonstrations on the streets of Tehran. On 16 January 1979 the Shah was forced to flee Iran. Khomeini's supporters announced that the rule of the shahs had been abolished. The way was now open for Khomeini, then living in exile in France, to return to Tehran. On 1 February 1979 he arrived and four days later he appointed a new government for the country.

Iran was now to be ruled by a Revolutionary Council formed by Khomeini's supporters and by a prime minister who was not a clergyman. The CIA strove to hold talks at prime ministerial level and to influence the new government. However, these efforts came to nothing and an Islamic republic was set up in Iran under the religious and spiritual leadership of Khomeini. No CIA officer had dreamt that the Shah of Iran, who possessed unlimited financial resources, military power and a merciless and well-equipped intelligence service, would be overthrown by an aged clergyman and that a theocracy would be established in Iran. Bruce Laingen had started his career as a young diplomat in the US embassy in Tehran in 1953 and was the embassy's most senior member when the revolution took place. He later described how over the years he had seen many US ambassadors and CIA station chiefs socialising with the Shah. They had all been intoxicated by his caviar and champagne, losing their ability to make an objective analysis.[4]

As the street protests and chaos grew, thousands of US citizens living in Iran and most of the personnel of the embassy were sent out of the country as a security precaution. On 18 March 1979 Howard Hart, the CIA station chief in Iran, was stopped at a checkpoint by Khomeini supporters and badly beaten up. He was then placed in the back of a car and was taken to an unknown destination on the grounds that he was a CIA agent. Understanding that his end might be near, Hart shot his captors dead with his pistol. Years later, he still recalled the hatred with which the young followers of Khomeini had looked at him.[5]

President Carter was obliged to give way to pressure from close friends of the Shah and Henry Kissinger in particular and allow the Shah to come to the United States. Carter feared that that the new regime in Iran would take revenge and so the decision was not easy for him. He asked, 'What will we do if the Iranians find a way to take twenty American marines hostage and shoot one of them at dawn each day?' and added, 'Let the Shah go and play tennis in Acapulco rather than California.' But the American friends of the Shah, who had been spoilt for years with presents from him, eventually managed to persuade the president and the Shah arrived in the US. No one in the White House had even bothered to ask the CIA what it thought on the subject.[6]

Two weeks later, a group of Iranian student supporters of Khomeini occupied the US embassy in Tehran and took all the embassy staff hostage. For the remaining 444 days of Jimmy Carter's presidency, fifty-three embassy officials would suffer an unbearable hell.

The Hostages from the American Embassy

Washington's situation was difficult. At headquarters a small committee was set up to work on rescuing the hostages. Communications with the CIA centre in Tehran had been cut off and the CIA had to make do with information it received from friendly services. If a rescue operation was to be carried out, it needed up-to-date and accurate information. Someone had to go to Tehran from headquarters and work there temporarily. This would be a dangerous mission, one that might end in death, but who could do it? Ruzi was an experienced and brave intelligence officer. He knew the region, the people of Iran and their religious customs and traditions very well. He was also a Muslim. There was no one else in the organisation who might carry out this difficult and dangerous mission as well as he could.[7]

When Ruzi was appointed to the crisis committee, he flew straight from Bonn to Tehran. He was instructed to go under an assumed identity, research the situation on the spot with the eyes of an expert, and then work out a rescue operation together with the other members of the committee.[8] The CIA had two plans to free the hostages. Ruzi was at the centre of one, while the other focused on Tony Mendez, an extremely talented CIA technical operations officer and specialist in false identities. Many years later, the incident would become the subject of a film called *Argo*. The film did not mention Ruzi's presence in

Tehran and his role in the operation, but without his information gathered on the spot, Mendez's operation could not have succeeded.

Six State Department officials from the US embassy in Tehran had managed to take refuge in the Canadian embassy, in a different part of the city. In January 1980 the CIA managed to rescue these six people in an extremely successful operation. Mendez set up a fictional film company in Hollywood called Sixth Studio. Full-page advertisements appeared in *Variety* and the *Hollywood Reporter* in Los Angeles, announcing that a fantasy film called *Argo* was going to be made and that it would be partly shot in Iran. Mendez prepared false passports and make-up materials for six supposed actors in this film, obtained the necessary visa for himself from the Iranians and flew to Iran. He checked into the Tehran Sheraton that Saturday afternoon and on the Monday got into a taxi and went to the Canadian embassy. There the CIA agent went to work and succeeded in transforming six white Americans into Africans, Asians and Arabs. The disguise was so successful that they had difficulty recognising themselves.[9] The six Americans then used their false passports to go through the Iranian border controls and board a Swissair plane that bore the name of the Swiss canton of Aargau—strikingly similar to the name of the decoy film. One of the six Americans said in astonishment to Mendez, 'Good lord, what a perfect operation. The name of the plane and the name of the film are exactly the same. You've planned even that.'[10]

Ruzi was the first US citizen to visit Tehran after the members of the embassy had been taken hostage, travelling on a fake German passport as an Afghan carpet merchant. In Tehran he checked into the Intercontinental Hotel, one of the finest in the city. There were very few foreigners staying in the hotel and most of them were journalists from countries other than the US. Many were Germans, and Ruzi began making friends with some of them.

Every day thousands of youngsters would gather round the US embassy, demonstrating and shouting slogans. The German journalists would also go to the embassy each day and try to learn what was going on. Ruzi went along with the correspondent of the *Frankfurter Allgemeine Zeitung* who had become his friend, as if he was a member of the same team.[11] He noticed that the German journalist gave cigarettes to the policemen outside the embassy and spoke with them, and the next day he also took a few packs of cigarettes with him. He handed them out to the police and chatted with them. As his acquaintance with them grew, Ruzi began to extract important information. The foreign newspapers said at the time that the embassy staff had been blindfolded and taken out of the building to an unknown destination. The first thing Ruzi established was that in fact the hostages were still inside the building. The embassy had a very large garden, and at night the revolutionary guards would put members of the embassy staff into a vehicle one by one, blindfolded, and let them walk around the garden for half an hour.

The Iranians are masters of the art of miniatures. Although official papers in the US embassy in Tehran had been shredded, the Iranians pieced together the tiny shreds as if they were a jigsaw puzzle and then read them all. This meant that the new Iranian authorities were in possession of the contents of the entire recent correspondence between the embassy and Washington.[12]

Before arriving in Tehran, Ruzi had been required to make intense preparations for passing back information to headquarters. The CIA made an agreement with the British for their agents to meet Ruzi and send his information on. The meeting place was a bookshop in Tehran. Ruzi would put notes which looked like blank scraps of paper between the pages of one of the books. After he left, a British agent would pick up the book and remove the paper. When the blank paper was given a slight chemical treatment, the notes on it would become visible.[13]

Ruzi learned that there was a restaurant in Tehran frequented by Azerbaijani Turks, and he began to have his meals there rather than in the hotel. In the Azerbaijani restaurant he got to know interesting people and picked up important information about the situation of the hostages and the new government of Iran. In that restaurant Ruzi also met the governor of Tabriz. He was still serving in his post but expected to be dismissed and arrested at any moment. In the evening he would sit with the governor, eating and talking with him about the situation in Tabriz, although he did not reveal his real identity. Not long after Ruzi departed from Iran, the governor of Tabriz did in fact leave the country and settle in Switzerland.[14]

One night just after Ruzi had fallen asleep in his hotel bedroom there was a violent knocking on his door. Ruzi was worried. Who could be calling at that hour of the night and why? He got up, tried to remain calm, and opened the door with a smile on his face. Armed Revolutionary Guards plunged into the room and, without a word to Ruzi, began searching under the bed, in the bathroom and in the cupboards. Ruzi noted that they had not looked at his official papers and documents and asked himself what they could be searching for. When they had gone, Ruzi got dressed and went down to reception and asked the clerks there what the Revolutionary Guards had been looking for. The young man at the desk grinned and said that they had been searching for women. Later, an Azerbaijani whom he met in the restaurant described a similar event. One night he and his wife and young son had been returning from a visit to a relative. His car was stopped by Revolutionary Guards, who asked him and his wife for their identity cards. His wife did not have hers with her. Then they wanted to see their marriage certificate. They did not have that with them either. The Guards detained the woman while her husband drove to their home—it was an hour's drive away—got the marriage certificate and came back. Only then did they release her.[15]

Washington ignores Ruzi's advice

During the time he spent in Tehran, Ruzi came to see that a military operation to rescue the hostages was impossible. Within eleven days he had carried out all the work required of him. He returned to Washington, where the CIA's director, Admiral Stansfield Turner, was waiting for him. He talked over all the details with Ruzi and then went to President Carter and passed on what he had learnt.[16]

After meeting the president, Admiral Turner returned to headquarters and sent Ruzi in a CIA aeroplane to a meeting at which several generals from the Pentagon were present, to discuss rescuing the hostages. Ruzi briefed the generals in detail about the situation of the hostages.[17] He was disturbed to hear the rescue plans outlined by two US generals, which he found boastful and unrealistic. The plan was completely detached from the realities of the region and Iran. It involved purchasing some large Mercedes trucks and taking soldiers into Iran via Turkey to raid the embassy and rescue the hostages. Ruzi's vehement opposition led to the plan being dropped. He said that such an operation would cost the lives of the soldiers taking part in it and make the situation of the hostages worse or even endanger their lives. He tried to explain that work had to be carried on through diplomatic channels. After the meeting, he went back to his post in Bonn.[18]

Ruzi's advice was ignored and a decision was taken to launch a new operation. US helicopters would take off from a temporary base in the desert and drop soldiers into the garden of the embassy to set the hostages free by force of arms. The operation culminated in major disaster and failure. One helicopter collided with a transport plane. Eight commandos lost their lives in the deserts of Iran. After this unsuccessful operation, the situation of the hostages grew worse.[19]

When Carter lost the 1980 presidential election, the hostages were released by the Iranian authorities on the day that Ronald Reagan was sworn in as the new US president. Ruzi had foreseen this long before the failed operation, which he had advised against.[20] Carter came to Frankfurt to greet the hostages when they were released. He appeared extremely tense, as if his dignity had been torn to shreds. Iran had insulted him and tried to give the American government a lesson.

The people of Iran had never forgotten how Mossadegh had nationalised the country's oil and how after supporting the ordinary people of the country he had been removed as prime minister by the CIA. Ruzi had long tried to explain to CIA headquarters that, unlike much of the Middle East, Iran was not a country that had come into being after the First World War. It possessed thousands of years of history and a civilisation that stretched back for millennia. It should be treated with respect.[21]

17

THE COLD WAR ENDS AND RUZI RETURNS TO UZBEKISTAN

What Sort of Soviet Union?

Ruzi had been born in the Soviet Union, had been educated in Soviet schools and had gained experience of the Soviet state in his youth. For years afterwards he had amassed information about the Soviet system and he knew its weak points extremely well. At a time when most people supposed that the Soviet state would endure for long years ahead, he perceived that the system was approaching its end, and he continued to strive with all the resources he possessed to make this process shorter.[1]

As Ruzi knew, the Soviet Union had overwhelming economic problems. The economy was regulated by central planning and was extremely unwieldy. In theory the system promised people happiness and prosperity, but it was unable to pay for either of these things. The state was only able to finance its massive military power at the expense of the welfare of the people. The leaders were totally cut off from ordinary people.

A technocrat of Uzbek background who had headed some of the largest Soviet industrial establishments one day shared a reminiscence with Ruzi that summed up the totalitarian system extremely well. With the permission of the state, members of the Soviet elite could travel frequently to Western countries. Before setting out, the final duty of every technocrat was to call in at their local KGB headquarters for directives. They were obliged to declare in the country they were visiting that the Soviet Union was a paradise, that there was no unemployment there, that they had reached the stage of setting up the ideal Communist system, that people there lived in heaven and that all the peoples of the Soviet Union were brothers; a new Soviet people had been created, and the Soviet system was the most perfect and highly developed which humanity had ever seen. When they returned from their journey, the first thing they had to do was to visit the local KGB headquarters again and report on what they had seen.[2]

The man who explained all this to Ruzi had gone to the KGB on his return from a trip to Austria. They asked him what he had seen and experienced and he told them everything, just as it had happened. He was then given the following statement: 'You were not comfortable in Vienna and did not see any prosperity: you saw hunger, poverty, long queues in the markets and protest marches by hungry and wretched working-class masses. You saw that Austria is on the verge of a socialist revolution.' So when his colleagues asked him at work the following day about his impressions of his journey, he did not tell them what he had really experienced and seen in Vienna, but only what he had been told to say in the KGB headquarters.

One of the most serious flaws of totalitarian systems was the way in which they encouraged two personalities to emerge within a single individual. Ruzi knew very well that many Communist Party members would spend their time by day in seminars, giving lessons on dialectical materialism, historical materialism and atheism. Then at night they would worship God secretly in their own homes. People who are atheists by day and invoke God at night may appear to be committed to the system, but what exists in reality is a society made up of people who do not believe in the system in which they are living. Over time the cadres of the Communist Party had lost contact with ordinary people and become a new class, one possessing many privileges. Lenin's socialist state had turned into a totalitarian police state which controlled the whole country and its people. The collapse of the system was inevitable, and this was exactly what happened. In the whole of human history, no empire had ever fallen in such a short space of time.[3]

In 1983 President Reagan had called the Soviet Union an 'evil empire'. Five years later the White House announced that Reagan would make an historic official visit to the Soviet Union in May 1988. The visit coincided with the launch of Mikhail Gorbachev's policies of *glasnost* and *perestroika*, 'openness' and 'reform'. Before making important visits, politicians do their homework carefully, and receive briefings from specialists on the countries they are about to visit. The objectives of the visit are specified and preliminary preparations for the agreements envisaged are conducted by diplomats on both sides. This was to be the fourth meeting between Reagan and Gorbachev.[4]

Ruzi was invited to the White House to deliver a briefing to the American president about the political situation in the Soviet Union and the nationalities problem.[5] Several generals had been summoned from the Pentagon who were to brief the president on the military situation. It would then be up to the president to assess that information.

Midnight Meeting in Washington With the Mayor of Tashkent

Although the vast majority of US experts thought that the Cold War was going to continue for many years, and designed strategies on that basis, Ruzi did not share their thinking. He followed developments in the Soviet Union closely, meeting Soviet citizens as often as possible and extracting information from them. Around this time the mayor of Tashkent, Shukrullo Raxmatovich Mirsaidov, arrived in the US. His city, one of the largest and most important of the Soviet Union, was to be twinned with the American city of Seattle.[6] Mirsaidov stayed for a few days in Seattle and then went on to Washington as a guest of the Soviet ambassador there, who gave a dinner in his honour. Mirsaidov was highly cultured and well educated, and had extensive knowledge in particular of the history of Central Asia. Ruzi had learnt that he had secretly given assistance to the families of members of the Uzbekistan Communist Party who had been arrested and accused of being bourgeois nationalists. He wanted to find a way to meet Mirsaidov while he was in Washington.

Ruzi was known to the authorities in the Soviet Union as someone who had been fighting for nearly half a century for the break-up of the Soviet empire and the independence of the Central Asian republics.

253

Many articles critical of him had been published in the Soviet press and harsh accusations made against him. He did not know if Mirsaidov would agree to meet him, but if he did, the employees of the Soviet embassy in Washington must not find out. Ruzi sent a small delegation of Uzbeks living in the US to welcome Mirsaidov. One of the members of this delegation whispered to Mirsaidov that Ruzi Nazar was in Washington and wanted to meet him. Later the mayor surreptitiously replied that he would return to his hotel as quickly as possible and would wait for Ruzi there.[7] And, indeed, after the dinner in the Soviet embassy he excused himself to the ambassador, saying that he was tired and wanted to go back to his hotel to rest. After everyone else had gone to their rooms, and making sure that he was not being followed, he got into a taxi with an Uzbek who was waiting for him in the lobby and drove to Ruzi's home, in the Falls Church district of Virginia. Ruzi and Mirsaidov had never seen each other before, but their meeting was like that of two brothers who had been separated for many years.[8]

Mirsaidov and Ruzi embraced emotionally, each attempting not to show the other that their eyes were full of tears. They talked for hours, listening to classical Uzbek music and sipping their drinks. Ruzi had a rich collection of Uzbek music, from 1920s recordings onwards. Uzbek melodies are generally melancholy, rather like the laments of a people who have endured much pain. Mirsaidov was astonished to find that someone thousands of kilometres away from his homeland, who had been separated from it for nearly half a century, owned a collection like this, the like of which no one in Uzbekistan possessed. Ruzi said that it was with this music that he tried to relieve, at least in part, his homesickness for the land where he had been born.[9]

Shukrullo Mirsaidov was born in 1939. He had been trained in economics in Soviet universities and then, while still young, became a member of the Communist Party and rose within the bureaucracy. As mayor of Tashkent, he was a member of the ruling class, and might have been expected to be a supporter of the system. But during their conversation, Ruzi could see that Mirsaidov knew all about the recent history of the colonisation and oppression of Central Asia.[10] His remarks confirmed the arguments Ruzi had been making for years. Intellectuals and party members in the non-Russian Soviet republics did not believe in the future of the Soviet state. Soviet propaganda was in direct contradiction with the facts. The economy was undergoing a massive crisis. The nationalities problem continued to be the state's greatest concern. The Soviet Union would only be able to survive if it became a union of states possessing equal rights; otherwise its break-up was unavoidable.[11]

A few days after this meeting with Mirsaidov, Ruzi went to the White House. The briefing meeting began in the morning and continued after lunch. Ruzi conveyed the things he had learnt about the Soviet system to the president.[12] He mentioned the situation of opponents of the regime, in particular the difficulties endured by Mustafa Djemilov, the leader of the Crimean Tatars. Drawing on his recent conversation with Mirsaidov, he told Reagan that the nationalities issue continued to be the Soviet Union's primary problem and that it could only be resolved if the Soviet state became a democratic state ruled by law in the Western sense. This would also be the only way in which the Soviet state would cease to be a security threat for the US and its allies.[13]

Reagan made his official visit to the Soviet Union in the closing days of May 1988. He gave a speech to students and faculty staff in Moscow University in which he dwelt on democracy, saying that it began and ended with free elections. Speaking in the Soviet Union where all the organs of the press were under state control, he explained that in the United States, with its 1,000 television stations, 8,500 radio stations and 1,700 daily newspapers, news and views were expressed every day without the slightest interference from the state. He stressed that governments did not have the right to restrict democracy and liberties but that, on the contrary, the principle of democracy and the rule of law should limit the actions of governments.[14]

Reagan had been elected president at a time when the US had suffered a succession of defeats in foreign policy, but he started an ideological counter-attack against the Soviet Union and constantly kept up the pressure. He was supported in this by the British prime minister, Margaret Thatcher. When Thatcher met Gorbachev on a visit to Moscow, Gorbachev remarked that a speech she had given shortly before was reminiscent of the aggressive language of American presidents and of Winston Churchill during the 1940s and 1950s. Her words had taken Gorbachev back to the days when the Truman doctrine had been proclaimed and Churchill had spoken of an Iron Curtain being created across Europe. The British prime minister counter-attacked without apologising. She replied that Gorbachev had apparently not abandoned the view that the Soviet Union's war with the West would continue until Communism was set up in the whole world. The West, she said, was confronted almost everywhere by Soviet aggression, in Yemen, Ethiopia, Mozambique, Angola and Nicaragua. Gorbachev smiled and softened the atmosphere by saying, 'How nice it is that we can discuss matters so frankly with each other.'[15]

The Soviet Union Collapses

The reforms begun by Gorbachev dealt a fatal blow to the Soviet Union. *Glasnost* and *perestroika* had the effect of getting the Soviet people to question the single-party dictatorship which had kept the state going for years and controlled every aspect of political and social life.

On 18 May 1988 an article by the Soviet economist Professor Vyacheslav Dashichev was published in *Literaturnaya Gazeta*, one of the country's most prestigious papers. Dashichev argued that the Brezhnev leadership of the 1960s and 1970s had interpreted history wrongly and so had caused the world's great powers to form a coalition against the Soviet Union. The result of this was an arms race which the country could not withstand. Two months after Reagan's visit, the Soviet foreign minister, Eduard Shevardnadze, repudiated the policies that the Soviet Union had pursued during the previous twenty-five years.[16]

Ruzi had always believed that it was necessary for the Soviet Union to break up in order for his country and his people to lead a more dignified life. After half a century of his life had passed in stormy adventures, he saw this goal at least partially attained. Each of the Central Asian republics achieved independence and became a member of the United Nations.[17] On 19 August 1991, opponents of reform within the Soviet Communist Party attempted to carry out a coup, supported by the KGB. Boris Yeltsin, the president of the Russian Republic, called upon the people to oppose the coup leaders, and on 21 August their bid ended with their defeat and arrest. On 21 December Yeltsin and Gorbachev published a joint declaration to the world announcing that the Soviet Union had been dissolved. The Central Asian republics had already declared their independence after the attempted coup in Moscow failed.

For fifty years, Ruzi had declared that the non-Soviet peoples of the USSR desired independence. Events had proved him right. The people who hoisted the flag of independence in the non-Russian republics were Communist Party functionaries who had composed the governmental cadres of the Soviet Union before 1991. Eduard Shevardnadze, the last foreign minister of the Soviet empire, was to become the second president of Georgia after it left the Soviet Union. Heydar Aliyev, a member of the Politburo and deputy prime minister of the Soviet state, became first the chairman of the Supreme Soviet in Nakhchivan Autonomous Republic in 1991,[18] and then president of Azerbaijan. In Kazakhstan, Nursultan Nazarbayev, who had been first secretary of the Kazakh Communist Party, became first president of his independent country.

In 1991 non-Russian party members who had spent their entire lives in the Communist Party hoisted the flag of independence in front of their own peoples. Within a few months, they had broken up an empire established over three centuries with warfare and bloodshed. The process of historical change vindicated Ruzi Nazar, who had worked for the cause he believed in for half a century.[19] When the Soviet Union was dissolved and the republics of Central Asia declared their independence, Ruzi felt the great calm of someone whose side has come out of a just war with victory.[20]

Ruzi meets his sister again

Thanks to the reforms which Gorbachev started in 1990, Soviet citizens were allowed to travel outside the country, and it became possible for former Soviet citizens to visit their homelands. But it was still unsafe for Ruzi to travel to the Soviet Union. He had been proclaimed an enemy by the Soviet state.[21] There were no direct flights to Uzbekistan. It was possible to go via Moscow, but it would have been risky for him to go to Moscow at a time when the KGB was still active. However, Ruzi was now getting old. In the 1970s, he had learnt of the death of his mother and been very upset. He now wanted to try to see his sister and embrace her while there was still time, as he had learnt that her health was not good. So Ruzi invited Shemsihan, her daughter, Dilberhan, and Dilberhan's small daughter and son to the US.

The relatives of someone like Ruzi could not even have dreamt of travelling freely during the Cold War years. None of the letters he had written to them had ever arrived. But Ruzi was an experienced intelligence officer and he used to obtain news of his mother, sister and other relatives quite frequently.[22]

One day in the autumn of 1990, a plane carrying his sister, his niece and her children touched down at Washington's Dulles Airport. Ruzi and his sister had not seen each other for nearly fifty years. Shemsihan had witnessed how their mother had prayed to God for her son's health and well-being virtually every day since Ruzi had left in 1941, right up to her death. Ruzi had never stopped thinking about them for even a day and they had done the same. When Ruzi and Shemsihan first met again, after so many years, they hugged each other tightly so that no one else might ever divide them again.[23] Ruzi felt that he was embracing not only his sister but his mother, his father and his brother, who had been executed. Through her, he knew the scent of them and of his homeland. His sister and her family stayed for two months in the US, during which time Ruzi told her about all the things he had lived through over the past half century, and she told him her story of those years, talking during the nights until morning. Finally the day came when they had to part again. Ruzi bade farewell to his sister and her family and they went back to Uzbekistan.[24]

In the spring of 1991, six months before independence was declared, the Uzbek government decided to hold a conference for international businessmen and investors in Tashkent. An organising committee was set up and participants from more than 400 countries outside the Soviet Union were invited.[25] However, the attendees would have to travel to Uzbekistan via Moscow.

The chairman of the organising committee was Shukrullo Mirsaidov, whom Ruzi had met in Washington in 1988. Then he had been mayor of Tashkent, but by 1990 he had become prime minister of Uzbekistan. Even though Ruzi was invited to the conference by Mirsaidov, he still preferred to wait until he could take a direct flight there. He sent his son, Erkin, in his place to the conference. In Tashkent Erkin was met by Ruzi's friends, and after the conference was over he went to visit his relatives in Tashkent. They were astonished to find that he knew the streets and buildings of Tashkent perfectly and even had detailed information on the Fergana irrigation canal. Erkin explained his extensive knowledge: 'From when we were small, my father used to tell us about the country and city where he was born, its streets and historical monuments, and the history of the city. Margilan may be 13,000 kilometres from the country we live in, but from all that my father told me, I had the opportunity to learn even the smallest detail of the city.' It was a small sign of Ruzi's love for his country and his longing for it.[26]

When Erkin returned to Washington, he told his father what he had seen and experienced in Uzbekistan, down to the very smallest detail. He said that intellectuals in Tashkent and leading politicians had shown great interest in him, that he had been the guest of some important figure every evening, and that they wanted to see Ruzi there as soon as possible.[27] Ruzi was very moved to think that the intellectuals of Uzbekistan had understood his struggle and that he was greatly loved in his homeland. Ruzi had marched forward for half a century, through a lifetime of wars and suffering but always in the same direction, and finally he had reached his goal. He knew that the time had come for him to return to his motherland and began to look out for a suitable opportunity.

Uzbekistan declared independence in September 1991 but Washington dragged its feet on the question of recognising it. At the start of 1992, the Uzbek government asked for Ruzi's assistance. This was to be one of Ruzi's final operations. He consulted with his colleagues and organised a secret delegation sent to Tashkent. The four-member team travelled via Istanbul. They were greeted at Tashkent airport by the prime minister and foreign minister of Uzbekistan. They held talks at the level of head of state, and a week after the delegation returned to Washington, the US recognised the Republic of Uzbekistan as an independent state.[28]

Direct flights between Istanbul and Tashkent began early in 1992. The republics of Central Asia had become members of the United Nations and had been recognised by many of the world's countries as independent states. Ruzi could now visit the country where he had been born and had spent his childhood and youth. Early in May that year, Ruzi travelled to Istanbul with Erkin. He was given a warm greeting at Istanbul airport by some of his Turkish friends. He was rather nervous. He had been forced to leave his homeland when he was a youngster; now he was returning to it at the age of seventy-five, extremely healthy in mind and body, but still an old man. He had seen hundreds of his friends lose their lives in the Second World War. An invisible power had protected him on every occasion. During the forty years of the Cold War, he had come face to face with death on many occasions, but in the end he had emerged unscathed.

How would he be received in Uzbekistan? During the Cold War he had been portrayed as an enemy of the people and the state, and as a bourgeois agent. True, the Uzbek citizens he met outside the Soviet Union had always embraced him with affection and respect, but he still wondered what the effect of half a century of propaganda might be. He wondered about the cities where he had spent his childhood and youth, about the friends he had left there. During the seventy years the Soviet Union had existed, the Communist Party had carried out one of the greatest social and political experiments in human history. He wondered what its consequences might be. He wondered about all these things while he was flying from Istanbul to Tashkent.[29]

He remembered how, before he left his own country, he had committed his father to the earth. The way in which his mother had waved to him with moist eyes at Margilan railway station appeared to him as clearly as if only a few minutes had passed. He remembered the loves and adventures of his early years. The words of a folksong written by the Azerbaijani poet Rashid Behbudov came into his mind. He liked it very much and had listened to it on lonely nights. Soundlessly he began to recite it.

> I can't sleep at night for thinking of you.
> I can't get the idea of you out of my head.
> I am unable to tell you anything.
> Separation, separation, alas, separation,
> From every pain comes mighty separation.
> The dark nights are long since you departed.
> I do not know where I will go in these dark nights.
> The nights hit me and wound my heart.
> Separation, separation, alas, separation,
> From every pain comes mighty separation.[30]

Then he remembered the dream he had had in Ukraine during the war. His mother had stretched out her hands to him, but the glass wall between them prevented her from reaching him. The dream had come true. Ruzi had never been able to reach his mother again. When he returned to his country, he would visit her grave and say prayers. By doing so he would try to still his longing for his mother.

THE COLD WAR ENDS AND RUZI RETURNS

After a flight of five and a half hours, the pilot announced that the plane was beginning to make its descent. A large crowd greeted Ruzi in Tashkent airport. Hundreds of people had come to meet him, among them the most famous poets, writers, artists and politicians, as well as professors and students. Islam Karimov, the president of Uzbekistan, had sent his chief adviser to greet Ruzi. As soon as Ruzi embarked from the plane, he tearfully kissed the ground of the country from which he had been absent for fifty years and gave thanks to God.

He wanted to go without delay to his birthplace, Margilan, to feel the presence of his mother in the house in which he had been born and to visit the graves of his mother and father.[31] However, he understood that he would have to stay in Tashkent for a while. The people who welcomed him told him that President Karimov wanted to meet him. Ruzi and Erkin went to visit the president and the foreign minister, Obeidullah Abdurazakov, who embraced Ruzi with affection and respect. It was the beginning of a warm friendship between Ruzi and Abdurazakov that continued until the latter's death.

During the four days he spent in Tashkent, Ruzi met large numbers of people and explained his views on the future of the country to them.[32] A new era was beginning. He offered them his advice. Tashkent State Television had made a half-hour documentary about Ruzi and it was shown repeatedly on television during his time in Uzbekistan. It explained Ruzi's struggles for the independence of his homeland and for its people's right to live in a free and democratic society.[33]

After fifty-two years Ruzi, the son of Jamshid Umirzakoghlu, the man who could work magic with silk, returned for the first time to Margilan, the city of silk and silk weavers. The first thing he did was to visit the house of his mother and father, where he had been born and where he had listened to his mother's lullabies and his father's advice. Ruzi was met by his relatives, some of his childhood friends who were still alive, and prominent figures from the town. As he came to the house, animals were sacrificed. Pure white hangings decorated his way and silken fabrics were spread out on the ground. Ruzi walked over them to the house where his life had begun. It was as if the father whom he had buried with his own hands, the mother who had passed away during his absence, the friends whom he had lost in the war and in years afterwards, were all there. Ruzi felt that even though they were not physically present, they were there in spirit.[34]

NOTES

FOREWORD

1. Robert Byron, *The Road to Oxiana*, Pimlico Edition, 2004 (first published 1937).
2. Ghalib Lakhnavi and Abdullah Bilgrami, *The Adventures of Amir Hamza*, London: Random House, 2008.
3. Peter Frankopan, *The Silk Roads: A New History of the World*, London: Bloomsbury, 2015.
4. Aleksandr Dugin, *The Foundation of Geo-politics*, Moscow, 1997.

1. CHILDHOOD IN TURKESTAN

1. *Uzbek Soviet Encyclopaedia*, 'Margilan', Academy of Sciences of the Uzbekistan Republic, Tashkent, 1976, 20–22.
2. Zahiruddin Muhammad Babur, *Vekayi*, 2 vols., Türk Tarih Kurumu, Ankara, 1943. In Uzbekistan today, the Yodgorlik Silk Factory still employs more than 2,000 workers who produce annually 250,000 square metres of high-quality dress silk using only traditional methods. Modern technology is utilised in the Margilan Silk Factory where 15,000 workers produce 22 million square metres of silk fabric each year.
4. Ruy Gonzales de Clavijo, *A Journey from Cadiz to Samarkand*, Turkish edition, Kesit Yayınları, Istanbul, 2007, 131–178.
5. 'The Usul-u Jedid (new method) schools which Ismail Gaspirali founded in the Crimea gave their name to all the subsequent reform movements in the Turkic-speaking world and as a result were described as "Jadid". Jadidism later began to be used as an expression which articulated all the demands for reform and change felt by Muslim Turkish groups living in Tsarist Russia.' Ahat Andican, *The External Turkestan Struggle from Jadidism to Independence*, Emre Yayınları, Istanbul, 2003, 25–27.

6. For competition between the British and the Russians in Central Asia, see: Arminius Vambery, *Central Asia and the British-Russian Border Question: Collected Political Writings* (in German), Brockhausen, Leipzig, 1873; W. Frick, *Antagonism between British and Russian Interests in Central Asia* (in German), Vienna, 1890.
7. Baymirza Hayit, *Turkestan in the 20th Century* (in German), C.W. Leske, Darmstadt, 1956.
8. Vasily Vladimirovic Bartold, *Cultural History of the Land of Turkestan* (in Russian), Akademiya Nauk, Leningrad, 1927; Hayit, *Turkestan*, 17.
9. Hayit, *Turkestan*, 21.
10. Krishovayn, Chief of Provincial Office Equipment, St Petersburg, 1913, 5.
11. See Pyotr Grigorevich Galuzo, *Turkestan-Colony*, Moscow, 1929.
12. Bartold, *Cultural History*, 135.
13. Hayit, *Turkestan*, 48–49.
14. See Hayit, *Turkestan*, passim; Galuzo, *Turkestan-Colony*.
15. Maxim Gorki, *Vsevolod V. Ivanov, Voyna v peskah*, Leningrad, 1935, 41ff.
16. Mustafa Çokayoğlu, *Fragments of Memories of the Year 1917*, Young Turkestan Publications, Paris, 1937, 22.
17. Interview with Ruzi Nazar.
18. Interview with Ruzi Nazar.
19. Hayit, *Turkestan*, passim.
20. Mikhail Frunze (1885–1925) was the Bolshevik leader who accompanied Lenin in the October 1917 Revolution and played an important part in the Russian civil war, defeating the White Army under Admiral Kolchak at Omsk. Towards the end of 1921, Frunze visited Ankara in Turkey and met Mustafa Kemal (Atatürk), leader in the Turkish War of Independence.
21. Joseph Castagne, *Turkestan after the Russian Revolution, 1917–1921* (in French), E. Leroux, Paris, 1922, 30.
22. Andican, *Turkestan Struggle* 46–67.
23. Hayit, *Turkestan*, 112–163. Zeki Velidi Togan, *Turkili (Turkestan) Today and Its Recent History* (in Turkish), Arkadaş, İbrahim Horozö and Güven Basımevi, Istanbul, 1942–7, 224ff. Bobodzan Gafurovic Gafuroc, *History of the Tajik People and Summaries* (in Russian), Moscow, 1949, 456ff. Castagne, *Turkestan*, 212–215.
24. See Baymirza Hayit, *Basmatschi: Nationaler Kampf Turkestans in den Jahren 1917 bis 1934*, Dreisam Verlag, Cologne, 1992.
25. Vladimir Ilyich Lenin, *Sochinenya [Collected Works]*, Vol. 34, Partizdat TSK VKP, Moscow, 1937, 326.
26. Joseph Stalin, *Marxismus und nationale Frage [Socialism and the National Question]*, Berlin, 1913. Verlag der Sowjetischen Militärverwaltung in Deutschland, 1946, 10.

27. The New Economic Policy was introduced by Lenin in 1921. During the period it was in force (1921–7), although large industrial enterprises remained under state control, small businesses and merchants were allowed to make profits along capitalist lines. The NEP stopped the practice of confiscating produce from farmers and in particular permitted private enterprise to operate freely in agriculture, light industries and the service sectors. The NEP was abandoned in 1927 and in its place came five-year plans devised by Stalin for industrialisation.

28. Ruzi Nazar. Ruzi encountered Tashpolat again during the Second World War in Bessarabia, and once more in 1992 when he revisited Margilan, his birthplace.

29. Ruzi Nazar. After the Second World War began, four new houses were established by the Margilan City Soviet to replace those that had been demolished and four families were settled in them.

30. Ruzi Nazar.

31. Enver Altaylı and Irfan Ülkü, *Büyük Oyundaki Türk* [*The Turk in the Great Game*], İlgi Yayınları, Istanbul, 2008, 124.

32. Ruzi Nazar.

33. See Joseph Stalin, *Golovokruzeniye ot uspekov, k voprosam kolkonozno dvjenyi*, Gosizdat Moskovki Rabotchi, Moscow, 1930.

34. Ruzi Nazar.

35. Hayit, *Turkestan*, 277–300.

36. Baymirza Hayit, *Die Wirtschaftsprobleme Turkestans: Ein Beitrag zur Wirtschaftskunde Turkestans, mit einem Rückblick auf ihre jüngste Vergangenheit*, Türk Kültürünü Araştırma Enstitüsü, Ankara, 1968.

37. Ruzi Nazar.

2. STUDENT YEARS IN STALIN'S CENTRAL ASIA

1. *Uzbek Soviet Encyclopaedia*, 'Tashkent'.

2. Ruzi Nazar.

3. Ruzi Nazar.

4. Ruzi Nazar.

5. Teahouses remain an important part of political and social life in Uzbekistan today. Uzbek pilaf is served and young people and the elderly alike gather to exchange ideas.

6. Abdulkadir Meragi (born in Meraga in 1360, died in Herat in 1435) was one of the greatest composers of classical Turkish music.

7. Ruzi Nazar.

8. Interview with Ibrahim Yarkın.

9. Rızkulov, 'Germanya'daki Okuvçularımız', *Turkestan*, 10 December 1923. For details of what happened to the young people from Turkestan who

were educated in Germany and what happened to them after they returned to their own country, their interrogation by NKVD agents and their distressing end, see Şirali Turdiyev, *Ular Germaniya'da Okugen idiler*, Tashkent, 2006.

10. Ahat Andican, *The External Turkestan Struggle from Jadidism to Independence*, Emre Yayınları, Istanbul, 2003, 279–280.

11. See the relevant entries in *Uzbek Soviet Encyclopaedia*.

12. Ruzi Nazar.

13. Ruzi Nazar.

14. Ruzi Nazar.

15. In the 1950s Nikita Khrushchev, first secretary of the CPSU, revealed as part of his disclosure policy that the Moscow Trials were show trials whose verdicts were decided in advance and which relied on confessions extracted by force.

16. The word 'province' in this context is more or less equivalent to 'city'. Just as in the Ottoman empire, a Soviet province was a large administrative unit named after the town at its centre and including several small towns as well.

17. Ruzi Nazar.

18. Boris Souvarine, *Stalin: Anmerkung zur Geschichte des Bolshewismus*, Bernard & Graefe Verlag, Munich, 1980, 539–542.

19. A. Avtarhanov, *Memoirs*, Posev, Frankfurt am Main, 1983, 42.

20. Souvarine, *Stalin*, 539–605.

21. Ruzi Nazar.

22. Ruzi Nazar.

23. Ruzi Nazar.

24. Ruzi Nazar.

25. Ruzi Nazar.

26. Baymirza Hayit, *Basmatschi: Nationaler Kampf Turkestans in den Jahren 1917 bis 1934*, Dreisam Verlag, Cologne 1992, 71.

27. Ruzi Nazar.

28. *Pravda*, February 1937.

29. See relevant article in *Uzbek Soviet Encyclopaedia*.

30. Baymirza Hayit, *Turkestan in the 20th Century* (in German), C.W. Leske, Darmstadt, 1956, 334–336.

31. Hayit, *Basmatschi*, 334–336; Feyzullah Hojayev, *Izbranniye trudy*, Tashkent, 1970; *I.V. Stalin Sochinenya*, Hoover Institution on War, Revolution and Peace, Stanford University, 1967.

32. For more information on Turkestanis executed at this time, see Hayit, *Turkestan*, 334–339.

33. Mustafa Shokay, *Yılı Hatıra Parçaları*, Paris, 1937.

34. Ruzi Nazar.

35. Ruzi Nazar.
36. Ruzi Nazar.
37. Ruzi Nazar.
38. Ruzi Nazar.
39. Uzbek proverbs can be found in Saidahmad Hudayberganov and Gafur Gulum, *Uzbek Halk Makolleri* [*Uzbek Popular Proverbs*], Adabiet ve Sanat Nasrieti, Tashkent, 1978.
40. A Turkish pasta dish somewhat similar to ravioli. In Central Asia the pieces of stuffed dough are made rather larger than those in the Turkish recipe, and they are steamed and then served without sauce.
41. Ruzi Nazar.
42. Islamic prayers, performed five times each day.
43. Ruzi Nazar.
44. For the view of religion taken by Party and state institutions in the USSR, see Alexandre Bennigsen and Chantal Quelquejay, afterwards Lemercier-Quelquejay, *Islam in the Soviet Union* (translated by Geoffrey E. Wheeler and Hubert Evans), Pall Mall Press in association with the Central Asian Research Centre, London, 1967.
45. Ruzi Nazar.
46. Ruzi Nazar.

3. RUZI IN THE RED ARMY

1. Ruzi Nazar.
2. Ruzi Nazar.
3. Robert Payne, *Stalin*, Gunther Verlag, Stuttgart, 1967, 495–504.
4. Ruzi Nazar.
5. Ruzi Nazar.
6. Ruzi Nazar.
7. Ruzi Nazar.
8. Ruzi Nazar.
9. Ruzi Nazar.
10. Ruzi Nazar.
11. For similar instances of discrimination, see Hüseyin İkram Han, *Bir Türkistanlının İkinci Dünya Savaşı Hatıraları*, İstanbul, 1999, 21.
12. For plans for Ukraine made by the German Ministry of the East, see Otto Bräutigam, *So hat es sich zugetragen: Ein Leben als Soldat und Diplomat*, Holzner Verlag, Würzburg, 1968.
13. Ruzi Nazar.
14. İrfan Ülkü, *Büyük oyundaki Türk: Enver Altaylı*, İlgi Yayınları, İstanbul, 2008, 125.
15. Ruzi Nazar

16. Ruzi Nazar.
17. Tamara Artyomavna Petrossian. See *Uzbek Soviet Encyclopaedia*, 'Tamara Hanım'.
18. Ruzi Nazar.
19. Ruzi Nazar.
20. Ruzi Nazar.
21. See Elizabeth-Anne Wheal, Stephen Pope and James Taylor, *The Meridian Encyclopaedia of the Second World War*, New York, 1992; Bryan Perrett and Ian Hogg, *Encyclopaedia of the Second World War*, Longman, Essex, 1989. SS units took part in the operation beside the army. See George H. Stein, *The Waffen-SS: Hitler's Elite Guard at War 1939–1945*, Cornell University Press, Ithaca and London, 1986.
22. See Jürgen Thorwald, *Die Illusion Rotarmisten gegen Stalin: Die Tragödie der Wlassow-Armee*, Knaur, Munich, 1995.
23. In the former Soviet Union, today's Commonwealth of Independent States, the period between Operation Barbarossa in 1941 and the final defeat of Nazi Germany in 1945 is still called the Great War for the Fatherland and commemorated on 9 May each year with a public holiday.
24. Percy E. Schramm, *Kriegstagebuch des Oberkommandos der Wehrmacht 1940–1941, Eine Dokumentation*, Vol. 2, Weltbild, Augsburg, 1996, 59. As of 10 July, the Army of the North had advanced 130 km. The Armies of the Centre had advanced 320 km towards Moscow and during this period took 500,000 captives. The Armies of the South had greatest difficulties advancing as they encountered stiff resistance in the Ukraine.
25. Payne, *Stalin*, 519–536.
26. Payne, *Stalin*, 525–534.
27. Ruzi Nazar.
28. Ruzi Nazar.
29. Rich peasants in Russia were known as kulaks. After the revolution kulaks were regarded as enemies of the regime, had their property confiscated and were exiled.
30. Ruzi Nazar.
31. Ruzi Nazar.
32. Ruzi Nazar.
33. Ruzi Nazar.
34. Ruzi Nazar.
35. A homemade vodka traditionally produced in Ukrainian homes, with a very high alcohol content.
36. Ruzi Nazar.
37. Ruzi Nazar.

38. Ruzi Nazar.
39. Ruzi Nazar.
40. Ruzi Nazar.
41. Ruzi Nazar.
42. Ruzi Nazar.
43. Ruzi Nazar.
44. Ruzi Nazar.
45. Ruzi Nazar.
46. Ruzi Nazar.
47. See Lenin, *Sochineniya*.
48. There were disagreements over plans for Russia between the German Ministry of Foreign Affairs and the German army. Consequently it is impossible to speak of a single German plan. See George Fischer, *Soviet Opposition to Stalin*, Harvard University Press, Cambridge, Massachusetts, 1952.
49. On the Ukrainian Volunteer Units, see Peter J. Huxley-Blythe, *Under the St Andrew's Cross: Russian and Cossack Volunteers in World War II, 1941–1945*, Europa Books, Bayside, New York, 2003; Samuel J. Newland, *Cossacks in the German Army, 1941–1945*, Routledge, London and New York, 1991.
50. Ruzi Nazar.
51. Ruzi Nazar.
52. Ruzi Nazar.
53. Ruzi Nazar.

4. SOLDIERS AND PRISONERS OF WAR

1. Tahir Çağatay, *Türkistan Kurtuluş Hareketi ile İlgili Olaylardan Sahneler*, Istanbul 1959, 23.
2. Çağatay, *Türkistan*, 23.
3. Ahat Andican, *The External Turkestan Struggle from Jadidism to Independence*, Emre Yayınları, Istanbul, 2003, 492. Hitler viewed the races of Asia as 'half-human, oriental, and barbarous'. Because of this it was unthinkable that they could be given weapons in the German army. See Hans Werner Neulen, *An deutscher Seite: Internationale Freiwillige von Wehrmacht und Waffen-SS*, Universitas, Munich, 17; for a handbill which the Nazis prepared on this topic, see *Der Untermensch: SS-Hauptamt, Schulungsamt*, Nordland Verlag, 1942. After 1941 there was a shift in Hitler's thinking on these matters in favour of the Turkic peoples. He said that he 'only trusted Turks who were real Muslims'. See Neulen, *An deutscher Seite*, 323.
4. Mariya Çokayoğlu, 'Eşinin Ağzından Mustafa Çokayoğlu', *Yaş Türkistan*, Istanbul 1972, 165.

5. Cengiz Dağcı, *Hatıralarda Cengiz Dağcı:Yazarın Kendi Kaleminden*, Ötüken Neşriyat, Istanbul 1972, 165.

6. Dağcı, *Hatıralarda Cengiz Dağcı*, 107–114.

7. On the death rates of Soviet citizens taken prisoner by the German army, see Christian Streit, *Keine Kameraden: Die Wehrmacht und die sowjetischen Kriegsgefangenen, 1941–1945*, Deutsche Verlags-Anstalt, Stuttgart, 1978, 128. Dr Werner Mansfeld writes that as of 19 February 1942, 1.1 million people from a total of 3.9 million Soviet nationals were still alive.

8. Rasim Ekşi, *Dr Baymirza Hayit Armağanı*, Turan Kültür Vakfı, Istanbul, 1999, 42.

9. Nadir Devlet, 'Çağdaş Türkiler', Supplementary volume of *Doğuştan Günümüze Büyük İslam Tarihi*, Çağ Yayınları, Istanbul, 1993, 116.

10. The father of Richard von Weizsäcker, who was president of the Federal Republic of Germany from 1984 to 1994, and the philosopher and physicist Carl Friedrich von Weizsäcker.

11. Hüsrev Gerede, Hulûsi Turgut and Sırrı Yüksel Cebeci, *Harb içinde Almanya 1939–1942*, ABC, İstanbul, 1994, 250–252.

12. For places that Mustafa Shokay and Veli Kayyum Han visited, see Andican, *Turkestan Struggle*, 495–496. For the Prisoners of War Commission set up for the Turkestanis, see Joachim Hoffman, *Die Ostlegionen 1941–1943*, Verlag Rombach, Freiburg, 1986, 86–87.

13. See Ahat Andican, *Osmanlı'dan Günümüze Türkiye ve Orta Asya, Doğan Kitap*, İstanbul, 2009.

14. Jürgen Thorwald, *Wen sie verderben wollen: Bericht des grossen Verrats*, Steingruben Verlag, Stuttgart, 1952, 71; The commissioners charged with setting up the Turkestan Units officially began their work on 13 January 1942. See Document no. 1520-PS, 'Notes about a Discussion with the Führer at the Führer's Headquarters', 8 May 1942, Avalon Project, http://avalon.law.yale.edu.

15. Çokayoğlu, 'Eşinin Ağzından Mustafa Çokayoğlu', 140. Andijan, *Turkestan Struggle*.

16. Patrick von zur Mühlen, *Zwischen Hakenkreuz und Sowjetstern: Der Nationalismus der sowjetischen Orientvölker im Zweiten Weltkrieg*, Droste Verlag, Düsseldorf, 1971, 79–80. Gerhard von Mende, *Der nationale Kampf der Russlandtürken: Ein Beitrag zur nationalen Frage in der Sovetunion*, Weidmann, Berlin, 1936.

17. Known as Nuri Killigil after the introduction of surnames in Turkey in 1932.

18. Feridun Kandemir, *Enver Paşa'nın Son Günleri*, Güven Yayınevi, İstanbul, 1965, 79–80. Abdullah Recep Baysun, *Türkistan MillîHareketleri*, Istanbul, 1943, 109–115.

19. Mühlen, *Zwischen Hakenkreuz*, 83.

20. Documents on German Foreign Policy, 1918–1945, Department of State, Series D, vol. 13, 'The War Years', US Government Printing Office, Washington, 1964, 571–575. Andican, *Turkestan Struggle*, 511.

21. Erkilet held his first meeting with the Turkestani units on 26 October 1941. H. Emir Erkilet, *Şark Cebhesinde Gördüklerim*, Istanbul, 1943, 198–199.

22. Mühlen, *Zwischen Hakenkreuz*, 70.

23. Report on '45 Days in Hitler's Headquarters', submitted to the Turkish General Staff by Hüseyin Hüsnü Erkilet.

24. Ministerstvo Inostrannih Del, *Alman Dışişleri Dairesi Belgeleri: Türkiye'deki Alman Politikası (1941–1943)* Havass Yayınları, Istanbul, 1977, 17. (Hereafter referred to as *Türkiye'deki Alman Politikası*).

25. TBMM Zabıt Ceridesi, Devre 6, 27, içtima: 3, 24–25. Cited in Andican, *Turkestan Struggle*.

26. For the full text of Khrushchev's speech to the 20th Congress of the CPSU on 25 February 1956, in which he criticised Stalin and the cult of Stalin, see 'The Cult of the Individual', *Guardian*, 26 April 2007, http://www.guardian.co.uk/theguardian/2007/apr/26/greatspeeches1.

27. *Türkiye'deki Alman Politikası*, 68; Andican, *Turkestan Struggle*, 586.

28. *Türkiye'deki Alman Politikası*, 70. There was no agreement in government circles about plans for the Soviet territory occupied by the Germans. The Nazi Party, the Ministry of the Orient and the Ministry of Foreign Affairs all had differing views. For details, see Alexander Dallin, *German Rule in Russia, 1941–1945: A Study of Occupation Policies*, Palgrave Macmillan, New York, 1981; Jürgen Thorwald, *Die Illusion: Rotarmisten gegen Stalin—Die Tragödie der Wlassow-Armee*, Knaur, Munich, 1995.

29. Konstitutsiya CCP, Moscow, 1978, Article 72, 27.

30. *Türkiye'deki Alman Politikası*, 81.

31. For the memorandum presented to Hitler by the Minister of the East, Rosenberg, see Hoffman, *Die Ostlegionen*, 30. The command to establish the first legion was given on 30 December 1941. See Oleg Valentinovich Romanko, 'The East Came West: Muslim and Hindu Volunteers in German Service, 1941–1945' in Antonio Munoz, ed., *The East Came West*, Axis Europa Books, New York, 2001, 48.

32. Charles Warren Hostler, *Türken und Sowjets: Die historische Lage und die politische Bedeutung der Türken und der Türkvölker in der heutigen Welt*, Metzner, Frankfurt am Main and Berlin, 1960, 214–215.

33. Hostler, *Türken und Sowjets*, 215; Hoffman, *Die Ostlegionen.*, 26; Sergei Drobyazko and Andrei Karashchuk, *Vostochnye legioni i kazachi chasti v Vermakhte*, Ast, Moscow, 1999, 3; Romanko, 'East Came West', 47.

34. Oskar Ritter von Niedermayer (1885–1948).
35. See Hoffman, *Die Ostlegionen*, 61. According to an instruction issued on 4 July 1942, Niedermayer, as commander of the 162nd Infantry Division, was to go to the legion camps at Khorol and Lubny, where prisoners would be separated into groups by nationality. See Hoffman, *Die Ostlegionen*, 88. The Aufstellungstab (Installation Staff) in Mirgorod began work in May 1942. As of 12 December 1942 there were 35,000 men in the 162nd Infantry Division in Ukraine. See Neulen, *An deutscher Seite*, 331–332.
36. Hostler, *Türken und Sowjets*, 215; Hoffman, *Die Ostlegionen*, 88.
37. TBMM Tutanak Dergisis (Transactions of the Turkish Grand National Assembly), Vol. 9, 204, Session 101 of 18 July 1951. For the speech by Şevket Mocan, deputy for Tekirdağ, see Vol. 9, 205, Session 101 of 18 July 1951. See also Andican, *Turkestan Struggle*, 612–615.
38. Ruzi Nazar.
39. Ruzi Nazar.
40. Ruzi Nazar.
41. Ruzi Nazar.
42. Andican, *Turkestan Struggle*, 492. Interview with Baymirza Hayit. See also Hüseyin İkram Han, *Bir Türkistanlının İkinci Dünya Savaşı Hatıraları*, Bedir, İstanbul, 1999, 80–83.
43. Mühlen, *Zwischen Hakenkreuz*, 460–479.
44. For Nazi theories of race, see Alan Bullock, *Hitler: A Study in Tyranny*, Penguin Books, London, 1962.
45. İkram Han, *Bir Türkistanlının*, 81–83.
46. On the Nazi genocide of the Jews, see Eugen Kogon, *Der SS-Staat: Das System der deutschen Konzentrationslager*, Kinder Verlag, Munich, 1974.
47. Ruzi Nazar.
48. George Fischer, *Soviet Opposition to Stalin*, Harvard University Press, Cambridge, Massachusetts, 1952, 44; Alexander Dallin, *German Rule in Russia*, 440. The number of Soviet prisoners before November 1941 is given as 2,053,000. But in Rosenberg's letter this number rises to 3.6 million. Dallin, on page 427, however, gives the number in 1941 as 3,335,000 and 1,653,000 in 1942. According to Streit, *Keine Kameraden*, 356, the total number of volunteer soldiers in the German army at the end of 1942 was nearly one million. See Fischer, *Soviet Opposition*, 45. Hayit gives the total number of Turkestanis as 181,402: see Baymirza Hayit, *Turkestan im Herzen Euroasiens*, Studienverlag, Cologne, 1980, 103. As of 4 October 1944 the number of Turkestani soldiers in the German army is given as 110,000. The number up to 24 January 1945 was 45,000. See Antonio J. Munoz, *Hitler's Eastern Legions*, vol. 2, *The Osttruppen*, Axis Europa Books, Bayside, 1997, 5.

49. Veli Kayyum Han, *Mustafa Çokayoğlu Esleş*, *Millî Türkistan Mecmuası*, No. 70–71, 22. Andican, *Turkestan Struggle*, 494.
50. Ali Kantemir, 'Mustafa Bey Çokay Hakkındaki Hatıratım', *Millî Türkistan*, No. 99 A, 23–24; Andican, *Turkestan Struggle*, 498.
51. See Andican, *Turkestan Struggle*, 501.
52. For uniforms, see Document no. 1520-PS, 'Notes about a Discussion with the Führer at the Führer's Headquarters', 8 May 1942, Avalon Project.

5. RUZI AND THE LEGIONS' WAR AGAINST SOVIET RUSSIA

1. On weapons, see Sergei Drobyazko and Andrei Karashchuk, *Vostochnye legioni i kazachi chasti v Vermakhte*, Ast, Moscow, 1999, 5.
2. On pay, see G.N. Vzvarova, 'Turkestanskie Legionen', *Voyenno-Istoricheskiy Jurnal*, vol. 2, 1995, 41.
3. Ruzi Nazar.
4. Ruzi Nazar.
5. See Joachim Hoffman, *Die Ostlegionen 1941–1943*, Verlag Rombach, Freiburg, 1986, 33.
6. On the setting up of the committee, see P. von zur Mühlen, *Zwischen Hakenkreuz und Sowjetstern: Der Nationalismus der sowjetischen Orientvölker im Zweiten Weltkrieg*, Droste Verlag, Düsseldorf, 1971, 94ff.
7. Mühlen, *Zwischen Hakenkreuz*, 97.
8. For the official text sent by Ergesh Shermet on behalf of the NTUC to the TMB's representative Abdulvahap Oktay on 8 November 1952, see Ahat Andican, *The External Turkestan Struggle from Jadidism to Independence*, Emre Yayınları, Istanbul, 2003, 573.
9. Ruzi Nazar.
10. Ruzi Nazar.
11. Ruzi Nazar.
12. Ruzi Nazar.
13. On the life of Oskar von Niedermayer, see Matthias Friese and Stefan Geilen, *Oskar von Niedermayer: Deutsche in Afghanistan*, Aqua Verlag, Cologne, 2002.
14. Edward W. Said, *Orientalism*, Pantheon Books, New York, 1978.
15. Ruzi Nazar.
16. Ruzi Nazar.
17. Ruzi Nazar.
18. Ruzi Nazar.
19. Information from the father of Enver Altaylı, resident in Adana.
20. Archive of Professor G. von Mende.
21. David Littlejohn, *Foreign Legions of the Third Reich*, R. James Bender Publishing, California, 1987, 253.

22. Mühlen, *Zwischen Hakenkreuz*, 149–150.
23. Ruzi Nazar.
24. Interview with Baymirza Hayit.
25. Ruzi Nazar.
26. Ruzi Nazar.
27. Ruzi Nazar.
28. Ruzi Nazar.
29. Ruzi Nazar.
30. Ruzi Nazar.
31. Ruzi Nazar.
32. On the battles of Prokhorovka, see Dieter Brand, 'Vor 60 Jahren Prochorowka' in *Deutsche Österreichische Militärische Zeitschrift*, No. 6, 2003, http://www.bmlv.gov.at/omz/ausgaben/artikel.php?id=158.
33. Ruzi Nazar.
34. Ruzi Nazar.
35. Ruzi Nazar.

6. THE TIDE TURNS AGAINST GERMANY

1. See Earl F. Ziemke, *Stalingrad to Berlin: The German Defeat in the East*, US Army Center for Military History, Washington DC, 2002.
2. Ruzi Nazar.
3. Ruzi Nazar.
4. Ruzi Nazar.
5. Ruzi Nazar.
6. Interview with Baymirza Hayit.
7. Ruzi Nazar.
8. Ruzi Nazar.
9. Sergej Frölich, *General Wlassow: Russen und Deutsche zwischen Hitler und Stalin*, Marcus Verlag, Cologne, 1987, 23–52.
10. Fröhlich, *General Wlassow*, 23–52
11. Fröhlich, *General Wlassow*, 23–52.
12. Fröhlich, *General Wlassow*, 23–52.
13. See Otto Bräutigam, *So hat es sich zugetragen: Ein Leben als Soldat und Diplomat*, Holzer Verlag, Würzburg, 1968.
14. See *Türkiye'de Alman Politikası*, 90.
15. Veli Kayyum Han, 'Türkistan'ın Yeni Millî Siyaseti Üstünde', *Millî Türkistan*, No. 31, 1943, 3.
16. 'Türkistan'ın Millî Askerleri ve Siyasî Yol', *Millî Türkistan*, Nos. 19 and 20.
17. 'Millî Kongre'nin 8. Yıllığı', *Millî Türkistan*, No. 79, 1952, 9. The Turkestan Legion was recognised by the German authorities as the

official army of Turkestan and the NTUC as the provisional government. See Hüseyin İkram Han, *Bir Türkistanlının İkinci Dünya Savaşı Hatıraları*, Bedir, İstanbul 1999, 133.

18. 'Millî Kongre'nin 8. Yıllığı', 9.

19. Hermann Raschhofer and Theodor Oberländer, *Der Fall Oberländer: Eine vergleichende Rechtsanalyse der Verfahren in Pankow und Bonn*, Schlichtenmayer, Tübingen, 1962, 97. The German High Command told the volunteer units on 11 September 1942 to be ready for combat. For information about their mobilisation, see Joachim Hoffman, *Die Ostlegionen 1941– 1943*, Verlag Rombach, Freiburg, 1986, 38.

20. Fröhlich, *General Wlassow*, 193.

21. Alexander Dallin, *La Russie sous la botte nazie*, Fayard, Paris, 1970, 417; Ahat Andican, *The External Turkestan Struggle from Jadidism to Independence*, Emre Yayınları, Istanbul, 2003, 566.

22. Fröhlich, *General Wlassow*, 193.

23. P. von zur Mühlen, *Zwischen Hakenkreuz und Sowjetstern: Der Nationalismus der sowjetischen Orientvölker im Zweiten Weltkrieg*, Droste Verlag, Düsseldorf, 1971, 21.

24. Andijan, *Turkestan Struggle*, 562–563.

25. For detailed information on the Normandy landings, see Stephen Ambrose, *D-Day, June 6 1944: The Climactic Battle of World War II*, Simon and Schuster, New York, 1995; Alex Kershaw, *The Bedford Boys: One American Town's Ultimate D-Day Sacrifice*, Da Capo Press, Cambridge, Massachusetts, 2003; Cornelius Ryan, *The Longest Day: June 6 1944*, Simon & Schuster, New York, 1959.

26. Interview with Baymirza Hayit.

27. Ruzi Nazar.

28. Fröhlich, *General Wlassow*, 194–197.

29. Sir Olaf Caroe, *Sömürülen Topraklar*, Tercüman, Istanbul, 1972, 346.

30. Interview with Baymirza Hayit.

31. Andijan, *Turkestan Struggle*, 568.

32. Ruzi Nazar.

33. Ruzi Nazar.

34. Ruzi Nazar.

35. Interviews with Ruzi Nazar and Baymirza Hayit. On Olzscha's plan and activities, Meyer-Mader's initiatives and work at SS headquarters on this issue, see Mühlen, *Zwischen Hakenkreuz*, 141–157.

36. Andijan, *Turkestan Struggle*, 567.

37. Interview with Baymirza Hayit. See also Mühlen, *Zwischen Hakenkreuz*, 155.

38. Interview with Baymirza Hayit.

39. For the terrible, indeed intolerable, life of convicts in these camps in

Siberia and the camp conditions in general, see Anne Applebaum, *Gulag: A History*, Arkadaş, Ankara, 2008, 182–215.

40. Research by Enver Altaylı in the town of Andijan in Uzbekistan where Gulam Alim lived.

41. Oskar von Niedermayer, the former commander of the 162nd, had been arrested for criticising Hitler's eastern policies. Despite the attempts of his friends to get him freed, Niedermayer remained in Torgau prison until the Allies occupied Germany. In May 1945 he was released by the US army, but was captured by the Red Army at a road-block. He was tried in Moscow and sentenced to twenty-five years' hard labour, dying in his prison cell of tuberculosis on 25 September 1948.

42. 'The Heygendorff Report' in Mühlen, *Zwischen Hakenkreuz*, 55, 44n.

43. Bräutigam, *So hat es sich zugetragen*, 592; Mühlen, *Zwischen Hakenkreuz*, 39n.

44. Von zur Mühlen, *Zwischen Hakenkreuz*, 65 n.32.

45. Ruzi Nazar.

46. Ruzi Nazar.

47. Ruzi Nazar.

48. For the Crimea under Nazi occupation, see Edige Mustafa Kırımal, *Der nationale Kampf de Kirimtataren*, Verlag Lechte, Emsdetten, 1952, 307.

49. On Aryan racial theory, see Ernst K. Bramsted, *Goebbels und die nation-alsozialistische Propaganda 1925–1945*, S. Fischer Verlag, Frankfurt am Main, 1971.

50. Ruzi Nazar.

51. Ruzi Nazar.

52. Ruzi Nazar.

53. Ruzi Nazar.

54. Ruzi Nazar.

7. ESCAPING FROM THE JAWS OF DEFEAT

1. Ruzi Nazar.

2. Ruzi Nazar.

3. Ruzi Nazar.

4. Ruzi Nazar.

5. Ruzi Nazar.

6. Ruzi Nazar.

7. Ruzi Nazar.

8. The full text of the Yalta Conference is available at the Avalon Project: 'The Yalta Conference', http://avalon.law.yale.edu/wwii/yalta.asp,

accessed on 8 February 2011. For the Additional Protocol on prisoners of war, see 'Agreement Relating to Prisoners of War and Civilians Liberated by Forces Operating under Soviet Command and Forces Operating under United States of America Command, February 11 1945', http://avalon.law.yale.edu/20th_century/sov007.asp. See also University of Wisconsin Digital Collections Foreign Relations of the United States, http://digicoll.library.wisc.edu/cgi-binFRUS/FRUS-idx?id=FRUS.FRUS1945.

9. Ruzi Nazar.
10. Now Mariánské Lázně in the present-day Czech Republic.
11. Interview with Baymirza Hayit. Ahat Andican, *The External Turkestan Struggle from Jadidism to Independence*, Emre Yayınları, Istanbul, 2003, 174.
12. Ruzi Nazar.
13. Ruzi Nazar.
14. A *Soldbuch* (literally 'paybook') was a small notebook, rather like an identity card, which soldiers were obliged to carry in time of war.
15. Ruzi Nazar.
16. Ruzi Nazar.
17. Ruzi Nazar.
18. Ruzi Nazar.
19. Ruzi Nazar.
20. Interview with Baymirza Hayit.
21. Ruzi Nazar.
22. Ruzi Nazar.
23. Ruzi Nazar.
24. Ruzi Nazar.
25. Ruzi Nazar.
26. Ruzi Nazar.
27. Ruzi Nazar.
28. Ruzi Nazar.
29. Interview with Hussan İkram Han.
30. Interview with İkram Han.
31. Hüseyin Ikram Han, *Bir Türkistanlının İkinci Dünya Savaşı Hatıraları, Bedir,* İstanbul 1999, 148–154
32. Ikram Han, *Bir Türkistanlının*, 148–154.
33. Ikram Han, *Bir Türkistanlının*, 166.
34. Ikram Han, *Bir Türkistanlının*, 363
35. Ikram Han, *Bir Türkistanlının*, 167.
36. Ruzi Nazar.
37. Ruzi Nazar.
38. Ruzi Nazar.

39. Ruzi Nazar.
40. Interview with Hussan Ikram Han.
41. From notes on conversations between the author and Baymirza Hayit and Veli Kayyum Han, 1968–1977; Andican, *Turkestan Struggle*, 170.
42. On 11 May, the First Division of the Russian Liberation Army had surrendered to the Americans.
43. Sergej Frölich, *General Wlassow: Russen und Deutsche zwischen Hitler und Stalin*, Marcus Verlag, Cologne, 1987, 193.
44. Interview with Baymirza Hayit.
45. Interview with Baymirza Hayit.
46. Interviews with Baymirza Hayit and Veli Kayyum Han.
47. Reply by Rükneddin Nasuhoğlu, minister of justice, TBMMTD, c.9, session 101, 18 July 1952, 204.
48. A district of Istanbul.
49. Speech by Şevket Mocan, deputy for Tekirdağ, TBMMTD, 9.101, 18 July 1952, 205.
50. Andican, *Turkestan Struggle*, 177–8 and 179n.
51. Quoted in Andican, *Turkestan Struggle*, 573.

8. REFUGE IN ROSENHEIM

1. Ruzi Nazar.
2. Interview with Hussan Ikram Han.
3. Ruzi Nazar.
4. Ruzi Nazar.
5. Hasan Ali Karasar, *National Identity and Regional Integration in Central Asia: Turkestan Reunion* (unpublished doctoral thesis, Bilkent University), 197; Ahat Andican, *The External Turkestan Struggle from Jadidism to Independence*, Emre Yayınları, Istanbul, 2003, 569; P. von zur Mühlen, *Zwischen Hakenkreuz und Sowjetstern: Der Nationalismus der sowjetischen Orientvölker im Zweiten Weltkrieg*, Droste Verlag, Düsseldorf, 1971, 96–97 and 164.
6. Ruzi Nazar.
7. Hüseyin İkram Han, *Bir Türkistanlının İkinci Dünya Savaşı Hatıraları*, Bedir, İstanbul, 1999, 168.
8. Ruzi Nazar.
9. Ikram Han, *Bir Türkistanlının*, 169.
10. Interview with Hüseyin Ikram Han.
11. Interview with Hussan Ikram Han.
12. Ruzi Nazar.
13. Ruzi Nazar.
14. Interviews with Ruzi Nazar and Hussan Ikram Han.

15. Ruzi Nazar.
16. Ruzi Nazar.
17. Interviews with Ruzi Nazar and Hussan Ikram Han.
18. Ruzi Nazar.
19. Interview with Hussan Ikram Han.
20. Interview with Hussan Ikram Han.
21. Ruzi Nazar.
22. Ruzi Nazar.
23. Ruzi Nazar.
24. Hüseyin Ikram Han, *Bir Türkistanlının*, 170–173.
25. Andican, *Struggle*, 572–573.
26. Ruzi Nazar.
27. Ruzi Nazar.
28. Ruzi Nazar.
29. Ikram Han, *Bir Türkistanlının*, 178.
30. Ikram Han, *Bir Türkistanlının*, 179.
31. Interview with Hussan Ikram.
32. Interview with Ruzi Nazar and Hussan Ikram.
33. Interview with Hussan Ikram.
34. Interview with Hussan Ikram.
35. Ikram Han, *Bir Türkistanlının*, 178.
36. Ruzi Nazar.
37. Ruzi Nazar.
38. Interviews with Ruzi Nazar and Hussan Ikram.
39. Hüseyin Ikram, *Bir Türkistanlının*, 179.
40. Ikram Han, *Bir Türkistanlının*, 190.
41. Ikram Han, *Bir Türkistanlının*, 179–181.
42. Ikram Han, *Bir Türkistanlının*, 179–181.
43. Ikram Han, *Bir Türkistanlının*, 179–181.
44. Ikram Han, *Bir Türkistanlının*, 180–181.
45. Ikram Han, *Bir Türkistanlının*, 182–183.
46. Ikram Han, *Bir Türkistanlının*, 182–183.
47. Ikram Han, *Bir Türkistanlının*, 182–183.
48. Ruzi Nazar.

9. THE COLD WAR AND THE NEW ESPIONAGE

1. Ruzi Nazar.
2. Interview with Baymirza Hayat.
3. Ahat Andican, *The External Turkestan Struggle from Jadidism to Independence*, Emre Yayınları, Istanbul, 2003, 628.
4. For details of the postwar international environment, see *Sowyetsystem und demokratische Gesellschaft*, Freiburg, 1972, 600–614.

5. Comintern, in Russian *Kommunisticheskiy Internatsional*, is the abbreviation for the Third International. It was founded by Lenin when the Second International ended in disagreement in 1916. Lenin was opposed to the First World War and when the Communist parties in other countries supported their countries' entry into the war, he began a dispute with them. Later, Trotsky claimed that the Comintern was dominated by Stalin, and a group of which he was the leader set up the Fourth International in 1938. But Stalin and the Communist parties which followed his line rejected this organisation. For detailed information, see Michael K. Florinsky, 'World Revolution and Soviet Foreign Policy', *Political Science Quarterly*, 47, 4, June 1932, 204–233: Lorna L. Waddington, 'The Anti-Comintern and Nazi Anti-Bolshevik Propaganda in the late 1930s', *Journal of Contemporary History*, 42, 4, October 2007, 573–594. For speeches made at the First Congress of the Communist International, see 'The Organisation of the Communist International', www.marxists.org/history/international/comintern/1st-Congress/index.htm. The Comintern was dissolved by Stalin in May 1943. After the Paris Conference of 1947 and the launching of Marshall Aid, the Cominform was established by Stalin to act against the West. For detailed information about the Cominform, see Vojtech Mastny, 'Stalin and the Militarisation of the Cold War', *International Security*, 9, 3, Winter 1984–5, 109–129; Geoffrey Roberts, 'Moscow and the Marshall Plan: Politics, Ideology, and the Onset of the Cold War, 1947', *Europe-Asia Studies*, 46, 8, Soviet and East European History, [1994], 1377–1386.

6. These were short-lived states under Soviet control established after the Second World War. The Azerbaijan People's Republic or Republic of South Azerbaijan was set up in September 1945 as the result of a coup staged by the Red Army. The Mahabad Republic was officially founded in December 1945. When, as a result of pressure from Western governments, notably the United States, Stalin withdrew from the territory he occupied, these two states both collapsed. For detailed information, see Gary R. Hess, 'The Iran Crisis of 1945–1946 and the Cold War', *Political Science Quarterly*, 89, 1, March 1974, 117–146. For records in the Soviet archives to do with this subject, see Woodrow Wilson International Center for Scholars, Cold War International History Project 'Collection: 1945–46, Iranian Crisis'.

7. For the Russian demands, see Norman Stone, *The Atlantic and Its Enemies: A Personal History of the Cold War*, Basic Books, New York, 2010, 21.

8. William M. Hale and Petek Demir, *Turkish Foreign Policy* (in Turkish), Arkeoloji ve Sanat Yayinlari, Istanbul, 2003, 113–114.

9. See Stone, *The Atlantic and Its Enemies*, 21. For detailed information on the Marshall Plan and the situation in Europe, see Jussi M. Hanhimaki

and Odd Arne Westad, *The Cold War: A History in Documents and Eyewitness Accounts*, Oxford University Press, Oxford and New York, 2004, 105–137.

10. For the views of the Soviet Union on the Cold War, see R. Osgood, *Organichennaya voyna*, Moscow, 1960, 78; W.D. Sokolovski, *Voyennaya strategiya*, Moscow, 1969, 120–130.

11. *Sowjetsystem und demokratische Gesellschaft*, 3, 466ff. Also see A.W. Dulles, 'Disarmament in the Atomic Age', *Foreign Affairs*, 25, 1947, 204–216; H.S. Truman, *Memoirs*, Bern and Stuttgart, 1955 and 1956; John Burnham, *Die Strategie des Kalten Krieges*, Stuttgart, 1950; Ernst Nolte, *Marxismus, Faschismus, Kalter Krieg: Vorträge und Aufsätze*, Deutsche Verlags Anstalt, Stuttgart, 1977, 211–375.

12. On the *Oprishchina* see Gunther Stökl and Manfred Alexander, *The Russian State in the Middle Ages and Early Modern Period*, Steiner, Wiesbaden, 1981.

13. On the KGB's structure and activities, see John Baron, *KGB*, Bern-Munich, 1976.

14. Weiner, *CIA*, Fischer-Verlag, Frankfurt am Main, 2008, 27.

15. Weiner, *CIA*, 54.

16. Weiner, *CIA*, 55.

17. For George Kennan's thinking about the Cold War, see G. Kennan (alias 'Mr X'), 'The Sources of Soviet Conduct', *Foreign Affairs*, 25, 1947, 56–583; G.F. Kennan, *American Diplomacy, 1900–1950*, Chicago, 1951.

18. Weiner, *CIA.*, 59.

19. Ruzi Nazar.

20. Ruzi Nazar.

21. Ruzi Nazar.

22. Ruzi Nazar.

23. Ruzi Nazar; interview with Baymirza Hayit. Among the Turkestanis working in this centre were Veli Kayyum Han, Baymirza Hayit, Ergesh Shermet, Hussan Ikram Han, Malik Omeri, Ismail Tacibay, Mumin Teshebay, Mahmut Maksut Bek, Dama Kasim, Inayeti Haksever, Makam Omari, Aman Berdimurat, Abdullah Tolegen and Arkam Azim.

24. Ruzi Nazar.

25. Ruzi Nazar.

26. Ruzi Nazar.

27. Ruzi Nazar.

28. Interview with Baymirza Hayit.

29. Ruzi Nazar.

30. Interviews with Ruzi Nazar and Baymirza Hayit.

31. Weiner, *CIA*, 59.

32. Weiner, *CIA*, 60; see also Robin Winks, *Cloak and Gown: Scholars in the Secret War, 1939–1961*, Yale University Press, New Haven, Connecticut, 1987, 451.

33. Wiener, *CIA*, 68.

34. Andican, *Turkestan Struggle*, 635.

35. Declaration by the National Turkestan Unity Committee, 28 August 1951.

36. Andican, *Turkestan Struggle*, 635.

37. Ruzi Nazar.

38. On the murder of Bandera by the KGB, see Franz Wilhelm Seidel, *The Collaboration 1939–45*, Herbig, Munich, 1995, 60–61.

39. Ruzi Nazar.

40. See Nasimand Yaqublu, *Abdurrahman Fatalibeyli-Dudanginski*, Adiloğlu Neşriyatı, Baku, 2008.

41. Ruzi Nazar.

42. See issues of *Quick* and *Der Stern* at this date.

43. Weiner, *CIA*, 75–76.

44. Weiner, *CIA*, 78–79.

45. Weiner, *CIA*, 79.

46. Weiner, *CIA*, 80.

47. John Limond Hart, *The CIA's Russians*, Annapolis, Maryland, 2002, 136–137. In his memories, Hart mentions the exceptional damage which Angleton did to the CIA.

48. Weiner, *CIA*, 79.

49. On Philby, see S.J. Hamrick, *Deceiving the Deceivers: Kim Philby, Donald Maclean, and Guy Burgess*, Yale University Press, Connecticut, 2004; Philip Knightley, *The Master Spy: The Story of Kim Philby*, Knopf, New York, 1989.

50. See Michael Howard Holzman, *James Jesus Angleton, the CIA, and the Craft of Counterintelligence*, University of Massachusetts Press, Amherst, 2008; Tom Mangol, *Cold Warrior: James Jesus Angleton: the CIA's Master Spy Hunter*, Simon & Schuster, New York, 1991.

51. Weiner, *CIA*, 83.

52. Detailed information about Turkey's NATO membership can be found on the NATO website. See http://www.nato.int/archives/ismayrep/text.htm#6.

53. Ruzi Nazar.

54. Ruzi Nazar.

55. P. von zur Mühlen, *Zwischen Hakenkreuz und Sowjetstern: Der Nationalismus der sowjetischen Orientvölker im Zweiten Weltkrieg*, Droste Verlag, Düsseldorf, 1971, 229–230.

56. Ruzi Nazar; see also Stalin, *Works* (German edition), vol. 5, 1921–23,

Stuttgart, 1952, 268–269: speech made by Stalin at the consultative meeting in Moscow of the Russian Communist Party between 9 and 12 June 1923, with the participation of authorised functionaries from the national republics and regions. In his speech, Stalin said that the Uzbek functionaries Hojanov and Ikramov had not made bad speeches, but that Ikramov had said that there was no difference at all between the Turkestan of Tsarist times and the present Turkestan—only the signboard had changed. 'If this is not a slip of the tongue, if it is a thought-out claim, then in this situation the Basmajis were right and we must be wrong. In this case, it is not us who should be trying Sultan Galiyev but he who should be trying us. Then I want to ask these people, why did you not join the Basmajis? Comrades, Turkestan today is very different from the Turkestan of the Tsarist era. In this connection I would like to say this to these comrades: Let them please take some trouble, puzzle over what they have said, and put their errors right.' Stalin never forgot the words of Ikramov and Hojanov and in 1938 had them both executed.

57. Ruzi Nazar.
58. Professor Dr Theodor Oberländer was an expert in political economy and agriculture and had been a faculty member in the universities of Königsberg, Greifswald and Prague. Before becoming a reserve officer in the intelligence arm running special operations, Oberländer had worked on the political and economic problems of the Soviet Union and Eastern Europe. Thanks to his wide travels, particularly in the Caucasus, he had got to know this region very closely. During the Second World War he directed special operations with the Bergmann and Sonderbergmann Units. See Joachim Hoffman, *Die Ostlegionen 1941–1943*, Verlag Rombach, Freiburg, 1986, 28–30.
59. Ruzi Nazar.
60. Karis Kanatbay, 'Bizning Maksad' ['Our Aim'], *Türkeli Mecmuası*, No. 1, 1951, 4; see also Karasar, *National Identity and Regional Integration in Central Asia* (PhD thesis, Bilkent University, 2002); Mühlen, *Zwischen Hakenkreuz*, 229.
61. *Millî Turkestan*, No. 83, 87.
62. *United Caucasia*, No. 26, 28; Andican, *Turkestan Struggle*, 644–646.

10. RUZI GOES TO AMERICA

1. Ruzi Nazar.
2. Archie Roosevelt, *For Lust of Knowing, Memoirs of an Intelligence Officer*, Little Brown, Boston, 1988, 444–448.
3. Ruzi Nazar.

4. Ruzi Nazar.
5. Tim Weiner, *Legacy of Ashes: The History of the CIA*, Doubleday, New York, 200782–83.
6. Ruzi Nazar.
7. For the numbers of those in the concentration camps and the terrors they experienced, see Anne Applebaum, *Gulag: A History*, Arkadaş, Ankara, 2008,579–589; Robert Conquest, *The Great Terror: A Reassessment*, London, 1992, 485; V.N. Zemskov, 'Arkhipelag Gulag: glazami pisatelya i statistika', *Argumenti I Fakty*, No. 45, 1989, 6–7.
8. Ruzi Nazar.
9. Ruzi Nazar.
10. In 2010 a book appeared which made many claims about Professor Mende with only a very slight connection with the facts: Ian Johnson, *A Mosque in Munich: Nazis, CIA, and the Muslim Brotherhood in the West*, Mariner Books, Boston and New York, 2010. The son of Professor Mende, Professor Erling von Mende, has written a sixty-page text refuting the distortions contained in this work.
11. Ruzi Nazar.
12. Ruzi Nazar.
13. Ruzi Nazar.
14. Ruzi Nazar.
15. Ruzi Nazar.
16. Ruzi Nazar.
17. Ruzi Nazar.
18. Ruzi Nazar.
19. Ruzi Nazar.
20. Mikhail Eisenstadt-Jeleznov had been born in Moscow and sought asylum in New York in 1924. See University of Minnesota, Immigration History Research Center, 'Eisenstadt-Jeleznov, Mikhail, Papers', http://www.ihrc.umn.edu/research/vitrage/all/ea/ihrc613.html.
21. Ruzi Nazar.

11. FIRST VISITS TO THE MIDDLE EAST

1. Ruzi Nazar.
2. Ruzi Nazar.
3. Ruzi Nazar.
4. Ruzi Nazar.
5. Ruzi Nazar.
6. Ruzi Nazar.
7. Anouar Abdel-Malek, *Ägypten: Militärgesellschaft: Das Armeeregime, die Linke und der soziale Wandel unter Nasser*, Suhrkamp Verlag, Frankfurt 1971, 45–90.

8. Anouar Abdel-Malek, *Ägypten*, 91–92.

9. Ruzi Nazar.

10. Ruzi Nazar.

11. Interview with Baymirza Hayit.

12. Private papers of Gerhard von Mende. See also P. von zur Mühlen, *Zwischen Hakenkreuz und Sowjetstern: Der Nationalismus der sowjetischen Orientvölker im Zweiten Weltkrieg*, Droste Verlag, Düsseldorf, 1971, 39, 228.

13. Ruzi Nazar.

14. Ruzi Nazar.

15. In Islam, the Hadith are all the collected sayings of the Prophet, written down to enlighten believers about events in his life and possible questions. They express the sense of various verses of the Koran in a more open manner. Sunnah is the name given to the Prophet's actions and words on any topic, which are a model for Muslims to follow in their own lives.

16. The best known of these were Imam Muhammad ibn Ismail al-Bukhari (810–870), author of the Ṣaḥīḥ al-Bukhārī, and Abu Isa Muhammad ibn Isa at-Tirmidhi (815?–892?), author of the collection known as the Jami'at-Tirmidhi. Their works are considered the most reliable of the six collections of Hadith known as the Kutub al-Sittah.

17. Ruzi Nazar.

18. Ruzi Nazar.

19. Ruzi Nazar.

20. Ruzi Nazar.

21. Ahat Andican, *The External Turkestan Struggle from Jadidism to Independence*, Emre Yayınları, Istanbul, 2003, 646–647. In May 1953 Baymirza Hayit set off on a five-month tour of Turkey, Syria, Jordan, Egypt, Saudi Arabia and Pakistan. He met many Turkestanis in Turkey, among them Abdurrahman Kavuncu Hoca Efendi, the mufti of Bahçe and Osmaniye. Abdurrahman Hoca Efendi went on the hajj later in the same year and was able to assist Baymirza Hayit in his work in Mecca and Medina by translating for him. (Information supplied by the late Abdurrahman Kavuncu Hoca Efendi, the author's maternal grandfather.)

22. Interview with Baymirza Hayit; see also Andijan, *Turkestan Struggle*, 651.

23. Ruzi Nazar.

24. Ruzi Nazar.

25. Ruzi Nazar.

26. Ruzi Nazar.

27. Ruzi Nazar.

28. Ruzi Nazar.

29. Ruzi Nazar.
30. Ruzi Nazar.
31. Ruzi Nazar.
32. For Atatürk and the Turkish War of Independence, see Erik Jan Zürcher, *Turkey: A Modern History*, I.B. Tauris, London, 2005; Lord Kinross, *Ataturk: The Rebirth of a Nation*, Phoenix Press, London, 2005.
33. For Turkey's relations with Turkestan in the Turkish War of Independence, see Mehmet Saray, *Atatürk'ün Sovyet Politikası*, Veli Yayınları, Istanbul, 1984; Zeki Velidi Togan, *Hatıralar: Türkistan ve Diğer Müslüman Doğu Türklerinin Milli Varlık ve Kültür Mücadeleleri*, Türkiye Diyanet Vakfı, Ankara, 1999. For assistance given to Turkey during the War of Independence by the People's Republic of Bukhara, see Nurettin Hatunoğlu, *Rusların Türkistan İşgalinde Son Perde: Buhara Hanlığı ve Alim Han*, Ötüken Neşriyat, 2011, 286–294.
34. Ruzi Nazar.
36. For details of the Turkish position during the Second World War and its foreign policy, see Baki Öz, *Bıçağın Sırtında Siyaseti İkinci Dünya Savaş'ında Türk Dış Politikası*, Can Yayınları, Istanbul, 1996; Edward Weisband, Kayabağ, Örgen Uğurluö-, *İkinci Dünya Savaşı ve Türkiye*, Örgün Yayınevi, Istanbul, 2002. See also *Stalin, Roosevelt ve Churchill'in Gizli Yazışmalarında Türkiye 1941–1944 ve İkinci Dünya Savaşı Öncesi Barış Çabaları ve Türkiye 1938–1939*, Havass Yayınları, Istanbul, 1981.
37. Interview with Veli Kayyum Han.
38. Interview with Veli Kayyum Han. See also Andican, *Turkestan Struggle*, 592.
39. On the transition to a multi-party system in Turkey and the Democrat Party government, see İlter Turan, 'The Recruitment of Cabinet Ministers as a Political Process, Turkey 1946–1979', *International Journal of Middle East Studies*, 18, 4, November 1986, 455–472; Frank Tachau and Mary-Jo D. Good, 'The Anatomy of Political and Social Change: Turkish Parties, Parliaments and Elections', *Comparative Politics*, 5, 4, June 1973, 551–573. For further information, Sina Akşin and Ali Berktay, *Kısa Türkiye Tarihi*, Türkiye İş Bankası Kültür Yayınları, Istanbul, 2007, and Feroz Ahmad, *Turkey: The Quest for Identity*, Oneworld Publications, Oxford, 2003.
40. See 'Law No 5886 on Turkish Accession to the North Atlantic Treaty Organisation', *Resmi Gazete* (Turkish Official Gazette), 19 February 1952. Turkey and Greece had acceded to NATO through a protocol agreed in London on 17 October 1951. On Turkey's entry into NATO, see Baskin Oran, ed., *Türk Dış Poltikası: Kurtuluş Savaşından Bugüne Olgular, Belgeler, Yorumlar*, İletişim Yayınları, İstanbul, 2009, vol. 1, 543–544.

41. Andican, *Turkestan Struggle*, 286, n. 57.
42. A short-lived Tatar republic set up by the non-Russian peoples of Kazan in 1922 and eventually suppressed by the Bolsheviks.
43. Andican, *Turkestan Struggle*, 286, n. 59.
44. A Sufi lodge or convent.
45. See 'Kurtuluş Savaşı'nın Kahraman Tekkesi', 19 December 2005, http://hurriyet.com.tr/gundem/563843.asp?gid=0&srid=0&oid=0&l=1, accessed 20 February 2011; Abdurrahman Dilipak, 'Bilinmeyen Yönleriyle Özbekler Tekkesi', *Vakit*, 22 December 2006, http://www.tumgazeteler.com/?a=18625548=1, accessed 20 February 2011.
46. Ruzi Nazar.
47. Ruzi Nazar.
48. Interview with Professor Ibrahim Yarkın. See also Andican, *Turkestan Struggle*, 594.
49. Ruzi Nazar.
50. Ruzi Nazar; interview with Professor Ibrahim Yarkın.

12. THE BANDUNG CONFERENCE

1. The Asian-African Conference, generally known as the Bandung Conference, was held between 18 and 24 April 1955. Twenty-nine national delegations participated, representing more than half the world's population. See Britannica Online Encyclopaedia, 'Bandung Conference', http://www.britannica.com/EBchecked/topic/51624/Bandung-Conference. See also George McTurnan Kahin, *The Asian-African Conference, Bandung Indonesia, 1955*, Cornell University Press, Ithaca, New York, 1956.
2. For the speech to the conference by Jawaharlal Nehru, prime minister of India, see *Modern History Source Book*, 'Speech to the Bandung Conference Political Committee, 1955', www.fordham.edu/halsall/mod/1955nehru-bandung2.html. For the speech by President Sukarno of Indonesia, see *Modern History Sourcebook*, 'Speech at the Opening of the Bandung Conference, April 18, 1955', http://www.fordham.edu/halsall/mod/1955Sukarno-bandong.html.
3. Ruzi Nazar.
4. Ruzi Nazar.
5. Ruzi Nazar.
6. Ruzi Nazar.
7. Ruzi Nazar.
8. Ruzi Nazar.
9. Ruzi Nazar.
10. Ruzi Nazar.

11. Ruzi Nazar.
12. Ruzi Nazar.
13. Ruzi Nazar.
14. Ruzi Nazar.
15. Ruzi Nazar.
16. Ruzi Nazar. See too *China and the Asian African Conference*, Chou En-lai, University Microfilms Intl., Ann Arbor, 1998; National Committee for the Commemoration of the Thirtieth Anniversary of the Asian-African Conference (India), *Pictorial Record of the Asian-African Conference*, National Committee for the Commemoration of the Thirtieth Anniversary of the Asian-African Conference, Jakarta, 1985.
17. Ruzi Nazar.
18. For detailed information about East Turkestan, see İsa Yusuf Alptekin, *Unutulan Vatan: Doğu Türkistan*, Seha Neşriyat ve Ticaret, Istanbul, 1992; Osman Kubilay Gül, 'Doğu Türkistan'dan Türkiye'ye Hazin bir Göç Hikayesi', *Turkish Studies*, 2/1, Winter 2007, 252–273; Chiara Beta, *Xinjiang or Eastern Turkestan? The Conundrum of Chinese Central Asia*, Institute of International Economic Relations, Athens, 2001.
19. Ruzi Nazar.
20. Ruzi Nazar.
21. Ruzi Nazar.
22. Ruzi Nazar.
23. Baskın Oran, ed., *Türk Dış Poltikası: Kurtuluş Savaşından Bugüne Olgular, Belgeler, Yorumlar*, İletişim Yayınları, İstanbul, 2009, 537, 731, 813.
24. Ruzi Nazar.
25. For the final communiqué of the Bandung Conference and other statements issued during it, see *European Navigator (Fact Sheet, Text no. 556)*, 'Final Communiqué of the Asian-African Conference of Bandung (24 April 1955)', http://www.ena.lu/final_communique_asian_african_conference_bandung_24_april_1955_020000556.html.
26. Ruzi Nazar.
27. Ruzi Nazar.
28. For the opening speech made by Anwar Sadat on 26 December 1957 to the conference of the Organisation for Solidarity for the People of Africa and Asia, see *Modern History Sourcebook*, 'Afro-Asian Solidarity and the World Mission of the Peoples of Africa and Asia 1957'.
29. Ruzi Nazar.
30. Ruzi Nazar.
31. Interviews with Ruzi Nazar and Professor Ibrahim Yarkin.
32. Ruzi Nazar.
33. Ruzi Nazar.
34. Ruzi Nazar.

35. Ruzi Nazar.
36. For general information about General Qassem, see Uriel Dann, *Iraq under Qassem: a Political History, 1958–1963*, Praeger, New York, 1969; Avshalom H. Rubin, 'Abd al-Karim Qasim and the Kurds of Iraq:, Centralisation, Resistance, and Revolt, 1958–1963', *Middle Eastern Studies*, 43, 2, 2007, 353–382.
37. Ruzi Nazar.

13. UNDERCOVER WORK IN INTERNATIONAL CONFERENCES

1. Ruzi Nazar.
2. Ruzi Nazar.
3. Ruzi Nazar; Interview with Obeidullah Abdurazzakov. Abdurazakov is of the opinion that Murtazayev was liquidated because of his nationalist feelings.
4. Ruzi Nazar.
5. See Aynur Öz, 'Zülfiye—Hayatı ve Eserlerinden Seçmeler', *Türkiye Dışındaki Türk Edebiyatları: Antolojisi Özbek Edebiyatı*, 15, 2, Ministry of Culture, Ankara, 2000, 394–398; Zülfiye, *Eser Toplamı*, Tashkent, 1995; 'Zülfiye' in the *Uzbek Soviet Encyclopaedia*.
6. Ruzi Nazar.
7. *Uzbek Soviet Encyclopaedia*, Vol. 2, 301–302.
8. Ruzi Nazar.
9. *Uzbek Soviet Encyclopedia*, Vol. 2, 301–303; Ruzi Nazar.
10. The information given here about Mufti Sadreddin Han comes from my father, Şakır Altaylı, who was his assistant. The mufti sought asylum in Afghanistan from the Soviet Republic of Tajikistan in 1937. My father became suspicious of Aykarli and warned the mufti about this but could not convince him. As he would not work in the same committee as Aykarli, he left Afghanistan and, with the help of Memduh Şevket Esendal, the Turkish politician and writer who was then serving as Turkish ambassador in Kabul, he came back to Turkey. An intellectual Turkestani Muslim clergyman, the mufti took part in the establishment of the Turkestan National Autonomous Government in Kokand in 1918 and participated in the setting up of the Tashkent branch of the Committee of Union and Progress (the Young Turk Party). Then he went to Istanbul and met Young Turk leaders including Enver Pasha and Talât Pasha. He took part in the armed movement for Turkestani independence. He was arrested by the Cheka and sentenced to death, but escaped from prison and crossed into Afghanistan and carried on with his struggle there. He became a close friend of Memduh Şevket Esendal, the Turkish ambassador in Kabul.

11. For further details of Mustafa Aykarlı's life, see Mariya Çokayoğlu, *Eşinin ağzından Mustafa Çokayoğlu*, Yaş Türkistan, İstanbul, 1972.

12. The Turkestani wars of independence that started in 1916 against Tsarist Russian rule.

13. Ruzi Nazar.

14. Ruzi Nazar.

15. Interview with Obeidullah Abdurazzakov.

16. Ruzi Nazar.

17. Interviews with Ruzi Nazar and Obeidullah Abdurazzakov.

18. Ruzi Nazar.

19. Interviews with Ruzi Nazar and Obeidullah Abdurazzakov.

20. On the creation of the Turkish Communist Party and its structure and activities, see George S. Harris, *The Origins of Communism in Turkey*, Hoover Institution on War, Revolution and Peace, Stanford, 1967; Aclan Sayılgan, *Türkiye'de Sol Hareketler*, Doğu Kütüphanesi, Istanbul, 2009; Mete Tuncay, *Türkiye'de Sol Akımlar*, İletişim Yayınları, Istanbul, 2009.

21. Ruzi Nazar.

22. Ruzi Nazar.

23. For detailed information, see Lütfü Akdoğan and Mustafa Barzani, *Mustafa Barzani Anlatıyor: Ortadoğu'da Çanlar Kimin için Çalıyor?*, Arkaplan Müzik, Istanbul, 2007; Massoud Barzani and Ahmed Ferhadi, *Mustafa Barzani and the Kurdish Liberation Movement*, Palgrave Macmillan, New York, 2003; Hulûsi Turgut, *Barzani Dosyası: Osmanlı İmparatorlupu'nu ve Türkiye Cumhuriyeti XIX Yüzyıldan Berş Meşgul Eden Bır Kürt Aşiretinin Belgeseli*, Doğan Kitap, Istanbul, 2008.

24. Michael S. Volensky, *op. cit.*, 254–293

25. 'Kommunistecheskiy universitet trudyaschihsya Vostoka' in *Bolshaya Sovetskaya Entsiklopediya*, http://www.cultinfo.ru/fulltext/1/001/008/063/468.htm, accessed 27 February 2011.

26. Ruzi Nazar.

27. Ruzi Nazar.

28. Ruzi Nazar.

29. See Vera Tulyakova Hikmet, *Bahtiyar Ol Nâzım*, Yapı ve Kredi Yayınları, Istanbul, 2008; Vera Tulyakova Hikmet, *Nâzımla Son Söyleşimiz*, Everest, Istanbul, 2002.

30. Stephen Lee Crane, *Survivor from an Unknown War: The life of Isakjan Narzikul*, Diane, Upland, Pennsylvania, 25–45.

31. Ruzi Nazar.

32. Crane, *Survivor*, 100ff.

33. For more information about Gulam Alim, see Antonio J. Munoz, *Hitler's Muslims: Muslim Volunteers in Hitler's Armies, 1941–1945*, Europa

Books, Bayside, New York, 2009, 77; Oleg Valentinovich Romanko, 'The East Came West: Muslim and Hindu Volunteers in German Service, 1941–1945', in Antonio Muñoz, ed., *The East Came West*, Axis Europa Books, New York, 2001, 88.

34. Crane, *Survivor*, 137ff. There is interesting information in this book about how Isakcan and his friends saved the lives of Warsaw Jews.
35. Crane, *Survivor*, 117ff.
36. Ruzi Nazar.
37. Ruzi Nazar.
38. Ruzi Nazar.
39. Ruzi Nazar.
40. Ruzi Nazar.

14. RUZI IN TURKEY: SOLDIERS, PLOTS AND POLITICS

1. Nuri Killigil, the brother of Enver Pasha.
2. Better known as Celâl Bayar, president of Turkey from 1950 to 1960.
3. Today known as Gaziantep and Kahramanmaraş.
4. Ruzi Nazar.
5. See Alparslan Türkeş and Hulûsi Turgut, *Şahinlerin Dansı: Türkeş'ın Anıları*, ABC Basın Ajansı Yayınları, Istanbul, 1995, 210–211.
6. A late nineteenth- and early twentieth-century political and cultural movement to unite all the Turkic, Tatar, and Uralic peoples of Asia.
7. Türkeş and Turgut, *Şahinlerin Dansı*, 210–211.
8. Interviews with Ruzi Nazar and Alparslan Türkeş.
9. Ruzi Nazar.
10. Interviews with Ruzi Nazar and Alparslan Türkeş.
11. Ruzi Nazar.
12. Ruzi Nazar.
13. *İsmet İnönü'nün TBMM'deki Konuşmaları (1920–1973) ö TBMM Kültür Sanat ve Yayın Kurulu*, Vol. 2, Ankara, 1992, 300. On the 27 May 1960 military coup, see Şevket Süreyya Aydemir, *İhtilâlın Mantığı ve 27 A İhtilâli*, Remzi Kitabevi, Istanbul, 1973; Abdi İpekçi and Ömer Sami Coşar, *İhtilâlın İçyüzü*, Uygun Yayınevi, 1965. For memoirs of some of the principal personages involved: Celâl Bayar, *Kayseri Cezaevi Günlüğü*, Yapı ve Kredi Yayınları, Istanbul, 1999; Talât Aydemir, *Talât Aydemir'in Hatıraları*, Akşam Kitağ Kulübü Yayınları, Istanbul, 1968; Türkeş and Turgut, *Şahinlerin Dansı*.
14. Ruzi Nazar.
15. Oran, *op. cit.*, 511–521.
16. Cüneyt Akalın, ed., *Askerler ve Dış Güçler: Amerikan Belgeleriyle 27 Mayıs Olayı*, Cumhuriyet Kitapları, Istanbul, 2000, 108.

17. Ruzi Nazar.
18. The purge of the officers became known as the 'Incident of the Fourteen'.
19. Ruzi Nazar.
20. For Turkish–American relations at this period, see Baskın Oran, ed., *Türk Dış Poltikası: Kurtuluş Savaşından Bugüne Olgular, Belgeler, Yorumlar*, İletişim Yayınları, İstanbul, 2009, 522–575.
21. Ruzi Nazar.
22. Türkeş and Turgut, *Şahinlerin Dansı*, 185–186.
23. On the morning of 27 May 1960 a group of academics from Istanbul University went to Ankara by military plane and presented a report to the National Unity Committee. The report, dated 28 May, began with the sentence: 'It is not correct to consider the situation in which we find ourselves today as an ordinary and political government coup.' It claimed that the Democrat Party government had lost its legitimacy and that the 27 May movement against it had therefore been legitimate. See Kemal Gözler, *Türk Parlamenterler Birliği*, 'T.C. Anayasası—1961', http://www.tpb.org.tr/dokuman-arsivi/161-tc-anayasas-1961.html, accessed 24 February 2011. See also Erik Jan Zürcher, *Modernleşen Türkiye'nin Tarihi*, İletisşim, İstanbul, 1995, 353.
24. Açık Radyo, '27 Mayıs Darbesi Özel Program Dizisi, Bölüm 3', 27 May 2010, http://www.acikradyo.com.tr/default.aspx?_mv=a&aid=26669&cat=100 (radio documentary programme in Turkish about the 27 May 1960 coup).
25. Türkeş and Turgut, *Şahinlerin Dansı*, 115–116.
26. Türkeş and Turgut, *Şahinlerin Dansı*, 269.
27. Ruzi Nazar.
28. Türkeş and Turgut, *Şahinlerin Dansı*, 209–210.
29. Ruzi Nazar.
30. Ruzi Nazar.
31. Ruzi Nazar.
32. Ruzi Nazar.
33. The Teşkilat-ı Mahsusa was set up in the early years of the twentieth century. It was much more successful and better designed than contemporary intelligence services in Western countries. It was established forty years before the CIA and was the first modern intelligence service to carry out successful operations outside its own country. See the Princeton doctoral thesis on the Teşkilat-ı Mahsusa by Philip Stoddart, published in Turkish as *Teşkilat-ı Mahsusa*, Arba Yayınları, Istanbul, 2003.
34. Interviews with Alparslan Türkeş and Ruzi Nazar.
35. Türkeş and Turgut, *Şahinlerin Dansı*, 210–211.

36. The Yassıada Trials tried members of the former Democratic Party government and President Celâl Bayar and passed death sentences on the prime minister, Adnan Menderes; the foreign minister, Fatin Rüştü Zorlu; and the minister of finance, Hasan Polatkan.

37. Erdal Şimşek and İlhan Bahar, *Türkiye'de İstihbaratçılık ve MİT*, Kum Saati Yayınları, Istanbul, 2004, 272–273.

38. Ruzi Nazar. Also Milli İstihbarat Teşkilatı (Turkish National Intelligence Organisation), 'Milli Emniyet Reisleri Biyografiler, Ziya Selışık (1900–1966)', http://www.mit.gov.tr/must-biyog-meh1.html. For the conversion of the Turkish National Operation Service into the National Intelligence Organisation, see Milli İstihbarat Teşkilatı, 'MAH'ın Milli İstihbarat Teşkilatına dönüştürülmesi', http://www.mit.gov.tr/tarihce/ikinci_bolum_F.html.

39. Türkeş and Turgut, *Şahinlerin Dansı*, 220–222.

40. For the activities of Mihri Belli, see Aclan Sayılgan, *Türkiye'de Sol Hareketler*, Doğu Kütüphanesi, Istanbul 2009, 241–289.

41. Ruzi Nazar

42. JUSMAT: Joint United States Military Mission for Aid to Turkey. It was based in Ankara, its role being to provide training support for the Turkish armed forces.

43. Ruzi Nazar.

44. Ruzi Nazar.

45. For the Teşkilât-ı Mahsusa, see İlhan Balhar, *Teşkilât-ı Mahsusa'dan MİT'e*, Kum Saati Yayıncılık, Istanbul, 2009; Arif Cemil Cenker, Metin Martı, *Birinci Dünya Savaşı'nda Teşkilât-ı Mahsusa*, Arma Yayınları, Istanbul, 2006; Stoddard, *Teşkilât-ı Mahsusa*.

46. Şimşek and Bahar, *Türkiye'de İstihbaratçılık ve MİT*, 244–249.

47. Ruzi Nazar.

48. Personal communication from Fuat Doğu to Enver Altaylı.

49. Ruzi Nazar.

50. Conversations with Fuat Doğu at various times. One of the students sent abroad by him was Enver Altaylı, the author of this book.

51. See 'Fuat Doğu Has Left His Secret Memoirs to MIT', *Sabah*, 22 December 2007, http://arsiv.sabah.com.tr/2007/12/22/haber,00BB2926B3904376A47D3B8C578796DB.html.

52. Şimşek and Bahar, *Türkiye'de İstihbaratçılık ve MİT*, 331–332.

53. Personal communication in 1972 from Nurettin Ersin, then Undersecretary of MİT, in his office to the author of this book, Enver Altaylı.

54. Ruzi Nazar.

55. Ruzi Nazar.

56. Ruzi Nazar. The so-called 'Turkism Trial' took place over sixty-five hearings. There were twenty-three accused, among them Fethi

Tevetoğlu, Fazil Hisarcıklı, Hüseyin Nihal Atsöz, Zeki Velidi Togan and Reha Oğuz Türkan. Thirteen of the accused were acquitted, but ten of the defendants were held under arrest until 26 October 1945. They included Zeki Velidi Togan, Alparslan Türkeş, Nihal Atsız, Reha Oğuz Türkan, Fethi Tevetoğlu and Nejdet Sancar. For details of cross-examinations and defence statements during the trial, see Yavuz Bülent Bakiler, *1944–1945 Irkçılık-Turancılık Davası'nda Sorgular, Savunmalar*, Türk Edebiyat Vakfı, Istanbul, 2010.

15. FROM TURKEY TO BONN

1. Ruzi Nazar.
2. Ruzi Nazar.
3. Ruzi Nazar.
4. Ruzi Nazar.
5. Ruzi Nazar.
6. Ruzi Nazar.
7. Ruzi Nazar.
8. Ruzi Nazar.
9. Ruzi Nazar.
10. 'In the name of God, who embraces all living things with love and compassion.'
11. Ruzi Nazar.
12. Ruzi Nazar.
13. Ruzi Nazar.
14. Traditional Turkish parties of family and friends for occasions like engagements and weddings.
15. Ruzi Nazar. Doğuş Holding, the conglomerate which Ayhan Şahenk founded, today is one of Turkey's largest businesses, with a turnover of billions of dollars.
16. On the attempted assassination of the pope, see Paul B. Henze, *The Plot to Kill the Pope*, Scribner, New York, 1983; Edward S. Herman and Frank Brodhead, *The Rise and Fall of the Bulgarian Connection*, Sheridan Square Publications, New York, 1986; Nigel West, *The Third Secret: The CIA, Solidarity, and the KGB's Plot to Kill the Pope*, HarperCollins, London, 2000; 'Was Gunman Mehmet Ali Ağca Part of KGB Plot?', *The Australian*, 19 January 2010, http://www.theaustralian.com.au/news/world/was-gunman-mehmet-ali-agca-part-of-kgb-plot/story-e6frg6so-1225821002394.
17. Ruzi Nazar.
18. Ruzi Nazar.
19. On intelligence organisations and their importance, see Dovydas

Vitkauskas, 'The Role of a Security Intelligence Service in a Democracy', *North Atlantic Treaty Organisation, Democratic Institutions Fellowships Programme* 1997–1999, June 1999; Federation of American Scientists, *The Role of Intelligence*, http://www.fas.org/irp/offdocs/int006.html.
20. Ruzi Nazar.
21. Tim Weiner, *Legacy of Ashes: The History of the CIA*, Doubleday, New York, 2007, 399–400.
22. *Sowjetsystem und demokratische Gesellschaft*, Freiburg, 1972.
23. Ruzi Nazar.

16. UNDERCOVER IN IRAN DURING THE HOSTAGE CRISIS

1. Tim Weiner, *Legacy of Ashes: The History of the CIA*, Doubleday, New York, 2007, 487.
2. SAVAK (Sazeman Attelat ve Emniyet Keşvar) was the national intelligence organisation set up in 1957 by the Shah with American and Israeli advice. It was officially closed in 1979 when Ayatollah Khomeini took power.
3. Weiner, *Legacy of Ashes*, 489.
4. For an interview with Bruce Laingen giving his views on Shah Reza Pahlavi, see 'Ambassador Bruce Laingen', *Association for Diplomatic Studies, Foreign Affairs Oral History Program*, Lauinger Library, Georgetown University, http://www.library.georgetown.edu/dept/speccoll/laingen.htm.
5. Weiner, *Legacy of Ashes*, 493.
6. Weiner, *Legacy of Ashes*, 490ff.
7. Ruzi Nazar.
8. Ruzi Nazar.
9. Weiner, *Legacy of Ashes*, 490ff.
10. Weiner, *Legacy of Ashes*, 492–493, 803.
11. Ruzi Nazar.
12. Ruzi Nazar.
13. Ruzi Nazar.
14. Ruzi Nazar.
15. Ruzi Nazar.
16. Ruzi Nazar.
17. Ruzi Nazar.
18. Ruzi Nazar.
19. Weiner, *Legacy of Ashes*, 492–493, 803.
20. Ruzi Nazar.
21. Ruzi Nazar.

17. THE COLD WAR ENDS AND RUZI RETURNS TO UZBEKISTAN

1. Ruzi Nazar.
2. Interview with Obeidullah Abdurazakov.
3. Interviews with Ruzi Nazar and Obeidullah Abdurazakov.
4. On Reagan's visit to the Soviet Union, see Gerald M. Boyd, 'Raze Berlin Wall, Reagan Urges Soviets', *New York Times*, 13 June 1987.
5. Ruzi Nazar.
6. Ruzi Nazar.
7. Ruzi Nazar.
8. Ruzi Nazar.
9. Ruzi Nazar.
10. Interview with Shukrullo Mirsaidov.
11. Interviews with Ruzi Nazar and Shukrullo Mirsaidov.
12. Ruzi Nazar.
13. Ruzi Nazar.
14. TO COME.
15. Margaret Thatcher. *Downing Street No. 10: Die Erinnerungen*, Econ Verlag, Duesseldorf, 1993, 679.
16. Henry Kissinger, *Diplomasi*, İş Bankası Yayınları, İstanbul, 1999, 778–779.
17. These countries became UN members in 1992.
18. An exclave area of Azerbaijan, lying between Armenia and Turkey in the Caucasus.
19. For details of the manner in which the Central Asian republics became independent, and the attitudes of the former Communist Party leaders, see Edward Allworth, *Central Asia, 130 Years of Russian Dominance: An Historical Overview*, Duke University Press, Durham, 1994; Olivier Roy, *The New Central Asia: The Creation of Nations*, New York University Press, New York, 2000.
20. Ruzi Nazar.
21. Ruzi Nazar.
22. Ruzi Nazar.
23. Written information provided to the author by Ruzi's niece, Dilberhan, in 2010.
24. Ruzi Nazar.
25. The author of this book was a member of the organising committee.
26. Interview with Erkin Nazar.
27. Interview with Erkin Nazar.
28. Ruzi Nazar.
29. Ruzi Nazar.
30. Ruzi Nazar.

31. Ruzi Nazar.
32. Ruzi Nazar.
33. Ruzi Nazar.
34. Ruzi Nazar.

INDEX

INDEX

Antep, Turkey, 211
Anti-Bolshevik Bloc of Nations
 (ABN), 146, 147, 152, 153
apricots, 9
Arab League, 171
Arabic, 2, 3, 19, 28, 158, 172,
 196, 197, 199
Ardahan, Turkey, 76, 137
Argo, 245, 246
Argus, 165–6
Arlington, Virginia, 211, 213
Armenia, Armenians, 6, 11, 60,
 89, 156, 211, 234
Armenian–Azerbaijani War
 (1918–20), 211
Arnavutköy, Turkey, 116
Artukov, Israil, 28
Aryan race, *see* racial theories
Asia Corps, 53
Asia Solidarity Organisation, 191
askiye, 19, 45
Astrakhan Khanate (1466–1556), 5
Atajan Hashim, 22
Atatürk, Kemal Mustafa, 39, 176,
 211, 224, 264
Atatürk Forest Farm, Ankara, 229
atheism, 9, 15, 35, 174, 252
atomic bomb, 136, 151–2
Augsburg, Germany, 142
Austria, 48, 87–8, 102, 105,
 107–9, 111, 120–21, 201–10,
 236, 252
Austria-Hungary (1867–1918), 7,
 73
auxiliary units, 48, 61
Avicenna, 3
Avtarhanov, Abdurrahman, 152,
 171
Ayasofya Museum, Istanbul, 180
Aybek (Musa Tash
 Muhammedoghlu), 29
Aydemir, Şevket Süreyya, 205

Aydemir, Talât, 214
Ayit Bey, 87
Aykarli, Mahmut, 198–9, 201
Azerbaijan, Azeris
 and Afro-Asian People's Solidarity Organisation, 195
 anti-Bolshevik movement, 154,
  212, 231
 Armenian–Azerbaijani War
  (1918–20), 211
 and Committee for the Liberation of the Russian Peoples,
  145, 154
 Democratic Republic (1918–
  20), 96, 99
 Fethalibeyli assassination (1954),
  147–9
 First World War (1914–18), 53
 in Iran, 247–8
 National Committee, 97–9, 114,
  146–9
 and Nazi Germany (1933–45),
  48, 55, 60–61, 63, 74, 77,
  88–9, 95, 98–9, 161
 poetry, 207
 Republic of South Azerbaijan
  (1945–6), 136, 137, 138, 280
 and Russian Empire (1721–
  1917), 6, 228
 and Russian Revolution (1917),
  205
 Soviet Socialist Republic (1920–
  91), 99, 230
 and United States, 156, 159
Azerbaijan, 147
al-Azhar University, Cairo, 171,
 196, 201

Babakhanov, Ziyaeddin, 197–8, 200
Babur, Mughal Emperor, 91, 94
Babur, Zahir-ud-Din Muhammad,
 2, 32

300

INDEX

INDEX

INDEX

INDEX

INDEX

INDEX

INDEX

INDEX

INDEX

INDEX

INDEX

INDEX